Shape-shifter

An Awakening
on the
Paths of Art and Gender

Shannon Belthor

Lumenhorse Press

LCCN: 2010907194
ISBN: 978-0-9845567-1-7

First Edition

First Printing, July, 2010
10 9 8 7 6 5 4 3 2 1

Printed in USA

Published by Lumenhorse Press
Portland, Oregon
Lumenhorse.com

Front cover image:
Shamanic Seeds: Cadence of Blessed Surrender
© 2009 Shannon Belthor

Author photo: Barbara McIntyre

Acknowledgements

In stepping away from a life steeped in creative solitude, it's been a joy and a blessing to have the support of a wonderful team in the shaping of this book. With rivers of gratitude, I'd like to acknowledge: Charity Heller of Mighty Pen Editing for her enthusiastic support of the third draft of the manuscript upon my return from Bali. The numerous readers, including Nancy Parent, Janet Unitan, Jeff and Janice Godfrey, and my brother, Christopher, who sifted through earlier and later drafts, and generously shared their impressions; in particular, Georgiana Nehl, artist, dancer, and teacher, for her exquisitely thorough reading and insightful notes. Twig Deluge of Bare Bones Press, for his good-humored help with the interior design and layout, and invaluable insights into the rapidly changing world of publishing. Bryan Coffelt, for his calm, can-do spirit in setting up the website that hosts the companion images online, and creating the e-book version of this volume. And thanks to my circle of friends, who have ridden the roller-coaster of progress with me through the many phases, and offered encouragement along the way.

For Brooke,
whose friendship
has graced my life.

Life is a strange and wondrous thing,
and even one who would naturally sit quietly
in a cabin in a forest, or a desert, or by the sea
and contemplate the exquisiteness of existence
might feel called as well to pack her things
and set forth to share the story of her awakening.

Color images for each chapter are available at:
shannonbelthor.com

Introduction

From the equator, the moon seems wrapped in translucent velvet—set softly in a warm cushion of night, amid stars like fields of candles. I've seen through the crystalline light in the mountains of New Mexico the milk in the Milky Way, and felt the unfathomable vast between those stars and these eyes.

But here in Bali, I want to lie in that warm field, rub my cheeks against the nearness of it all, and nestle with the cosmos as one would a lover. In this embrace, the journey here—to this island, and to this earthly plane altogether—seems not so far.

I waken to Agung's ten-year-old son singing a Balinese folk song to the entire compound, to a background of clanging pans being washed by his sister, Sri, at five-thirty in the morning. Dreaminess scatters as light meets eyes once again in the haze of dawn, and I seem to be a white, bamboo mat-ceilinged room... No, I seem to be a body laying on an ancient, sunken mattress *in* this room. I urge this body to sit up, and look blearily around: a few baskets, a desk, a laptop... a story waiting to be unfurled.

One must start somewhere, so I rise, make tea, and meditate. After breakfast, I sit with the laptop and language amid the wash of nearly fifty years, and invite the unknown.

From a source I consider to be quite reliable, I hear there's an infinity of worlds into which one might arrive in the course of one's evolution, and that as worlds go, this is one of the denser. I find that last part remarkably easy to believe, though I must confess to finding belief, in and of itself, highly over-rated. I prefer a more direct sort of knowing, and having seen the gist of what this orb has to offer, this high-density rating seems reasonable enough.

There's a stunning array of matter absorbing a great deal of attention here, and I'm certainly not alone in noting the obvious: Beneath the fascination with things, there's a deep longing for the more rarefied end of the spectrum: freedom, peace, joy, light... and yes, love.

But perhaps that's the point: We muck around in the heavier parts until finally we say, *Enough already with all this suffering!* and start looking around for a better way. It may take a staggering number of visits to this earthly world to get it, but sooner or later, we look down at those muck-caked boots, and begin to consider the benefits of lightness of Being—of accepting the calling of one's longing toward a fuller, more joyous life.

I must have passed this way a few times before, because this time around, I seem to have landed here with an orientation toward the lighter side pretty much out of the chute. While this blessing certainly didn't present itself with a "Get off the Karmic Wheel of Suffering Free" card, it has lent some balance through the many challenges, and stands out to this day among the waves of blessings on which I continually shower gratitude.

One of the finer things in having gathered a bounty of journeys around the sun is a vantage point from which to look back and see the wellspring of this earthly version of who, and more essentially, *what* one is. Right there in plain sight is the ebb and flow of one's own set of traits and impulses like ocean swells across one's life.

If we feel blessed as adults, it may well be that we're firmly in the company of the finer qualities with which we landed—that they have not been subsumed by difficult circumstance—and they are yet richer for the ride and handsomely ensconced in wisdom.

When I reflect on the rhythms of traits across my version of earthly time, the one most essential is a sense of residing in a spectrum of worlds—of existing at a threshold, with the blessing of access to a spacious range inside and out. It's at the core of my being gender-variant, of my being an artist, and of freedom of the vastest sort.

When I think of the sacred role of the artist—which is to stand at the threshold and introduce the unknown to form and form to the unknown—I see, too, the messy practice of engaging the vision with the moving of materials and tools.

It is, after all, one's Doing in the constant stream of Now which in retrospect describes the arc of one's life—the uniquely odd rub of one's Being here in this dense realm. In a heartbeat, I can draw a line—a long curvaceous one to be sure—between this writing in the shade of the tropics and youthful explorations in pine-forested woods, which wends right across the years of creating in studios: from sea-level ghetto, to perched in the Southwestern sky; from humble chicken coop to gauzy walls of light.

As a sculptor, I know to gather in advance the materials I will juxtapose—the better to weigh them awhile by hand and eye, and let the conversation between them kindle. So I embark upon my stream of impressions with the start of my stay on this whirling blue orb, not out of duty to chronology, but because one must start somewhere, and there are bits and pieces back there in the far corners which might as well be dragged out, dusted off, and reacquainted with the light of day.

This inclination to dive in and knock out the heavy lifting is most certainly among those traits and impulses, and one which, as you'll see, cuts deeply across my well-labored sojourn in this matter-strewn world.

From this womb of light in Bali, it's rather like perusing it all from the vantage point of an afterlife in which, having passed from this well-used body, there's room aplenty to root around back there in the dustbin of memory. I imagine there, as here, one eventually finds that the value gleaned from such sifting of remembrance can only be appreciated and applied in the timeless Now. Perhaps, in the light of such awareness, we step away from the story we tell ourselves and others of who we are, and into presence... into simply Being.

As I reach back to tell this story of shape-shifting and awakening, the present insists on room for its lighter voice—on lapping at those earlier roller-coaster times with its own stream of contemplations. So there are every now and again in the landscape of these pages lightly-toned fields of text: what I've come to call *Ubud Interludes*, in which this state and place from which I write has its say, too.

One might see this book as an entwined pair of journals: one focused more on a creative life unfolding, the other on the unfurling Now. This wafting between narrative and present voices reflects what seems to me to be the gist of being at peace in this form-obsessed world: that regardless of what happened back there, one's attention is trained on this present moment spilling afresh from the font of Stillness.

Eventually, the story finds me right here, like a cat chasing its own tail, and together we go off into the sunset—the ongoing unfolding of this adventure and the moment hand-in-hand.

I

Germination

Odd Duckling

I began the tripped-out, tuned-in, turned-on Sixties by being born, and ended them by turning ten. In other words, I pretty much missed the social revolution. But even in the little New England town nestled in the hills of central Massachusetts, it would have been difficult not to catch some glimpses—we did subscribe to *Life* magazine, after all— and there were plenty of long-haired guys, gingham dresses, and bell-bottoms to go around.

But the *real* Sixties—when the social magma blew the top right off the cultural volcano—seemed to have happened *out there*, beyond the borders of our backwater town, where movies would finally arrive late and exhausted, having played, apparently, at every other movie house in the world. As a preadolescent, I lamented having missed the action, and quietly cursed my luck at having been born too late. Though I had only clues at best as to what this action might have actually entailed, I'm quite sure now it was for the best, as there was plenty on my plate without the psychedelics.

Before we moved into the center of the town of twenty-five hundred people, we lived in a cottage nestled in the rolling hills amid farms, forests, and meadows. My earliest memories reside there: of playing ball with our collie named Gent, who later died from a neighbor's rat poison; of the white, rose-covered arbor on an expanse of vividly green lawn; of Weeping Willows shimmering in the breeze by the pond. I had two brothers and a sister, and was—for the first five years—the tail end of the family pack.

There's another memory of perhaps the most formative experience of my life, from around the time my younger brother, Christopher, was born. We moved into town when I was five, so I couldn't have been older than that when I was standing alone one day in the den. I'd just come around the corner of the couch, when suddenly I was having a vision in which I was a ninety-three-year-old man laying in bed with my head propped steeply on a pillow.

I knew I was drawing my last breaths, but I wasn't ready for death. Looking back over the arc of my long life, I was deeply dissatisfied because I hadn't done what was in my heart to do. It seemed as if I'd been in a trance—done what felt safe, what was expected of me—and now, at this last moment, a feeling of anguished failure gripped me, nauseating me to the core of my Being. I felt sickeningly helpless in realizing what I would have done differently, just as I was out of time to do anything about it.

As suddenly as I'd fallen into the vision, I was standing again in the den. The unsettling lament had followed me back into my little body, where it lingered for days. Over the next months and years, I'd still get a little nauseous when I recalled the experience, but it gradually drifted with time into memory, and a deeply ingrained, barely conscious message etched into my Being:

Don't die having done only the expected.
Live your life fully.

Little wonder, then, that every major choice-point, I've gone down the more difficult road if it seemed it would better serve in my unfolding.

Germination

The summer of 1967—the Summer of Love—was the last one for decades in which I could trust my vocal chords, and if I'd known ahead, I might have talked nonstop the whole time just to get in what I could. That fall in the second grade, as I sat one Tuesday with my classmates around the piano, I tried to say my teacher's name: *M...M...M...M...M...* I stopped, bewildered. It was as if the assumption that I could simply open my mouth and speak my thoughts had spontaneously leapt out of my throat, flown out the window and over trees... and disappeared.

As the stuttering increased, so did my self-consciousness, and I took refuge where I could: alone in the fields, meadows, and woods bordering our land. We were a hard-working family, and there were lots of activities with three brothers and the neighborhood kids, but when I could escape unnoticed, I'd go to where I was free to stretch out and be my curious self, far away from the serial humiliations that often plagued my dealings in the human realm.

The trees and animals had no need for me to speak—though oddly, I found in the company of nature I could say whatever I wanted right out loud. The wind found me frighteningly funny indeed; but then, it didn't stick around for the difficult parts.

Under the canopy of pines, I'd tread as quietly as possible—*Quiet as an Indian...* I was thinking—so the birds and animals wouldn't scurry away. In this attempt at silence, I first discovered the song of trees. There, it was the song of pines—the whistling, rustling whisper unique to wind through bristled boughs. And housing an ever-changing universe, there was a pond at the edge of the woods in which eye-like, gelatinous orbs grew tails to my astonishment, and still later, legs and deep-throated voices—apparently free of hesitation. In the natural world, I discovered a consciousness beyond my own—a deep, peripheral mystery like a well you could see a little way down, but not nearly to the bottom.

Fertilized by generous helpings of horse droppings, the fields were a riot of grasses taller than I, and wildflowers: Queen Anne's lace, goldenrod, Indian paintbrushes, milkweed, and so many more. I've always smelled things—much like a cat—to get a better sense of them, and on the aroma of growing things, I was transported to a primal realm I thought of as *the jungle place* because I felt like an animal—instincts and senses interwoven, acutely alive. Lying in the fields, intoxicated by fragrances of the wild, I'd watch clouds pass in a view framed by tasseled grasses that seemed to reach right up and touch them. Jimi Hendrix kissed the sky, and so did I.

Every now and then, we'd all pile into my father's mint-colored pickup truck and drive off across the countryside to retrieve a pile of bricks to add to the stockpile that fed my mother's insatiable appetite for yet another patio or walkway in the yard. This was not a volunteer mission. It was, though, fairly representational of our primary familial bond: we worked together, like it or not.

Sometimes we'd show up to a neat, stacked pile, but more often than not, it was a collapsed chimney with chunks of mortar still intact. These were invariably cheaper, as was child labor, so we'd descend on them like an ant colony, knocking off the mortar and loading them into the truck. We'd relax on the way back. Lest we rest on our laurels, though, as soon as we arrived home the truck would back up to the designated spot, and we'd hop right out and unload the bricks in stacks of four, five, or six.

On one occasion, we were undertaking a large patio on a terrace just outside the kitchen door. The perimeter was a stone wall about seven feet high, and we were tossing the bricks up to my brother on top, who made piles which were then carried away by someone else. The system worked quite well until one of those piles wobbled, and a brick fell, striking me on the head. Then it was my turn to wobble as I was brought, still stunned, into the house.

My mother leapt into nurse-mode: I remember her calming me while we sat in the kitchen, her red hair perfectly coiffed, as always, her hands parting my auburn locks to have a better look at the damage. She washed away the blood with a warm cloth, and the tears with funny asides and assurances of my long-term wellbeing.

It's an image right out of a Norman Rockwell painting, but it was in fact quite out of character for her. This approximation of warm, nurturing attention was reserved for such injuries and

Germination

serious aliments, while more minor ones rated the pat response: *Well, if it's not better in two weeks, tell me about it.*

I sat there swinging my feet amid the dizziness and pain, soaking up the rarity of warm attention, and feeling oddly lucky. For evidence of the power of emotional patterns engrained in childhood to ripple through one's life, I need only observe the warm glow of anticipated nurturance that immediately arises with the occasional injury forty and some years later.

One shimmering mid-morning, with the fragrance of greenery rising with the last pockets of dew, I was standing on the sloping land below the house, looking across the field. Flocks of birds erupted into the sky as if forsaking land forever, while others leapt from trees, descending as if discovering earth for the first time. Grasses rustled; Queen Anne's lace and goldenrod nodded in the warm breeze.

I reached out to touch something, and as I looked up once again across the field buzzing with life, an intense feeling of passionate love seized my whole Being. Not the choirs-of-angels-singing-the-glories-of-nature sort, but the exquisitely painful I-think-my-heart-is-being-torn-out-of-my-chest kind of love.

Along with the feeling, an image of a faceless Being in flowing robes with a gentle, but powerful female essence appeared—not distinctly in the field or in my mind, but somewhere between. The passion quickly reached a crescendo, at which point I became acutely aware of separation—like a knife cutting right through me.

I stood there, out of time, disconnected from place, with the clearest sense of a lover's rapture and hunger. This realization of severance from essential connection was my first conscious taste of deep longing. Several decades would pass before I saw the connection between this longing for the androgynous female, and the seemingly inevitable course of my life.

Something extraordinary had happened—something alien to the events of my then eight years. In the following days, I thought about this opening quite intently. Until then, I'd assumed one's life amounted to a stockpiling of experience and learning, and this was what you could draw from as you grew up and matured. But this theory couldn't account for the vision, so there seemed to be just two possibilities: One was that I'd lived before, and this was a memory from an earlier life. *Proof*, I wondered, *of reincarnation?* The other was more open-ended: Maybe there was simply more to whom I was than all the things I'd seen, and heard, and touched.

This was 1968—perhaps the air that day was part zephyr, part zeitgeist.

One memory releases another: this one of a hot, sunny afternoon when a bunch of us were playing on the merry-go-round at the grade school playground. There was a game of some sort involving opposing sides, which I recall having to do with one group trying to spin the ones aboard so fast they'd fly off. The clearest impression I have is of holding on to the chest-high bar and spinning at a dizzying speed with a few others, while the other team stood on the ground around it, pushing on the bars as they circled around to make it go faster and faster.

Eventually, someone had to go home, and we needed to even up the teams. I got moved to the other side, which was no big deal—it was just a game, and the sides were arbitrary.

But the act of changing sides had a profound effect on me. I thought about it afterward, especially in the context of a soldier changing allegiance—his realizing in one clear, life-altering moment that his heart-true home is *over there*. In my mind's eye, I saw through his eyes, and felt his world crumble and renew simultaneously. Although I didn't have the words for it then, I was left with the sense that one's identity might be so essential that it could mean having to go against everything one had been raised with in order to be true to oneself.

Germination

Not long before, I'd seen an episode of *Star Trek* in which someone had faced a dilemma—a choice of conscience—involving the possibility of losing all his friends and colleagues. In the days and weeks after the merry-go-round game, a question persistently resurfaced: *Would I risk the scorn and loss of those close to me to go to my true home?* At first, I kept pushing the question away; I felt disloyal and ashamed even to be contemplating it. As I dared to peel away the feelings of guilt and imagined loss, I could sense the uncomfortable truth: Y*es, I would take the risk, and do what I had to do to be true to myself.*

As far back as I can remember, I've had a conscious sense of experiencing life through this body—of this being an exploratory mission of sorts—and that I could just as well have had other, completely different circumstances. Most of the time this sense resided in the background, but at times it would surface in an intense feeling of presence and attention.

In one situation, I was in the Catholic church we attended on Sundays. We stood at one point in the Mass, and I looked around at the congregation and thought, *Ok, so this is my tribe, and this is what they believe...* It was just pure, objective information, and I felt like I could have been with any group, taking in what I saw without feeling any need to accept or reject what I was observing; I was simply taking stock of my reality.

Another time, I was standing in the midst of a 4th of July event in my small hometown. The parade had culminated at the park in the town's center: The veterans of World War Two and Korea were about to pierce the air with a multi-round salute, and the boys would scramble for the prized brass casings. It occurred to me to turn slowly and "scan" what was going on around me. With senses wide open and the mind at full attention—but not thinking—I simply turned all the way around as though I were recording every detail.

In the midst of this extraordinarily rich experience, I felt as though something was looking through me—through my senses. I joked to myself that it was an alien borrowing my perceptions (though I didn't know this word) and wondered if my mind would store it—if I'd be able to retrieve it later when I was much older, or have a really clear kind of memory movie to see when I was dead. I had no idea at the time that this way of Being and seeing would become one of the most essential and valuable practices in my life—in general, and in the practice of art.

Instead of My Mother

My mother had a long, thin strip of black leather folded in half, which she called *the strap*, and getting this stinging pair of well-worn whips vigorously applied to one's behind was near the top of an intricate hierarchy of punishments.

One day she ordered me to the laundry room for some infraction, and told me to put my hands as usual over the edge of the round washing machine opening; she put the cover lightly down over my hands, so I couldn't instinctively reach back to protect myself. As she was strapping me, I reached inside, grabbed some core part of me and sent it hurtling across the universe to get it away from her; I remember seeing star clusters passing by as I streaked away.

When she said twenty years later, reflecting back in a rare moment of warmth, *You always were a good kid*, I wanted to ask her, *Then why did you hit me?* But I knew all too well by then she'd just crumble—the abuser would simply morph into victim, and escape on the charge that I'd upset her. There was no healing to be had in bringing it up, and it was as clear as ever that peace with her version of mothering would only be found within.

Germination

We all took what seemed to be random turns landing on what we called *Mom's shit-list*, but my sister was on it permanently. We may never know precisely what motivated my mother's seemingly bottomless resentment of her. Marie was even named after my mother's older sister, with whom my mother had what appeared to be a unilateral rivalry and jealousy going back to childhood. It seems in her insecurity she saw her daughter, too, as competition, and my mother's insatiable need to be in control—and to be *seen* to be in control—was unleashed on her without mercy.

One of my mother's favorite punishments—besides an elaborate web of fines—was to have us write repetitive sentences, such as *"I will respect my elders,"* a hundred or more times, and we were considered grounded until we had them done. Marie had an insurmountable number of sentences backlogged—literally, in the tens-of-thousands—so year after year she was grounded. We'd be out playing or working, and she'd be in her room writing sentences, or inside doing chores. She was constantly at risk of being accused of one offense or another, for not doing something exactly as my mother would, or for just simply Being.

Later in life, she'd spend many years in therapy, and it's remarkable she didn't end up completely warped in the process of growing up in the deep end of this toxic environment. My sister's treatment haunts us still; in a family devoid of bonds, it lends a tragically unpleasant semblance of one: We'd all like to flush that insanity away into the furthest recesses of the past.

My father, while not the perpetrator, failed to step forward in the midst of abuse visible enough to cause murmurs in town. Why didn't he stop my mother? I suspect he was hiding, too, from her storm of insecurity-driven need for control. He seemed not to be an introspective man by nature, and the culture of the Great Depression era in which he was raised certainly didn't condone inward-looking contemplation, especially in men.

Perhaps as a means of escape, he focused on his work, and when he could, his boat. All he wanted—all he needed to be happy—was a modest house, a boat, and a presentable wife, but he ended up with a well-poised, tremendously insecure woman with an ever-expanding need to impress and be right, at whatever cost, to herself and those around her.

What is clear, though, is that he did the best he could, given the circumstance and emotional tools at his disposal in those days. It warms my heart to know that in his remarried life, he's found a great deal more warmth, and opportunity for another sort of redo. My brother, Christopher, wrote recently: *I think of him now with his Down's Syndrome grandchild—the two madly love each other and the interaction between them brings tears of joy.*

Walking home from school on a fall day in the sixth grade, kicking the long piles of windblown leaves drifted along stonewalls and picket fences, I was lost in thought. For four years I'd been routinely frustrated, embarrassed, and humiliated by the unpredictability of my speech. If I could just understand what caused it, maybe I could change something and make it better. It was a slippery, terrifying issue to contemplate, but I had to know: *Was it psychological or physiological?* Maybe there was hope if it was one or the other.

Feeling around inside me, I tried to find the glitch that turned sounds into walls. But it wasn't precisely in my mind, or my body, either; when I focused on one, it seemed to be partly in the other. It was simply too nuanced and complex to get a hold of, and there seemed to be no way out—except for the faint hope that in the sea change from there to adulthood, it might be outgrown.

Back in the recesses—born of hope, and perhaps some foresight—I had a hazy vision of adulthood, wherein I was, in a way, someone else— someone who didn't stutter at all. Every now and then, a gauzy glimpse of speaking fluidly to an audience floated through...

A good deal of the time, I lived in terror of the next sound wall. Speaking was like walking down the street, having a transparent wall suddenly show up right in front of me, and walking straight into it. Sometimes, I'd catch a glimpse of it just in time and get around it by choosing another word that seemed easier to say. This often worked, but at times it spun me off into convoluted rephrasing. I never told jokes, because the focus on the punch line guaranteed my vocal chords would lock up. The safest thing was to simply not talk unless I had to.

My mind would reel with the answers I didn't give in class and the conversations I shied from, or were shattered midway. So I quieted my frustrations by revisiting the situation later, saying it to myself just the way I would've wanted. Even though it was after the fact and silent, it lent some dignity to my flailing sense of communication. And if there were an essential part of me that didn't know the difference between encounters in the physical world and those imagined, I wanted to give this innocent part of me a gift of the experience beyond the splintering concerns of fluency.

Many years later, I asked my mother why she'd sent my older brother to a speech therapist when he'd started stuttering just two years ahead of me—but not me. She said she simply didn't notice I had a problem—that the first time it came to her attention was when a family friend pointed it out. I knew from those difficult years in her home how emotionally detached and controlling she was, but it was still shocking as an adult to hear that any mother could be so out of touch with a child who was very much in her vicinity. It left me speechless; I didn't bother to ask why she didn't help me then, after her friend had told her.

There had been whispers in the family closet over the years of a nervous breakdown in 1967, yet my father says she changed from one day to the next—that she was suddenly righteous and controlling. But there's a ghost in the closet, too: I remember all of us kids being terrified of the third floor of the house we'd moved to in town, and especially of the oil portrait of Mrs. Burl that still hung in one of those small rooms. We shivered in the stern presence that seemed to be watching us from the wall, and I wonder now if the deceased Mrs. Burl had a personality like what my mother's became.

My older sister, Marie, remembers a different mother before then—one warm and fun and loving. I have one tender memory that especially comes to mind: As we were sitting on a wooden pew in church, I wrapped my six-year-old hand around my mother's thin-gloved thumb, felt the warmth of the soft, smooth leather. She placed her other hand over mine; I looked up as she gazed over at me for a moment, love streaming from her eyes.

Once, in the field next door,
I flew a kite so high
it became just barely a speck
against the blue and white-streaked sky.
The string was so long,
its weight pulled it into a bellied curve
that seemed like a lesson in levitation.

Space at the end of the string;
gravity calling me home to dinner.

Rummage Tale

The neighbor's chickens cluck their way down the steps and through the gardens, interjecting their rummaging into mine. Their priority list seems to be short and to the point: 1.) find insects among the fallen leaves, and 2.) avoid humans at all cost. You'd think by the way they scatter at the slightest movement they're afraid that out of the blue, one of us is going to grab them, ring their feathery necks and eat them... Which, come to think of it, is not an unreasonable concern at all here in Indonesia.

Jolted from the stream of memories and impressions, I take off the reading glasses, and rub my eyes. I've rarely peeled back the layers of time and delved into the recesses of those at-times wondrous, often hell-tinged days. It's been a long time, too, since I recalled my childhood wish to become someone who wouldn't stutter; I want to reach back to him, hold him, and whisper: *You may find this hard to believe, but what terrifies you now turns out to be a hidden treasure. You get your wish, and so much more.*

Amid squawking and scurrying, I make my way to the small, open-air kitchen building that elevates food preparation to a few notches above camping, and make tea, grateful for the simplicity. While it steeps, I lean against the doorjamb, soaking in the flowering trees and dragonflies navigating the warm, moist air. I'm feeling grateful, too, for the ability to speak—and the solitude in which I don't have to.

These days, I'm focused on just Being—not getting caught up in the sometimes random, sometimes repetitive treadmill of mind—as much as possible, but reaching back and unearthing the past has opened a mental spigot. It leaves me to deal with the cascading thoughts and feelings, and I feel blessed for the sanctuary of silence and stillness I've found within—and which is reflected, too, all around me.

Tea in hand, I leave my sandals on the steps of the veranda and take up my writing post on the pillow-laden, bamboo lounge. Settling in, I find the stream of past where I left it, and immerse myself again. In this reaching back, I want to dash right through the more unpleasant childhood circumstances—giving a broad sense of them, but leaving the grittier parts in the dark. As I search around inside, I realize the concern is not about being unwilling to look directly at them, but about setting up an unpleasant experience for the reader.

I sit back and look at the scope of what I'm doing more objectively: The calling of the moment is to pluck out those bits relevant to the later unfolding, and from this bird's-eye-view, I see that one can't very well describe a spectrum of Being with the verity of one end missing. And how does one share the joy of passing through the doorway of suffering without describing the darker side of the portal?

Schism Stew

My siblings and I were certainly well provided for in a material sense, in the form of nice houses, cars, boats, and so on. But the experience of family and community—which one would hope would lay at least a reasonably healthy foundation for one's relationship with humanity at large—was squelched into an ethic of duty and productivity. As kids, we used to joke about the five of us being the *child unit*: We received virtually no individual attention unless it involved a work project, or unless we were being singled out for some infraction of the well-laid-out rules.

My father never did get our names straight—he'd go through the list until our eyes lit up in recognition of our own. We did our best to get ourselves out of eyesight as much as we could to avoid being drafted for more work; one reason I loved the fields and woods so much was that I could be out of earshot, too.

Being raised in a family headed by what could've been a poster-couple for Type-A personality meant taking on a good deal of responsibility at a young age, and this meant there wasn't much time for exploring the natural world. When we were younger, there were go-carts to be built and raced down the neighborhood hills, apple fights to be waged, and kickball games with brothers and the neighborhood kids, but by the time we were preadolescent, we were expected to do much more than the usual chores. In our house, we only used the word *bored* once, as we quickly learned its utterance was tantamount to daring to be given a long list of productive things to do.

We always moved to old houses in need of a lot of work, and we kids were trained in all aspects of remodeling. We didn't just help out: In most respects, we *were* the crew. My parents were big believers in instilling basic values, and for them, a strong work ethic and respect for the worth of money were central.

Chores were considered household duties, and we were expected to come directly home from school and work the two hours we *"owed the household."* As my parents were especially keen on addressing values around work and money, we were compensated nominally for any work beyond chores, and were expected to do some of that after

Germination

chores and on weekends. By about the age of twelve, we were also expected to pay for our own clothes and personal care items.

It was a rather Old World upbringing: We were apprenticed at home, and raised from an early an age with as many skills as possible—evidently, so that in the event of something fatal happening to our parents, we would be of use in the community. It was an obviously outmoded Dickensian vision applied to mid-twentieth century America, and I imagined myself taken in by the local blacksmith—not that I knew of one—and given room and board in trade for my labors.

I had plenty of experience under my belt when I was given some paint and rolls of wallpaper and told to *go do the kids' bathroom.* I was twelve years old, and needed no supervision.

There was no room for slacking. A neighbor once commented with amazement to my mother that we worked just as hard even when she wasn't around. The neighbor had no idea of the underlying reality: It was just so much easier to have the work done; not producing sufficiently was a kind of sin in the family.

Around the age of twelve, I made the radical suggestion, *Maybe we weren't put on this planet to work all the time.* I remember as the words were coming out of my mouth, being quite sure I sounded like a hippie to the rest of the family. We didn't actually work *all the time*, but what I really yearned for was unstructured time—room for exploring and absorbing—and some choice about how much of my time I sold to the household. I paid for my heresy by being considered lazy from then on, and became the butt of an endless stream of laziness jokes.

My mother—strong-minded and efficient—headed up the renovations. An extraordinarily creative perfectionist for whom "good enough" rarely was, she drove us nearly mad with her overseeing of every detail. It was an excruciating training in doing things right which would serve us well in our working lives later on, but at enormous emotional cost at the time. With the focus relentlessly on getting the work done, any ramifications for parent-child relations weren't even secondary—they simply didn't factor in at all. We had far more of a working relationship with our parents than an emotional one, and what emotion existed for us kids roiled in resentment. They were so focused on, and busy with, each project, there was time and energy only for preparing us to be competent, productive workers: what they would have called *"contributing members of society."* They did their best with the parental modeling with which they'd been brought up, but in the process, they raised five emotional orphans.

If I had a nickel for every time my mother accused me of being too sensitive, I'd have... well, quite a pile of nickels. In her old-school approach to parenting, it was her duty to toughen us up in preparation for being on our own. I remember wondering how a person could possibly be *too sensitive*; in the woods and fields, I was always trying to see more, hear more, sense more in every way I could. I wanted to experience what was beyond the obvious, and clearly, "toughening up" was worse than no help at all.

It seemed that too much sensitivity was only a problem when it involved people. Somewhere along the way, it occurred to me that sensitivity itself wasn't the issue—more inclusiveness always seemed better than less, even if it was at times distasteful. It seemed what we *did* with the information was what led to problems.

So as a child, I tried to be as open as I could inwardly, and to the natural world—which was, blessedly, in abundance all around— while fending off the boot-camp-like attempts to get me in line with a properly cynical view of the world and its human occupants. Those deep bonds with my inner landscape, and with the seemingly infinite layers of nature in those years of psycho-emotional abuse became the foundation of my later work as an artist.

My father, an unrepentant workaholic, was an inventor who drafted complex mechanical beasts of stainless steel in the office he kept at home. He had a prototype and small-production shop—which

Germination

we called *the plant*—and we were required to work there, too. While I disliked working on the houses, I detested the plant. Housed in a concrete-block building, the confluence of cold, hard materials; acrid stench of metal-cutting blades; and gritty gray film coating everything was diametrically opposed to my nature. Every moment spent there felt like a prison sentence.

On a break one day while working at the plant, I was standing on the loading dock; leaning against the block wall, I stared into the woods behind the building. From this threshold, with the harsh, metallic world behind, and the soft realm of wood ahead, I felt my essence.

A thought raced up from the subconscious as if riding the end of a long, lean whip: *I feel like a girl in this hard place.* It was the terrifying truth, and I did what most any twelve-year-old boy would do: I folded it up and stuffed it back down where it came from. But it wouldn't fit neatly away. Instead, it lurked about in my mind—for the most part keeping to the shadows, yet ready to leap out whenever there was corroborating evidence.

Landscape maintenance was headed-up by my father. With five acres of grass and numerous mature maple and oak trees, it was a considerable undertaking. My brothers and I did the mowing, weeding, and watering individually, but when it came time in late autumn to clean up the fallen leaves, we'd all join in.

We were gathering one morning for this epic project, and I was not in a good mood—which at first I thought was due to the crew work being anything but fun. But then, while getting some tools in the garage, part of a dream from the night before swept through me: *I was a grown woman. There were no clothes covering me, and I reached up and cupped my breasts; it was natural to have them, and they were part of a body that felt deeply familiar and exquisitely connected to the earth.*

The image faded, leaving me standing in the garage feeling

profoundly sad: I wouldn't grow up to be that. I was impossibly far away from what felt so natural, so right. What would have been just a sexy dream for most boys left me feeling exiled from my true nature. I tried to bury this, too, but it had cut straight to the core.

My inner world was getting complex; something else out of the norm was now going on, but my conscious mind just wasn't ready, or able, to deal with it. At the time, I had no idea these strange stirrings weren't unique to me—that I had a good deal of company dating back to prehistory—or that the culture at large was struggling with its own sexual awakening. I pulled myself together, joined the others in the yard, and merged with the work.

Every couple of weeks, my mother would drive the green Ford station wagon to the IGA supermarket and drop me off with a grocery list a foot long, and a signed blank check. I'd fill a couple of carts to the brim shopping for the seven of us, then call her to pick me up when I started to check out.

There was a rack of mostly rock-n-roll albums near the registers, and I'd leave time to sidle up to this window into worlds utterly alien to my rural life—alien, yet disconcertingly familiar. David Bowie's *The Man Who Sold The World* and his later *Hunky Dory* rocked my little world with images of a man basking in the feminine. I'd never seen anything like this. Part of me echoed the culture of the time and town, thinking, *What a faggot!* while another—far deeper and truer—was tantalized to the bone.

There was evidence on public display that said I wasn't alone. And the unabashedly mascara-laden image of Lou Reed on the cover of *Transformer* was backed up by the lyrics. *Walk on the Wild Side* was like a megaphone aimed straight at my ear, telling me I had company at that frightening edge. When it played on the radio once in a while, it felt like an anthem, while at the same time an invitation to queasy discomfort. I certainly wasn't alone in this, either.

Germination

Gatekeeper

I was blessed with the gift of an inborn sensibility that knew to play gatekeeper to my sensitivity—to protect my openness to What Is—and ward off any encroachments as best I could. Holding onto this opening was certainly at odds with the intense separation my siblings and I felt from an even remotely healthy foundation of family and community. It was as if I were standing beside an insurmountable wall between me and human belonging, and instead of futilely beating on it, I turned away and focused on what else the world had to offer.

I have no doubt I chose well, given that an experience of healthy family connection was clearly not forthcoming, and becoming less sensitive would have meant separation from my own essence, as well. In this semi-conscious choosing, I accepted the nature of What Is, and placed my attention on connecting with the natural forces fueling and nurturing my spirit. What I preserved back then later blossomed into the wellspring of my artistry, which has been my therapy. My path, too, around the wall of separation to the back door of community, and humanity at large.

We all have our work here in this difficult world, and what comes easily to one person may be a life's journey for another. I may never know to what degree solitude is simply inherent in my nature, but I do know its sanctuary has been a balm most sublime for the wounds of the past. While I'm certain I'll always turn to aloneness as a cherished respite, it's this pattern of self-protective retraction inherited from childhood that has called for healing and opening.

By the grace of contemplative meditation—the studio of the conscious heart—I've felt the calling to What Is, beyond the patterns engrained by the onslaught of unpleasant circumstance. Yet I know by the gift of self-compassion, there is no given amount to which I *must* unfold, and the degree to which I've already opened cannot be measured by some objective standard, because there is none—nor is such a thing relevant.

What matters is *that* I open in the moment, and thereby release my Self in even the smallest ways beyond the confines of retraction. In this blessed unraveling, I've found landscapes ever a bit larger, spaciousness all the nearer, and warmth of deeper connection like glowing coals.

Midwest Transplant

In the early Seventies, my father sold his business and began designing machinery for larger companies. Although none of us was particularly excited about the destination, we moved in 1973 from central Massachusetts to the Midwest. For my parents, both of whom were born and raised in the countryside, Omaha provided the kind of exposure and opportunity a small town simply couldn't. For me, the upside was that the wretched metal shop was gone forever; the downside was so, too, were the woods and fields.

I'd lost my refuge, and entered a terrifyingly unfamiliar social environment for my last year of middle school. To make matters worse, I was placed in a single-sex Catholic high school—which might not have been so bad, except it was the wrong sex. Surrounded by boys and priests, I was suffocating, feeling like an imposter sentenced to showing up for incarceration for a major portion of each day. When the guys bragged about their sexual conquests, or made rude comments about girls, I played along, not wanting them to know I found it all sad and depressing... I just couldn't help but hear them from the girls' point of view.

Having been raised with tools instead of sports equipment, I also lacked another essential way of bonding in the male world. I could wield a hammer for hours on end with considerable accuracy, but I lacked practice with hitting a moving object, and hadn't a clue what the rules of the games were. In touch football, they'd say, *Ok, you rush,* and while it was clear speed was involved, I hadn't a clue as to where to apply it, or for what purpose, and being seen as not knowing undermined one's masculinity. Needless to say, gym class was a nightmare of alienation and improvisation.

In all my male-bodied life, the only information I received about being masculine was in the negative: *Don't act like a girl. Don't say the kinds of things a girl would say. Don't move like a girl.* This wasn't communicated explicitly, but it was enforced by peer pressure, with teasing for even the smallest infractions. I was a good actor—and wasn't effeminate anyway—so passing as a regular boy wasn't difficult. But as I grew into adolescence, I was desperate at times for female expression, and it erupted in the only way it could—in my sexuality.

A considerable schism was forming by then between my inner and outer lives. The threat of stuttering had made me extremely self-conscious, so I tended to keep to myself. I liked girls very much, but my contact was pretty much limited to high-anxiety situations like school dances, and I had no idea what to do or say—even if I could get the words out. With my hormones raging, I did what most boys do: I masturbated a lot. At least in that fantasy world, I got to dress as a girl and have sex with them, too.

The only times the gender aspect of my inner and outer worlds met was when I cross-dressed—which was always in private, and rarely unhurried. But in those heightened moments, I felt a condensed sort of exquisiteness as the fabric touched my skin, and as the more fluid and revealing styles brought out my more female traits.

It was spellbindingly exciting to be so readily propelled to an attractive female version of me—though it was painful, too, because in feeling so close, I also felt most intensely the reality of separation from the form of my true nature. There was an uncomfortably compulsive drive to it: I'd feel a nearly overwhelming urge to play out my female side, but as soon as I had an orgasm, my ordinary consciousness took over, and I just wanted to put this part of myself away and not deal with it.

A cyclical pattern had developed: I'd go through a period of perhaps a couple or a few months of relative quiet when masturbating was enough of a release, then an intense phase, when a much deeper longing blazed through my whole Being. While these daunting times were extremely stimulating sexually, they were mostly a torturous burden.

My inner world was stirring—pushing at its boundaries—and wouldn't settle back into the recesses of my Being. During these phases, it seemed as if my secret world was hemorrhaging into ordinary life. I felt helpless, haunted by longing and despair. There was little to do but live with it, and wait for the tide to recede—for a while.

There was no one to turn to during these difficult times. At one such moment, I felt as if I were coming apart at the seams, and though I should have known better, I spontaneously turned to my mother one afternoon and told her I needed to talk. That alone provides a good sense of my desperate state of mind. She sat right down on the couch and said, *What is it?... You have five minutes*, without so much as a hint of concern.

Never mind, I said, *it's not important.* I wasn't at all surprised that she didn't register my pain and distress. Even with the emotional upheaval, I was actually relieved when she just stood up and walked away. I had no idea what I was going to say, and looking back, it was undoubtedly better for me it didn't get said.

The stuttering, too, cycled through phases of severity, and like the longing for femaleness, it never went away completely. It seemed natural they'd cycle together—especially with the increased anxiety during the times of longing. Perhaps if logic ruled in these realms they'd have meshed, but they had their own transitions, like weather in a difficult climate.

In moments of profound despair, I imagined flying away, and envied birds for their wings; I'd see them outstretched and feel the friction of air across them. I ached for their freedom to float on air to some better place. My oldest brother was away at college in California, and I envied him, too. I knew there would come a time to stretch out into a life on my own terms; but in the wash of teenage angst and hormones, it seemed like some other life altogether—one eternally far away.

With the house renovation project completed, I started landscaping for some neighbors. It was wonderful to spend time outdoors working with growing things, but the primary motivation was to get away from the house. My mother's obsessive need to be in control of herself and her environment left only slivers of room for us, and I often felt as if I were perched in her world.

There was a green plastic refrigerator magnet with gold-colored letters that pretty well summed things up: *The Golden Rule: He Who Has the Gold, Makes the Rules*. My mother thought it was quite amusing, which was not at all surprising since it reflected her philosophy quite nicely. It was her house, and she ruled it; if that didn't work for us, we should simply leave. To the degree I reasonably could, I did, and the positive response I got from the landscaping was truly refreshing. It was hard work, but it was under a wide-open sky, I felt appreciated and, best of all, no one was standing over me.

My parents consulted with each other on most everything, and it was decided—I'm sure at my mother's prompting—that my father should make some effort to connect with me, so I was assigned to crew for him on his two-person, Olympic-class sailboat. Behind his quiet exterior, he was quite competitive, and racing even in cold weather was his own sort of heaven. We were to race every other Sunday, and while this might objectively sound like fun, in my mind's eye, I saw two wisps of smoke rising from the right hand side of the calendar—two perfectly good days every month gone up in flames.

We'd set off like two strangers for the man-made lake set improbably in a flat, nearly treeless landscape. An hour-and-a-half later, we'd arrive and start assembling the boat, knowing nothing more about each other than when we'd left. He was emotionally unavailable and devoid of interest in me or in sharing himself; I felt like a squirrelly little alien around him, and had no idea where to start in connecting with him even if I'd wanted to try.

We seemed to have nothing in common—even after we nearly drowned together when the centerboard broke mid-race in high wind and waves, flipping the boat over and trapping us underwater in the mast shrouds. It didn't help that as far as I was concerned, the best part about sailing was coming ashore and putting on warm, dry clothes. We talked a little on the way down and back, but I have no recollection of anything we said. I vaguely recall an award ceremony in which we won something—he was a well-studied, excellent sailor—but at the end of the season we went about our lives as if the outings had never happened.

The one memory I have of being close with my father also had to do with water, which he loved being around. In the green hills of Massachusetts, we belonged to a boating club at a tree-lined lake, which had floating docks that led out to the slips where the boats were kept. The water on the outer side of the docks was well over my head, and I was terrified of it without a life jacket.

I'm perhaps six or seven: I see my father swimming on the deep side, and then I'm on his back with my arms around his neck having the best ride ever—feeling joyously safe as the water laps against us, and deliciously special, indeed.

Eastern Light

After three years of icebox winters and oven-hot summers in Omaha, my parents took a trip back East and visited Cape Cod—the long, thin part of Massachusetts which looks on a map like an arm flexing out into the Atlantic Ocean. They returned with the news that they'd bought a big old house by the water. As far as the two remaining brothers and I were concerned, we'd hit the jackpot: Living right at the ocean on beautiful Cape Cod was about as good as it could get. Except, of course, for the fact that we would still have to live in a cauldron of familial dysfunction.

We packed as the school year ended, and left for the Cape when it was through. I had a driver's license for all of four months when I got in my car and followed my father's to the East Coast. This was long before the advent of cell phones, and there were some really frightening moments on the way, such as driving through Chicago in the pouring rain at the tail end of dusk, knowing full well there was only the flimsiest contingency plan if we should get separated.

As we pulled into a rest area on the Cape, I wondered why we were stopping so close to our destination. We stepped out of our cars into the brilliant afternoon sun and briny air, and he said that he just wanted to tell me I'd done a great job of driving. I could see he was proud of me, and that I'd climbed a notch or two in his estimation. It's the only time I recall of him making a point of complimenting me.

With the help of a small crew of hired help, we renovated the house on the Cape over the summer. The work was a good distraction from my worries about the upcoming school year: I didn't know if I'd be in a stuttering phase, or how I'd fare socially at a coed public school.

The crew needed a gofer—as in "go fer this"—and I was very happy with the assignment, which got me out of the house and familiarized with the layout of the nearby towns. And since coming back with the right things was critical, the job entailed learning in detail about parts and materials for the electrical and plumbing trades, which served very well later. As always, we worked hard, but the seaside landscape was fabulous. It was, after all, a prime vacation spot, and we had front row seats on the water in a town so cute you could almost take postcard pictures blindfolded.

While the natural environment was spectacular, the social one at school was less inviting. When I arrived there in my junior year, the social cliques had long been formed. The new students gravitated toward the same lunch table and became an informal outcast support group, although, for the most part, we had little in common besides our recent immigrant status. Bill, whose family had just moved from Boston, was an exception. We hit it off right away, and formed a friendship that remained long after the group had dissolved into the social fabric.

He had the nicest sounding car stereo system I'd ever heard, and great music on high-quality cassette tapes. At the mention of eight-track tapes, he rolled his eyes, shook his head, and slid in a cassette. Crosby, Stills, Nash, and Young filled his little Capri with a depth and brilliance that had me instantly grinning and moving to the beat. Bill was much worldlier than I, and I think he enjoyed blowing down some of the walls of my sheltered life. I wouldn't have seen films like *Slaughterhouse Five* or *A Clockwork Orange* if he hadn't suggested going.

The quality of interaction in Bill's family was a revelation. I didn't have much contact with them, but I could tell from the way he spoke of his siblings and parents with warmth and appreciation, that they were close. His parents actually spoke to him as a person with feelings and concerns, and they shared their own. This could hardly have been more different from the authoritarian regime at home, and while the contrast was both stunning and saddening, it was still a fine glimpse of something much healthier.

Germination

My world was opening up, but I still had no idea how to relate with girls, and they seemed to have no interest in me. I certainly wasn't exuding sexual energy—at least not any they recognized. With a backlog of unexpressed femaleness, I had little enthusiasm for my male side. Besides the fact that being sexually assertive was simply alien to my nature, it didn't help that my year-and-a-half older brother was precisely the opposite. He'd circle like a bird of prey any attractive girl in his vicinity, and with his gift for jabber and a shiny, fast Camaro, I didn't stand a chance.

Paired with the conundrum of my sexuality and identity, were nice old-fashioned romantic ideals: You meet a nice girl, become friends, fall in love, and *then* make love. Those values alone were apparently enough to get me relegated to the "Friends" category on a permanent basis. Or, perhaps they thought I was gay—they wouldn't have been alone.

One night, Bill came by, and we headed into town in my car. When we got back to the house, we sat and talked in the car for a while until it got close to my curfew. I needed to be there early, as an alarm clock would be set for midnight outside my mother's bedroom door; if I didn't shut it off, and she had to get up, there would be, as she put it, *hell to pay*. I went in and started heading up the stairs, but was surprised to see her coming down. *What were you doing out there?* she wanted to know. Apparently, she'd been watching, but the bush by the car had blocked her view.

I was talking to Billy, I said cautiously, still a little buzzed from partying. I didn't want to say anything more than I had to. *Bill-y?* she taunted, smirking. I was really uncomfortable with where this was going. *That's what his family calls him*, I said, climbing up past her to my room, *and it's how he introduces himself sometimes.*

Are you sure about that? she retorted. As far as she was concerned, she had me figured out; anything more I might say would be construed as proof of her suspicions. She seemed to me right then like a cat playing with what she saw as a captured mouse.

The incident ricocheted through me for weeks. My hormones were raging, and I was perplexed enough as it was. I'd always been without support—emotionally, and for who I was in general—but my sexuality was part of my private, vulnerable inner world, and the person with whom I felt most unsafe had mocked it. I was used to protecting myself from her, but this time, I didn't see it coming.

My mother's jab got me wondering if I was so bothered by it because it might be true: While my sexuality clearly wasn't in the realm of expectation, I had no sense of its parameters. *What if I were attracted to men?* I decided to test the possibility the best way I knew, and if it were true, I would just accept it and deal with it. I figured that if it made me happy... well then, I'd be happy.

So the next few times I masturbated, I got myself excited, then conjured up the sexiest fantasies of men I could muster. But they just didn't do anything for me, and the excitement tapered right off. *Well*, I thought, *at least that's one attraction I don't have to be concerned about.*

Back in Omaha, I'd started playing the guitar, and this provided a connection with some musicians at school on the Cape. It became increasingly clear, though, that I had far greater enthusiasm for it than actual talent. At first I tried playing with them, but their abilities so outstripped mine it was just embarrassing. I soon stopped, and just hung out and partied with them in the little time I was allowed for socializing.

It wasn't easy to acknowledge, but I learned that being really good at some things is more than a matter of practice—they also require a deep, natural affinity. I'd tried playing the drums, too, and it was obvious I didn't have that sort of affinity with playing musical instruments. Disappointing as it was, coming face-to-face with the fact sooner, rather than later, was a relief: I could relax, enjoy the occasional rock star fantasy, and move on to exploring other things.

I graduated from high school without having joined a club, gone to a prom, or had a girlfriend. When I didn't go to the graduation ceremony, I was still a virgin, and it seemed quite likely I'd be one yet heading off to college in the fall. In the meantime, the landscaping business I'd started the summer before kept me occupied, outdoors, and out of the house.

On a weekend night, I'd usually go to a club to dance and, more importantly, explore the possibility of seceding from my virginal state. If that had been the sole purpose, it could have been arranged in some down and dirty fashion well before, but I still had visions of romantic love—and a first romp complete with emotional fireworks. Having figured out how to ask girls to dance, I was having difficulty with the next step—yelling small talk over the thumping music. There were two things working against me: small talk didn't come easily, and the big red "*V*" on my forehead.

Midway through the summer, I met a cute girl named Cindy who either didn't notice these setbacks, thought they were oddly attractive, or was kind enough to ignore them. I went home that night from the dance club with her name and number in her impossibly neat handwriting on a cocktail napkin tucked proudly in my pocket.

Cindy loved the color yellow; she liked sex even more. We went to a party where my friends were playing, and I lost my virginity among the amplifiers and instrument cases in a tiny room in which the only piece of furniture was a twin bed. It wasn't what one would necessarily think of as a romantic setting, but if I'd wanted to announce it to the world, there was at hand the equipment to reach at least half the town. That summer was a delightful period of making up for the loving touch I'd long been missing.

Gestation

The eight months I've been here in Ubud, Bali were initially a time of recovery from the wrenching two years it took to set up the conditions for this new life, but as the experience has deepened, it's become as well a healing from the prior forty-seven altogether. Going on nine months now, I'm rounding out what my British friend, Abi, might call a "proper" period of gestation, which seems to be unfolding on its own regardless of my not knowing what it's actually opening toward. And I'm blessed in not having to know right now how long this rebirthing will go on.

Amid the unknown pervading these thankfully open-ended days, I can say this with certainty: I'm blessed now with more clarity than I've ever had, I have a story to tell, and if I'm reading the intuitive impulses in my belly well, telling it has a great deal to do with what comes next.

Of the five basic elements—Earth, Fire, Water, Air, and Space—I've always been especially drawn by the spirit of my nature to the more rarefied ones: Air and Space. Feeling connected with the sky is important to me, but even more so the quintessence, or Space—the essence that permeates all the elements, all of nature. And for the ancients—who called it *Ether*—the heavens.

Yet, as I will share, while by nature I turn to Sky, by self-nurture, I've sought to ground myself—to feel a sense of connection and home in the solidity of Earth—though at times at the expense of my more flighted nature. I'm drawn at my core to a sense of balance, so I'm not surprised to find myself now in a kind of tropical sanctuary that feels as much of Earth as Air, gently embraces Fire and Water, and revels in wafting Ether.

There are plenty of places I could stay which have much more expansive views of rice fields, the volcano to the northeast, or the ocean to the south. But I found by serendipity a relatively quiet, more nestled place off Monkey Forest Road that lends itself very nicely to this process of gestation.

I rent the downstairs room and bath in a two-story, ornately Balinese building from a woman who spends most of the year traveling the world doing healing work with the sound of crystal bowls, and the whole place just resonates with good feeling. It's set into land sloping down to a small river, so my space feels like it's partially underground, though there's a large stonewall holding back the land in the rear. All around, large flowering trees, vines, and palm fronds form a jagged green shroud dotted with riots of colored flowers against Sky.

Between the shafts of brilliant tropical light that make their way around and through the plants and into the windows of my room, and the stones and shadows all around, there's a palpable balance of Sky and Earth that embraces my Being with vast Space. I feel sublimely held while I pupate toward lighter ways, as if I were a long-sought substance in a cosmic artist's hands.

□ □ □

Emancipation Approximation

In September of my eighteenth year, I went ecstatically off to college in western Massachusetts, arriving with some clothes, a few personal items, and a small mountain of psycho-emotional baggage with which to start a new life. I'd escaped the constrictions of home, but the left-brained coursework and intensely public life in the dorms were anything but fertile ground for the personal exploration I was quietly craving. It wasn't the wide-open emancipation I'd long dreamt of, but it was nonetheless a euphoric liberation.

There's no better indication of just how divorced I was then from my true nature than having signed up for the Business and Finance Program. It's hardly surprising, considering my family's entrepreneurial inclinations, the emphasis on pragmatism and money with which I was raised, and that it was the path of least resistance with my parents. But I still find the fact of it astonishing; I remember sensing my spirit, but having little sense of how to *live* it. This choice stands as a poignant marker on a landscape of What Might Have Been, and the vast spectrum of transformation between then and now is certainly one of my essential blessings.

With a four-and-a-half hour drive between us, visits with Cindy were sporadic. When we finally did get together, the backlog of desire poured out in marathon lovemaking sessions. For someone who'd never been allowed to sleep in, spending an entire day in bed—with delightful company—was a novelty of the loveliest sort. It's hard to think of her without hearing Leon Russell's sultry, raspy twang—we must have played *Lady Blue* hundreds of times.

I don't recall any variation I came up with that she wasn't up to trying, including my long-fantasized cross-dressing and having sex with a girl. As far as she was concerned, it was just good, kinky fun. I didn't dare tell her there was more to it for me—but then, I barely admitted this even to myself.

After a couple of years, I ended the relationship because she obviously wanted children, I didn't, and it seemed unfair to go on with it as if I might eventually give her what she desired. I knew in my heart what I really wanted—even if it was terrifying to glimpse—and she and that were worlds apart. In choosing an open-ended future, I broke her puppy-loving heart, and set myself up for a wide span of aloneness.

On Halloween of senior year, a bunch of us got together to dress up before going to some parties. I wanted to be an androgyne, so a friend's girlfriend volunteered to help with some makeup to offset my rather male-ish costume. Having had plenty of practice, I could have done it myself, but I went along with her offer, not wanting them to know. Besides, having a girl put it on was a novelty not to be passed up. She looked at my face—turning it from side to side—before deciding what she'd do.

After studying it briefly, she exclaimed: *You have such makeup-able eyes!* I mumbled something lame after a few moments like, *Oh, yeah?—*

trying to mask its cutting right to my essence, and revealing what I already knew to be true: When I cross-dressed, I actually looked nice. Liking the way I looked as a girl made it particularly painful because—as I'd experienced in cross-dressing alone—what appeared then to be so close felt all the further away. I pulled away from that emotional black hole almost as soon as it appeared, gathered myself, and focused on not appearing to enjoy the transformation as much as I did.

I was used to not connecting well at parties, but at least this night it was easy to understand why: People seemed not to know what to make of me, or how to interact with a person of indeterminate sex. Besides being outright androgynous in appearance, I can only imagine the mixture of energy I was exuding on my first venture out in drag— even if it was just quasi-drag.

Later, I went back to the apartment and talked to my roommate until he sauntered off to bed. I sat there awhile, not wanting the license of the night to end—wanting just a little more time out of the cage. Finally, exhausted, I surrendered in a stream of warm water and soap in the bathroom sink, and collapsed into bed.

Were I to choose a single word for my internal state in college, it would be *haunted*. A couple of times, friends said they'd seen me on campus, but didn't say hello because I looked angry. I told them I wasn't angry—just thinking. I wonder now, though, if while I was concentrating on some intense stream of thought, my exterior betrayed the inner pain: a lurking sadness, usually submerged, but always present.

There were times of reprieve from the stuttering, when thoughts would flutter from my tongue without concern for stumbling, and moments not plagued by the bottomless longing: for a body quite unlike my own, and for a sense of belonging with another person. But these respites were like the silence between musical notes—fragile, and sure to be soon disquieted.

Looking back, it's hard to comprehend the extent of my denial, but since I was completely without support for who I truly was, it's not surprising it was there. Surely, a very tentative, semi-conscious part of me knew what I needed to do, yet the part of me that was most conscious, most in control, just couldn't see the way to it. This was long before the Internet, when there was no ready way to reach out and find others of like ilk. Just a fraction of the information and community available now would have been so helpful.

The waves of longing had been breaking through with greater intensity, and at one point I felt subsumed. Shrouded by my state of mind at the time, I can't quite place the year of one event: Obviously in need of some help, I decided to go to Health Services to talk to someone. I remember being on campus, heading up a slope in the direction of the building.

I never got there; somewhere short of it, I talked myself out of going. Maybe it was embarrassment, or perhaps I figured they wouldn't understand—or both. I'll never know if it would've done me some good.

囗 囗 囗

Finding the Warm Pool

In earlier years, I'd found my soul's sustenance with the wild things—they seemed a part of me, both in rooting me, and freeing me into the world and beyond. By the time I was well into college, I'd lost touch for the most part with that natural refuge, despite the university being surrounded by forests no more than a short drive away.

It was certainly a heady place, and while so much emphasis on academics was a distraction, it was a symptom of something deeper: I'd forgotten to find sanctuary in nature—in the essence of the raw, physical world—in part because I was losing my bearings with my own physicality, and amid the lack of privacy, my innate sensibility. Along with a growing visceral discomfort, I'd gradually withdrawn into my mind and the labyrinth of inconsonant feelings. In that retraction from my physical self, I had displaced the natural sense of wonder and grounding I'd gotten from being consciously in touch with, and through, my senses.

While I'd drawn a bit as a kid, the real germination of my creative life began rather obliquely sophomore year, and became the saving grace of those discombobulated college days—as well as my life in general. I was sharing an apartment with my older brother—who was in his senior year—and we'd each put away a little money over the summer so each semester we could do something we'd never done before. We bought an airbrushing kit that fall and took turns playing with it, but it was tricky to get good results at first, and he soon lost interest.

Starting with canvas boards, I eventually began painting murals on the apartment walls. The work was extraordinarily satisfying, especially in stark contrast to the dry, imagination-numbing business courses to which I was dragging myself. It was a shifting of tides, too, as I'd grown up in my brother's shadow in many regards. As a kid, he could draw amazing, original characters, and one would have naturally figured that if one of us were to become an artist, he would be the one. I was beginning to get a truer sense of myself.

Over the winter break junior year, I bussed tables at a restaurant in Florida. Clearing up from a tour bus group one day, I looked down at the tray heaped with plates and cups, and suddenly it was twenty years later. With my feet up on the desk in my office, I was leaning back in a chair with my hands clasped behind my head.

It was the end of the day; I was tired, and daydreaming about my life. A thought floated through: *I've never really been happy being in business... I should've been an artist.* A pile of dirty dishes appeared once more in front of me, and Rip Van Winkle-like, I was twenty years old again. There was still time to do things differently!

Back at school, I did some research into the Business Program and found a little-known variation called "General Business and *blank*," which allowed me to insert an Art Minor. Since I'd worked hard early on and completed nearly all the necessary business credits, the last year-and-a-half could be devoted primarily to art classes.

In the beginning, I thought the combination might make me more well-rounded, and bring a greater sense of connection with the other students. It did indeed engender more balance, but as it turned out, the business students already thought I was too funky, and the art students thought I was too straight-laced. Socially, I didn't feel like I belonged in either world, but I was at home in the visual arts.

Studying Color Theory literally changed my life. I was introduced by a gentle, heartful man of about fifty-five to a world alive with spectral energy. Leaving class one gleaming spring day late in the semester, I stepped outside into a world ablaze with color. As if a gray veil had been lifted, everything came alive in the context of the things around it. I could feel my eyes being pushed and pulled around the landscape by the chromatic relationships we'd been playing with for weeks.

Driving home, I must've looked like a lunatic, staring at everything as if I'd never seen it before. I didn't care—I was seeing with a kind of innocence I hadn't known since I was a kid in the woods and fields.

The art classes I was able to work into the program were a godsend in relating creatively with the world. Finally, I was formally introduced to a visual language that deepened and broadened the sense of wonder and connection I'd always felt in, and with, nature. I started to recognize that Being is underscored by relationship—layers and layers of relationship: between qualities of form, form and light, light and spirit, spirit and essence, and on and on.

This was a language where vocal chords weren't gatekeepers, and the affinity was obvious. After years of struggling with playing music—with little to show for the effort but disappointment—exploring the visual arts was like diving into a warm, welcoming pool.

When I was creating, I didn't envy the birds—I was flying, too. While I clearly had some talent, I knew at the time I was still a fledgling; and while I might soar later, I lacked the depth of maturity I knew was essential to take me to the most sublime heights. But this was a way there, and like the longing to be physically a woman, it was a deep, resonant calling to home.

By the time I graduated, most of the walls in my apartment were covered in murals. I can't help but see my life then as being a lot like that apartment: intensely worked on the inside, but separated in many respects from the world outside. By the end of senior year, I was starving for room to spread my wings and explore; I wanted to grow and mature so I'd have layers of living to create with, and from.

I wanted, as well, to move to a city with old architecture and a progressive feeling—a place with a palpable sense of possibility. Standing on a windy, frigid subway platform while visiting a friend in Boston, I made a choice between moving there and the far-off city of San Francisco.

Hub of Stillness

I'm a Northern being, born and raised with the assumption that the year betides with varying amounts of sun, degrees of temperature, and all that this variance implies: For considerable swathes of year, things grow or cease to, one bundles up or sheds clothing, one longs for some other part of the cycle, or senses a desired one slipping inevitably away. The circularity of its presence brings the wheel of time to one's yard, one's days—to the rhythms comprising one's years.

Nearly a year now of skirting the equatorial belt, I'm not missing the rainy cold I know is descending on the city I left behind, nor the soon-to-come blowing snows in those places of earlier times. But the ingrained longing remains; it finds new avenues, as when it hungers across space rather than time for that shining something other. Or it attaches itself to fleeting glimpses of distant landscapes in their splendor, often sidestepping quite neatly the difficulties and discomforts of those moments it draws upon. I wonder if the Great Beyond is rather like this far more even-keeled place of small fluctuations of thermometer, and gently somersaulting states of rain or little rain—the better to savor the variables from the simplicity of relatively level ground.

From this perch, those northern places seem of a different world altogether, but the tendency toward marking my stay in this earthly realm in terms of recurring rhythms remains. It seemed when I was there, that every autumn was my own reaping in this world, every winter I lay fallow with the soil, that every spring was a rebirthing, and every summer a too-short blossoming amid warmth and radiant light. The seasonal handgrips on the year are all but gone; I turn now to my inner landscape for a sense of what it would be if I were there, or to my own seasons of change here.

And so, without the cue of September's slanting light to signal, once again, the surrender of embracing warmth; or that of March to herald growth to come, I must sense the wheel within. In the silence, I feel the round by subtler bearings, sense the changes in the landscape of the heart. This is, at last, the season I most longed for, like a June day stretching out across, engulfing the whole calendar—a hub of stillness from which to look back, unwind, and respool those seminal turnings.

2

Go West

Bay Area Renaissance

San Francisco still had a big-town feel in the early Eighties, yet it comprised a delicious array of cultures, urban offerings, parks, ocean-side beauty, and so much more. I wanted worldly exposure, and here it was compactly packaged and served up in an oh-so mild climate. Much as I'd found a home in the visual arts, the city suited me well beyond my imaginings. The juxtaposition of old architecture and progressive attitudes was similar to Boston, but here it was so much gentler, more relaxed and open. There was clearly room to be your non-mainstream self—even if you weren't ready to be it.

Across the Golden Gate Bridge was the quieter hamlet of Sausalito. I quickly gravitated toward its small-town-by-the-sea setting, and rented a room from the first New Age person I'd ever knowingly met: a tall, lean guy about ten years older than I with a broad, kid-like smile and manner. Vulker was studying healing with herbs and acupuncture, and his worldliness had outfitted him with at least four languages.

The setting could hardly have been more delightful, as it was right on the small boardwalk with a backdrop of steep, green hills and a view out across the bay to the city. Some nights, San Francisco floated like a crown of jewels on glistening black waters; on others, the obscuring fog that poured through the Golden Gate in the evening left a diffused orb of golden light hovering just above the horizon.

Living with Vulker introduced whole new realms: I experienced for the first time what a healthy, organic, vegetarian diet looked and tasted like, and met adults the likes of which I'd never experienced. Soon after I moved in, we went to a place where people *really* danced. There was no alcohol, and no social pretense or need to get drunk to dance—just movement for the joy of it!

I loved to dance; it was blissfully freeing to leave my socks and shoes to the side and just fly in my body with a room full of happy people. One of my fondest memories of Vulker is him bent at the waist, arms outstretched to the back like wings, flying about the place like an African dancer around a fire.

As the music didn't completely dominate the space, it was much easier to talk to people there than in the dance clubs I was used to. I met middle-aged people who had a delighted sparkle in their eyes like children, and easy, loving smiles. On the way home, I kept talking about them enthusiastically until I realized Vulker was looking at me oddly. *What's the big deal?* he asked, *They're just...people.*

I explained that I'd never met adults before who were so vibrant—who still had a sense of wonder—and how those I'd known back East seemed so retracted and afraid to be happy. He shook his head as he took it in, and looked back over at me like I was some kind of refugee. I just shrugged and looked back out through the windshield, happy to have made it to this new, extraordinary place that lent a greater sense of home than I'd ever felt.

⬜ ⬜ ⬜

Focus on Light

After graduation, I'd gone to Florida to raise money for the move west, and worked the summer for my brother, who'd graduated two years earlier and become a contractor. A few months into my stay in San Francisco, those funds were quickly dwindling, so I fell back on some of the trade skills I'd learned at home: painting, paperhanging, and carpentry. I made decent money working part-time, and it provided freedom to explore while I got a clearer sense of what to do next.

I'd bought a good manual 35mm camera and was having a wonderful time searching out and recording snippets of this wonderful corner of the world, which was still percolating with visual delights from studying color theory. I was a regular customer at a little photography shop in the Marina district, where I'd drop off at least a couple of rolls of film a week for processing. The manager, who'd stand just outside the door smoking on his breaks, noticed the stepladder on my car one day and asked if I was interested in some painting work.

He introduced me to the owner of the shop, who had some projects at his home—most of which were pretty small. After those, however, I began painting the front of a two-story apartment building he owned. I'd barely begun when a stiff wind blew across the façade while I was up high on a ladder, and the prospect of being slammed down onto the concrete below frightened me to the bone. I immediately got down, put the equipment away, and went right over to the store to speak with him.

He knew I was a regular there, so I told him about my interest in photography, and that, having just graduated from college, I had too much to lose to be hanging off the sides of buildings. Then I asked him for a job at the store. He had a good laugh, appreciating the nerve it took to walk away from a project and immediately ask for a job—nerve I may not have had if I hadn't just been shaken-up on that ladder.

A few weeks later, a position opened up, and the paintbrushes went into retirement. While I had a good grasp of the basics of photography, there was a great deal to absorb about the various types and models of equipment. But this steep learning curve didn't bother me at all—I was like a kid who'd just gotten a job at the candy store.

There were opportunities for exploration around every corner in the Bay Area, and I was ready to absorb, often with camera in hand. I walked a lot, visiting the compact neighborhoods, marinas and junkyards, downtown, Chinatown, Golden Gate Park, the Marin Headlands, Mt. Tamalpais, and even the Haight-Ashbury neighborhood—epicenter of the Summer of Love I'd missed out on fifteen years before.

The camera lent a gentle sense of mission on what would otherwise have been interesting, but rambling outings. Lenses and film don't see the world as our eyes do, and learning the differences and how to compensate for them—or accentuate them—taught me a great deal about the subtleties of perception while getting to know my adopted city and its gorgeous surround.

Photography offered a way of seeing the world—and Being with it—that felt like an outgrowth of the childhood times in the forests and fields. It called for being present—for seeing beyond the names of things—and being in rhythm with what was around. It was a reminder of how shimmering, sacred light makes love with form and radiates beauty in revealing its essence. With the camera, I could try to frame a slice of this and hold it outside the arc of time, or make a record of the moment to reveal the arc of time around it. Only a small percentage of the images succeeded in this regard, but the true value was in the space that opened up inside me in trying.

In retrospect, this was my first real art practice. Art was woven into my life, and my life into it. I came to realize that—past the awkward initial stages of getting familiar with the tools and materials—it was truly a practice when it informed my perceptions outside the studio, and I could see what was happening in the studio paralleling the rhythms of my life. This open-ended, ongoing relationship with creative practice has been a calling to me ever since—a common thread through the range of mediums and solo journeying over the years.

Working at the store offered access to equipment I otherwise wouldn't have been able to afford, and gradually, I assembled a really fine kit of camera and darkroom gear. In a rarefied medium concerned with the recording of light, the equipment had a taut, practical kind of beauty, and I found working with it quite grounding. I'd always been drawn to a balance of Earth and Sky, and there was a harmony for me here in the density of glass and metal amid the gathering of airy light to sensitive film.

I thrived creatively in photography's balanced draw from both left and right sides of the brain—in its being a blend of science and art.

While I truly appreciate the wonders of digital photography, I loved the hands-on making of images in the darkroom. There is certainly an art to choosing where and on what to aim the camera, and on framing and composing in the viewfinder, but the variables involved in creating a beautiful negative image, then physically creating a positive image from it in the womb-like dusk of the darkroom was, for me, a large part of what made it an artful process and practice.

With the enormous range of variables involved, you had to understand and control the physicality of it to operate with reasonable predictability, and that was where the science came in. This foundation in physical form was crucial for me in the practice of inviting formless creative spirit to flow into the work.

Having dipped into photography out of a joy of sensing color, I had little initial interest in working in black-and-white. As I became increasingly drawn to light itself, however, the early seduction by color gave way to intrigue with aspects more of the formless sort. I loved that black-and-white—or more accurately, the exquisite spectrum of light and shadow—eliminated the prettiness of color to reveal the beauty and essence of light, and left visual space for the subtlety of spirit. It was the start of a life-long, creative exploration of an ageless question:

How do I evoke the presence of spirit in form?

By the time I started working at the photography store, the stuttering had pretty much dissipated, though it was always perched in the periphery—a potent form of mild terror at the ready. Answering the phone was always a challenge—as the store's name was a stutterer's nightmare—so I'd quietly repeat it under my breath to get the vocal chords vibrating before I began to speak aloud. Behind the counter, I knew the equipment well enough to talk around any sound walls I saw coming.

I sought out the help of a speech therapist, and met with one who wasn't especially helpful in terms of what he could offer me directly. He did, however, provide a clue: Breathing had something to do with it—in combination with one's energy level. On the surface, it wasn't much to go on, but it got me curious about the subtleties of energy and breathing, and this led to the study of Zen and other teachings in the spiritual realm. But now I'm getting ahead of myself, because not long after I started at the store, I met a very lovely woman.

White Pickets

As much as I enjoyed the sort of dance experience Vulker had shown me, I still went to nightclubs as well. One night at a massive club in the city, I met on the dance floor a beautiful Filipino woman with big, dark eyes and a gorgeous smile. It was kismet with Lee from the moment our eyes met—the sort of effortless connection that leaves longing for good love firmly on the heap of past.

It wasn't long until I'd left the boardwalk and rented a flat with her in the city. We had the downstairs of a once-grand Victorian house that had been converted to a beehive of apartments. This was the part of the house built to impress visitors, with high, coved, and ornately trimmed ceilings, and huge windows allowing in generous daylight. We slept in the turret off the corner of the house—a little rounded space just big enough for my queen-sized futon.

This was a wonderful time: I worked four days a week, yet somehow easily paid for my portion of the overhead, and still had enough to put away for emergencies and the next item on an insatiable list of photo equipment. On many of my days off, I'd drop Lee off at the doctor's office where she worked, have a coffee at a favorite cafe, and go home to the practice of photography.

Lee had grown up in San Francisco, and introduced me to sides of it I hadn't yet found. We'd go to the Mission District, get beers on one side of the street, take them to a Mexican restaurant on the other, and order from menus completely devoid of English. She showed me out of the way corners on a magic carpet of companionship. Along the way, she gave me a much more personal sense of the city, and how it had changed over the years through her lovely eyes.

Once again, I was blessed with a lover who enjoyed my proclivity toward cross-dressing with sex. She was amazed that I knew just what to do to bring her to orgasm, but I wasn't about to tell her I simply knew innately because I had a woman's spirit, and that I was just well-disguised as a man; I still had difficulty facing this honestly myself. My love for Lee, and passion for creativity, hadn't quelled the upwellings of longing, or the deep current of sadness that ran below the surface of my happy life with her.

Now and again, I'd catch glimpses of transwomen—which, in San Francisco was not so unusual—and the actuality of such profound change would reverberate through me for days or weeks. It brought me face-to-face with the path I was struggling to suppress; yet, there it was, living and breathing in my world... and it was soulfully, erotically attractive.

In a black-and-white photography course, I met a man who would have a profound affect on the next few years of my life. Martin was teaching it, and exuded an appreciation for architecture, music, and literature. He was about twenty years older, and quickly became a friend, a mentor, and somewhat of a father figure as well. Perhaps because my father had been so left-brained and distant, I especially welcomed Martin's warmth, humor, and creative perspective. He was a natural teacher, and a commercial photographer who worked for a large non-profit company with an audio-visual department.

I'd been itching to leave the store, and felt comfortable in asking him if there might be a position for me where he worked. While there wasn't one at the time, he got me an interview, and they thought well enough of me to create the new darkroom position the photographers had been asking for. A couple of months later, I started—on a well-paying freelance basis—operating the darkroom, which made everyone happy: The photographers despised being down there, while I disliked shooting portraits of new-hires and buildings, and really enjoyed the simplicity of being tucked in somewhere alone.

About this time, Lee and I started looking for a house to buy, and we quickly found one across the bay in Oakland, in the blue-collar neighborhood where I worked. Very much a fixer-upper, it had been owned by the same family for fifty years and needed top-to-bottom renovation. I had romantic images of us working on it together, perhaps because that was the closest thing to a bonding experience within my family growing up.

As it turned out, she didn't like taking direction from me, or the dust and grit of work, so we fell into a pretty traditional arrangement: I did the renovations while she took care of the house, and did the laundry and cooking. For about two years, I worked on the house and at the darkroom, where there was always archival work if I wanted the extra income.

There was space to garden in the backyard, and the mild climate felt like a sweet invitation to embrace Earth and natural lushness. I accepted by rebuilding the soil, and planting jasmine, Chinese lantern, lavender trumpet vine, corkscrew willow, magnolia, fuchsia...

Shifting Currents

In the meantime, I was opening to realms that felt exquisitely expansive and deeply familiar: Buddhism (Zen, especially), traditional Native American ways, Taoism, various approaches to religion from India, and so on. Some of my favorite contemporary writers were Carlos Castaneda, Robert Pirsig, and Dan Millman, because they wove some of these profound teachings into the tangible experience of life. *A Separate Reality, Zen and the Art of Motorcycle Maintenance*, and *Way of the Peaceful Warrior* were just a few of the books lending new perspective in those early days of spiritual unfolding, and would make the journey ahead far richer and more rewarding than it would otherwise have been.

I loved feeling the undercurrents of writings that were, on the surface, radically different, yet resonated in common ground. The shimmering austerity of Zen Buddhism, for example, with its lean focus on mindfulness, balance, simplicity, stillness, silence, space, and effortlessness, contrasted beautifully with Castaneda's vivid depictions of spiritual adventures, energy dynamics, and psycho-spiritual experiences in desert landscapes. In one book, he undergoes an intensive process of what he called *recapitulation*—an intensive, thoroughly veracious life-review. I remember thinking this would be not only an extremely painstaking process, but an immensely valuable one as well... perhaps at some much later time.

Through the written word, I was finding communities of similar sensibility with lineages of practitioners stretching back many millennia. To have ignored this wisdom arcing across the generations would have meant reinventing the wheel to the degree I could—and missing out on the path-blazing of untold numbers of masters of consciousness.

I never assumed what I was reading was true; instead, I approached it with the openness I brought to the woods and fields as a child, and trusted my heart to gauge the worth and truth of what I was absorbing. Some of what I gleaned blossomed in my life directly, while other aspects lay like seeds for years, waiting to germinate when I was ready.

Gradually, my relationship with photography was changing: I'd set up a darkroom in the basement of the house, but my heart wasn't in the medium as it had been earlier. It certainly didn't help that the workspace had devolved from a lovely converted pantry off the big, open kitchen back in San Francisco, to a musty, low-ceilinged realm better suited to trolls—but it was more than this.

The professional darkroom work was a mercenary engagement, quite without the creative satisfaction that had previously impassioned my practice of photography. Though there was an element of burnout with the process and equipment on the surface, something more essential was going on: I was beginning to be drawn to a deeper connection with physical form. The medium of expression was shifting—foreshadowing profound change all around.

Color had brought me to the study of light and its relationship with form, and now I was feeling called to work with color in direct relationship *with* form. I'd always been very much in my head, and was intrigued by this invitation to become more grounded by way of creating objects. It was quite practical as well: I was inspired by a friend who'd shown me some basic furniture he'd made with a miniscule set of skills, the house certainly needed furniture, and applying the language of color to useful things fit right in.

The change from black-and-white recordings of light to working with colored form was a bounding leap nearly from one end of the spectrum of physical mediums to the other. Not so many pages ago, I noted the aspect of creative practice in which you find what's happening in the studio paralleling the rhythms of your life. As the mediums shifted, I had no idea how deep those rhythms would turn out to be. The tide was turning toward the physical, and the upwelling of longing for different form was breaking through.

Mooring

One of my practices these days is the art of presence—of being aware in the moment beyond the whirl of mind. Without such attentiveness, the near-constant percolation of random thoughts—many of which are spurred by fragments of memory and emotion—call out to more fragments to join in overwhelming the moment. While memory and emotion certainly have their place in the spectrum of awareness, I prefer they not run rampant, and override my consciousness—my sense of Being.

This practice in writing takes me necessarily through the past now, not just in recollection—that is, in writing *about* it; the real value in this can only be found in writing *from* it. Were it not for the underlying sense of higher calling in this recapitulation, I'd step away from the time-warping intensity of reaching back and herding words, and simply rinse myself clean of these reawakened ghosts.

Yet allowing their haunting to ring through me brings clarity to the landscape of psycho-emotional challenges of those earlier times. Suffering opens the door to choosing something else, and having explored so many of my shadows over the years, there is opportunity here in this engagement for far more choice than I've ever known. I'm discovering that in opening in the present to the difficulties that spawned those impressions of memory, they are most available for transfiguration in the light of acceptance and awareness.

This deep, long rest amid the warmth and spirit of this tropical place has cleared the room for coming home, finally, to higher Self... For feeling my bearings in the stillness, and bringing my soul—my essence—and its way in this dense world together: for surrender in the finest sense.

From this melding of inner and outer landscapes, I can now tell this story because it and I have ripened such, that the telling of it is part of this integration. And because the words spill through the heart—despite the lingering patterns of old ways—from a vast ocean of peaceful silence.

The Dam Bursts

There came a time amid those years with Lee when it seemed we'd naturally spend many more together, and for a while, we even talked about getting married. But not long after, it was as though the old man from the vision I'd had of dying when I was five years old sat right up on his death bed and declared, *For heaven's sake, you know the price of not really living your life, so get on with it!*

While I like to think of myself as having quite good recall, it's difficult to sort out the timing of certain events that happened next, given my psycho-emotional state at the time. It was, after all, a slow-motion meltdown of the lovely life with Lee, and of the complex composite of persona and physicality I'd presented to the world thus far. I reflect on those days now and find fleeting images of the ensuing cascade:

- The cross-dressing left the bedroom and began parading around the house, which prompted Lee to ask, *This is more serious now, isn't it?*
- I found a therapist who dealt with these issues, who promptly asked, *How long have you been having these feelings?*
- I went to a total of one trans support group meeting, after which I pondered, *Is this really where I'm going?*
- I debated some more with myself, wondering if I'd really given my maleness a full chance to represent my Being.
- I wandered the slopes of Mt. Tamalpais, looking at the possibility of taking small steps in the direction of change; but I could see where they inevitably led, and so—sitting in the lush grass, gazing out over the rolling hills to the sea—I finally surrendered to the natural course of my unfolding.

Go West

Soon after, while sitting in meditation, an indistinct image of the feminine—more like a body of light than anything else—came into my awareness, and I said, *Have your way with me*. Then an image of a group of faceless Beings arranged jury box-like appeared—with no feeling of judgment whatsoever—and they spoke with a single, telepathic voice: *If, at the end of this life, you could choose whether or not to come back in human form—and if so, in what form—could you make that choice then?*

I knew I'd be able to, so I quickly said, *Yes, I could*. There was a brief pause before they replied, *Very well, then... choose now*. I didn't have to think about it, since there was indeed another life to be lived: *I would come back as a graceful, beautiful, powerful woman who loves women*. The featureless face that spoke for all seemed to nod a bit. *Very well*, it said, *it will not be easy, but it will be possible*. I felt the blessing of the Universe in my journey, and from this point on, had no hesitation at all.

The talk of marriage had prompted the realization that my true nature would surface at some point. I imagined twenty years down the road to two scenarios: one in which I was miserably suppressing who I really was, and another in which our marriage—perhaps with children—was breaking up because I could no longer hold it back. Now that I was clear in what I needed to do, our worlds were, in every way, diverging. Mine was simultaneously imploding and opening to something altogether new and unknown, and her white-picket hopes for us suddenly seemed galaxies away.

I could have asked her to journey on with me, and I still wonder now and again how my life would be different if she'd gone along. But at the time, she didn't say she'd want to still be with me, and it didn't seem fair to ask her to stay. We'd shared true love, had some good, kinky fun, but she was not really a lesbian at heart.

We still lived together for many months, and it was extremely painful for both of us. She felt as though my choosing to go ahead with the change was her fault—that she'd somehow not been woman enough for me to want to stay a man. I assured her that what I was experiencing was an innate part of who I was, and my finally accepting it had nothing to do with who she was or how we'd related.

She started dating, which would have seemed more surreal, but what I was doing had already taken first prize in that respect. We'd been together for five years, and went through what amounted to a divorce— only without the marriage.

She was terribly angry for a long time afterwards, and told me at one point that no one would ever love me like she did. I don't think she meant it as a curse—or know if I took it on subconsciously as some sort of punishment—but I'd reflect on this, too, from time to time over many years, and hope amid the aloneness she wasn't right.

Having seen an endocrinologist who had a reputation for being particularly open to working with trans people, all I needed was a letter from a therapist saying I was in fact a bona fide transsexual. The one I'd seen earlier had moved away, and since I wasn't about to start the process all over again, I found one who had a great deal of experience with trans people, and who was willing to diagnose me in one session. I showed up prepared with a statement, which I wrote to clarify my state of Being to myself, as much as for anyone else.

A Transsexual Manifesto

I am an intelligent, introspective, and healthy person, blessed with a deep sense of who and what I am. For years I have nurtured a balance between my male and female elements. Yet, I can no longer deny the truth which has, since childhood, quietly struggled for acceptance in my conscious mind: my gender is female.

I have been cross-dressing since I first awoke sexually, accepting this as a natural expression of my feminine side. I would dream of being female, awaken with an aching sadness, and try to forget. Over the years, the desire for a female body would erupt into my consciousness with increasing frequency, strength, and duration. Eventually, I could not both repress it and retain my integrity.

Throughout this time, I have explored the sexual, psychological, emotional, and spiritual dimensions of this disparity in great depth; confronted the fears; and studied the ramifications—both alone and in therapy. I have carefully sifted through the thousand reasons not to make this change, as well as myriad alternatives.

Yet, despite the fact that any other option would be easier, less painful, less risky, impermanent, and have far fewer social ramifications, one undeniable truth remains: I desire to be female in form. This has been true since I first awoke sexually. The difference now is that I have accepted this desire, and with clarity of mind and heart born of intensive search, have chosen to undergo the process of aligning this truth and the reality of my physical being.

I don't fear what society will think. I realize there will be uncomfortable situations, but this is insignificant in light of the feeling that, after so long lost in doubt and fear, I am going home. I know the risks, I see the work; there is no path for me but this way home.

We had a wonderful talk, near the end of which she remarked, *Well, you certainly have a classic transsexual profile!* An image of the side of my head floated through my mind before I realized she didn't mean that kind... Yes, she'd be happy to write the letter for the endocrinologist, and could she keep my manifesto? As a sexuality educator, she wanted to share it with her students. I didn't know it at the time, but some months later, I'd end up speaking to quite a few of her classes.

I used to get anxious for the things I wanted to come right to me, and I'd be gripped with a mix of longing and excitement as I felt the gap of time between that moment and the anticipated one of arrival. Waiting to start the hormones trumped all this.

With the go-ahead from the therapist in hand, and an appointment to begin the hormones scheduled, I reflected on the upcoming changes while working in the darkroom one afternoon. I'd held back for so long, and more than anything else I'd ever desired, I wanted this change. In the intensity of that anticipated becoming, linear time seemed almost liquid, to lie back in a yawning gap as days swallowed years... I simply had no more or less than this moment to be in, with that dear outcome moving escalator-like toward me.

First Pill

With my first hormone pill in hand, I went to a favorite park up in the Berkeley hills. On the way up to a high hilltop, which I called the *Temple of the Pines*, I was very conscious of every step, every movement— my last, subtly yet profoundly, as a male being. I knew it would take some time for the changes to be evident, but symbolically, it was a momentous event.

I'd been waiting since getting the prescription filled the day before so it'd be more of a ritual, and I anxiously settled right away on the soft pine duff. I stared for a bit out over the whole Bay Area as if I could see my new life out there, then pulled the ovoid purple pill from my pocket, put it in my mouth and swallowed. A dam burst, and I was washed at last into the distant outskirts of the realm of the feminine.

A week later—as my body began to assimilate the hormones—I began what I've come to call *backwash*—the psycho-emotional aspect of reprogramming the body. I'd never experienced such intensity and tenacity of sadness and grief in all my life. Formerly, when I needed to cry, I just wept and soon reached what felt like the bottom of it, and was done. Now, there was no bottom. I felt as if I'd been specially picked to express the sadness and grief of this world, and there seemed to be an endless supply.

I'd had a fetish for bald women for some time; I don't need to know what it was about it—it just did something for me. Amid the hormone-induced onslaught of ungrounded-ness just after the first week, I got a little crazy one day and accidentally killed off that perfectly lovely fetish by shaving my own head. It was "fetishide" by over-indulgence.

Not only was it sad to lose a nice, benign little turn-on (one only gets so many really good quality ones like that), but it was a serious setback to my emerging female expression. There was a lesson in this rash action about the potential consequences of making major decisions from difficult states of mind. But as you'll see shortly, I apparently learned nothing from this in that regard.

I did soon learn how slowly my hair grows—at least the hair on my head; the rest of it was another matter. Electrolysis sessions soon started with a woman who hadn't worked on many transwomen. After a long while of excruciatingly painful work the first time I went to see her, she said quietly, *You must really want this...* I just nodded. She wasn't referring to the painful process, of course, but to the change itself. *Yes, with all my Being, I really wanted it.*

Coming Out

As the hormones began to take effect, I was still working at the darkroom. I'd begun to express more of my female side at home, yet would show up at work in my old male guise, with loose-fitting shirts to hide my emerging breasts. The female was oozing out at this point, and it was a challenge to keep her in check.

I'd had one ear pierced since the days at the photo store, and had recently gotten the other done as well. When I went to work one day, Marianne, the very cool receptionist, leaned a little forward at her desk and said in a hushed tone, *You may want to know that you're wearing two earrings...* I just smirked, said, *Oh, thanks!* and pulled one right out before anyone else noticed. Nowadays, a guy with both ears pierced is commonplace, but then it was fairly radical—and particularly in this semi-corporate setting, a definite no-no.

As a way of thinking and sharing about re-approaching my way of Being in the world, I imagined that we're handed a set of cards displaying our qualities when we're born, and after a significant portion of life, we have them arranged in a way that depicts who we are. I'd thrown those cards into the air, and would let my true nature rearrange them to fit my evolution as they fell. There was a powerful element of surrender in recognizing that what I was becoming was not for me to control—being authentically me was far more about discovery.

At first, only my closest friends knew I was starting the transition, but as the changes became more visible, I began sharing my process more widely. The women in my life were unabashedly supportive and excited for me. They had so many questions about what was going on internally, and what would be happening with my body.

On the other hand, my male friends struggled to be accepting—some of them even came right out and asked, *So, you really wanna have your dick cut off?* I explained to them that, for a man, this would be an unthinkable thing; but I wasn't a man, so I didn't share their fear of losing my penis. *And anyway*, I said, *it's not going to be 'cut off'—it'll be extensively remodeled.* They'd wince and shrug because, either way, it'd be gone.

A gay friend called one day and said he no longer wanted to be my friend, as there seemed not to be enough room for him—that I'd become self-centered. I tried to explain that this was a phase; I was on a staggering amount of hormones, and the only way I knew to maintain some semblance of balance was to focus on the center of my Self. But his heart was closed, and those words didn't reopen it. I was left to wonder if my surrendering aspects of my maleness was just too much for him to be around.

Coming out to my family was another matter, as we were by this time scattered around the country, and for the most part, only sporadically in contact—if at all. I waited until I'd been on the hormones for several months before I broached the subject with them, with the exception of my younger brother, Christopher. We'd had a similar world-view all along, and he was, not surprisingly, very supportive as soon as he knew it was my path—something I had to do to be who I am in the world. That he was losing a brother didn't seem to concern him at all; he saw my essence, and knew it was inherently intact.

With some considerable trepidation, I called my mother. I had no illusions of her suddenly transforming into someone supportive of my Being—let alone of my taking this radical step toward being authentically myself—especially since she'd always kept herself straight-jacketed by her perceptions of others' perceptions of her. Image was everything to her, and for me to reveal my inner world in this very public way would be, in her view, inconceivably foolish.

There was also an undercurrent of perceived loss in this for her, as she would be losing a son. Ideally, one would hope a parent would see, and accept, the change as a transformation—with the soul remaining a constant—so the loss would be healingly counter-pointed with a gain. But this would, at best, take time and some considerable doing on her part to open consciously to her own evolution; I held no expectations in this regard. In the meantime, for me, the floodgates were open, and I was awash already in waves of emotion-charged hormonal change, and there was little I could do but face the response, whatever its course.

My mother likes to tell her friends about my change, not out of respect for it, or because it might help spread a little more understanding in the world, but because it makes her seem more interesting. She likes to tell them how open she was to it, and has some pretty amusing anecdotes demonstrating her good humor about it all.

Unfortunately, her recollection is far more in tune with how she would like to present the awkward moment of my coming out to her as having gone, rather than how it actually went. She was, in fact, quite angry and unsupportive, and seemed to operate from the premise that her approval was somehow necessary for me—despite the life-long, unyielding stream of cynicism and criticism, and the obviousness of my being many years into adulthood.

She said of my big hands, *They'll always give you away...* and wanted to know why, with my mention of Zen-inspired acceptance over the years, I couldn't just accept myself as I was. I explained that sometimes acceptance means that one surrenders to the change to which one is called—but she was having none of this.

She'd long figured I was gay, so she wanted to know why I didn't just go ahead and be with a man. *You don't have to be a woman to do that,* she said—suggesting I really just lacked the courage, and was trying to approach it through the back door. I explained it wasn't at all about being with a man—that I was still only attracted to women, and was, in fact, becoming the lesbian I always was. Ever the headstrong pragmatist, this was not something she was going to take seriously, especially since it flew in the face of her long-held assumptions.

Eventually, she struck a thoroughly unpleasant balance of sorts, in which she humored my process on the surface, but would let it be known on a regular basis—in a relentlessly passive-aggressive manner— she still considered me a *he*.

Lee and I needed to sell the house—the renovation of which was a long way from complete—and she just wanted to be done with it and

Go West

gone. I needed money to take my next steps, and was concerned the labor I'd put into the place would be wasted if it were left partially done. So we researched what it was worth then, and agreed on how we'd split the equity. I would finish the work, sell it, and keep most of the difference.

I continued with the darkroom work until the physical changes were getting obvious. It so happened, too, the audio-visual department was moving to a new location downtown, and since that location seemed far too public, it was a natural time to leave. Then the focus was on the house full-time—which amounted to ten or twelve hours a day, seven days a week. It took a grueling seven months of increasingly stressful labor to complete the house. There was very little money to put into it, so I did nearly everything myself, all the while riding the psycho-emotional hormone roller-coaster. I had no idea one person could produce some many tears amid so much work.

Stillness Beyond the Layers

To rooster calls, Balinese children's voices, and the swooshing of Agung's bundled-branch hand broom gathering the night's fallen leaves and blossoms, I waken in the gauzy dawn light, make green tea, and sit to meditate. I don't decide to meditate; it's simply how I start the day. It's an opportunity to gather attention, feel the life force flowing through the body, tame the dream-wild mind, and nurture the blossoming of the heart. It's a date with my higher Self, and I sit with this active peacefulness a good while.

Engaging the mind from this spaciousness, I slide into contemplation—deliciously wafting between the higher mind and the infinitely vast field of knowing beyond it. From the stillness at the core of my Being, I look out over my way in the world and see the layers of programs looping through: engrained impressions from family, society, culture, emotion, feeling, perception, memory, karma, and so on—sifting, filtering, and coloring reality—cueing the compulsive composite we often call *personality* toward its habitual range of response.

The writing of the previous day has brought to the fore a contemplation of identity, and I'm shuffling through the program of memory, recalling the psycho-emotional ramifications of changing this body's chemical "software" from testosterone to estrogen: the greatly expanded emotional range, heightened feeling of empathy, lessening of aggression, overall softening of personality... Hormonal influence stands in the spotlight of awareness, and I see from this core of stillness how this program dovetails with the nature of my Being, and why I needed to set up the conditions for its realignment.

I knew from the outset of this journey that Being in alignment with my nature would allow me to better see past myself—past that set of programs—and become more intimate with What Is. I also recognized there would be much inner work along the way which had little or nothing to do with gender. Unfolding into my true identity simply allowed me to stop tripping over what had separated me so obviously from the nature of my Being, and focus attention more fully on those finer, lighter things: creativity, fulfillment, peace, joy, and love.

In the light of awareness, I know I was not a victim of some accident of birth, or some tragic cosmic joke, or a victim of any sort whatsoever. I incarnated in precisely the right body, so that in experiencing those shifts in gender and hormonal programs, I could see through that lens the Beingness that remained absolutely unchanged, shining like a lighthouse beacon on a storm-whipped shore. I could focus my attention then on letting go of identity with form—on transcending all illusion of separation from All That Is. Ultimately, the trans path has not been for me as much a homecoming to the female, as a process of transcending the illusory duality of gender altogether.

Out of memory arises the wonderful observation: *Wherever you go, there you are.* In taking on this homecoming to truer Being in form, I knew this path would set the groundwork for a lifetime of revelation, and far from being a deterrence, it seemed all the more worth embracing: A lifetime well spent, indeed. Wherever it would go, I'd find me there, nurturing a sense of balance inside and out—stepping in what ways I could in each moment toward wholeness.

From the stillness, I know that while I'm just being myself in the world, the higher Self goes about its simply Being—loving, and delighting in, this odd incarnation. I know in this still place I am, like All That Is, loved beyond comprehension or measure. And this is freedom—far truer and more delicious than traveling the world.

Ritual for a Small Death

About six months into both the house renovation and bodily transition (a fine analogy if ever I saw one), my friend Caroline helped create and enact a ritual I called a *Wake and Re-awakening*—a symbolic funeral for my former embodiment and expression, and a welcoming for the new one.

In the garden there was a seven-foot tall wooden stand I'd made earlier for a wonderfully earthy, rusty old bell that hung on an equally rusty chain. I turned the stand into a funeral litter on which I could be carried, and asked friends to bring something symbolic, or perhaps some words to be "buried" with the old me.

On the day of the event, rain threatened all morning. I suggested to Caroline that maybe we should have a backup plan in case it needed to be held inside. She turned right around and said, without any semblance of kidding, *It's not your decision, you're dead.* She was an actress and part-time priestess who could be quite fierce if necessary, and I loved that she was stepping right up and taking charge—allowing me to let go, surrender, and die.

A short while later, I laid on the litter, and my friends carried me out into the backyard under thick clouds. The moment they set it down, the sun came bursting out, and everyone gasped. Light had shown up, too, making the surrender all the sweeter.

Caroline danced and invoked the aid of the Divine before a large piece of black gauze cloth was placed over the litter to symbolize burial.

Friends took turns throwing what they'd brought—rather like you would flowers into an open grave—and sharing parting thoughts. After Caroline danced and performed more invocations, the black cloth was exchanged with a white one to welcome me back into the light.

I then "awoke" and stood up, and a friend who'd been chosen to be my gatekeeper stood the litter up on end, and hung the bell on it. I rang myself back into the world three times. There were beautiful flowers all around, and chocolate covered strawberries—and wine, of course. To this day, the gorgeous fragrance of tuberose has a special place in my heart, and I can't smell it without thinking of this wonderful day.

I had just one regret with the whole ritual: I didn't get a chance to see Caroline officiate; I heard it was quite a sight, as she wore only a belt of little bells. She said later that at one point, in midst of a particularly wild turn of dancing, she looked over at the sound of a garbage can lid being lifted, and there was my middle-aged African-American neighbor looking over the fence at this basically naked woman dancing around a shrouded litter, with a group of people respectfully looking on. We wondered if she'd concluded that, finally, she was privy to what white people do on Saturday afternoons.

▢ ▢ ▢

Stepping Out

Over the next month or so, I finished the house with Caroline's assistance. I was exhausted, and still tweaking details, as she literally pulled me out the back door as the Open House event began the day it was put on the market. We went out to the coast and spent the night out near Muir Beach.

I called the realtor the next day to see how the event had gone; she could hardly wait to tell me the place had sold for full price in one hour. There was just one condition from the buyer: He wanted to buy all the furniture I'd made for the house. It was wonderfully affirming of that direction with the work, and he got no argument from me.

Between then and closing, I went about focusing on my new life. I arranged to sublease an apartment for a few months on Dolores Street in San Francisco—just blocks from the Castro district—and moved what I didn't need there into storage. It was a brief, magical time of enjoying the beautiful home I'd created, resting from the onslaught of work and stress of the past months, and letting go into more of my female self in the world.

That summer was a delightful phase of reacquainting myself with living in the city. I spent many hours walking and riding the transit system to various neighborhoods, sometimes stopping in clothing boutiques to see if they had something for my new wardrobe. But mostly, moving about in the city was a way of exercising my liberated sense of Being, and the shopping was rather like my exploration with the camera those first months in the city, in that it provided a sense of purpose to the wandering.

Though I was between creative mediums, I didn't feel adrift as I usually would later, when one faded and the next hadn't yet blossomed. The house project had left me burnt-out—a little jaded from so much expenditure of energy with so little creative discovery in the process. With the inner shift toward the physical that had preceded the tumultuous change, the affair with photography had drifted off into a similar condition.

I wasn't feeling as though I was between mediums because, at this point, I *was* the medium. My body was literally changing form while my way in the world evolved exponentially, and the element of discovery—so essential to creativity—was there by the closetful.

At doctor's offices, I started filling out the "Sex/Gender" part on the patient information forms by putting circles around both options, and drawing a curving arrow from the top the *M* to the top of the *F*—like a gender-naut on a skyward trajectory from one planet to another.

□ □ □

Early on in the transitioning, I was quite surprised at the amount of attention I was getting. People would nudge each other, and I could see them mouthing, *Is that a man or a woman?*

In my male form, I'd been practically invisible because what I was physically in relation to my sensibility was a falsehood, and I had no interest in projecting a male presence. Within a few months of being on the hormones, I'd walk into a restaurant and there would be a sea of nudging and turning heads as I walked to my table. Little did I know when I'd dressed as an androgyne for Halloween back in college—and found people didn't know how to interact with a person of indeterminate sex—that this perplexity would become a major social theme in my life.

It was a remarkably Zen-like state of Being neither and both simultaneously, and though I was inching my way decidedly female-ward, I reveled in the realm between. One day, I was at the counter in the hardware store in the Castro—where every kind of gender-variant person passes through—and the young woman behind the counter, who was herself quite androgynous, called over to me: *Uh, ma'm... er, sir.. .ma'am, ummm...* With a laugh and a shake of her head, she waved me over, mumbling with some delight, *I can't tell...* She was on the observing end of the exchange this time, and enjoying the view from the other side. For me, it all seemed oddly comfortable: Betweenness suited me to a degree I hadn't thought to anticipate.

My favorite response occurred when I was looking for a bathroom at a movie theater. I hadn't realized yet that I needed to specify which one I was looking for, so when I asked an usher, *Where's the restroom?* he glanced up and down, and tactfully replied, *Well, there's one over there... and one over there,* pointing to the Men's and Women's rooms respectively. Give the man a prize! Perhaps only in a town like San Francisco would that just roll out of someone's mouth so naturally.

It wasn't pure bliss, though, as I'd ramped up to a staggering amount of hormones, and was getting regular, hours-long sessions of electrolysis. Back then, we didn't have antiandrogens, which block the body's production of male hormones—thereby minimizing the need for estrogen. I was on so much estrogen and progesterone because it was necessary to override the male hormones to tip the balance to the female side.

As I shared what I was experiencing with female friends, they'd sigh and say in one way or another, with a pained look: *Sounds like you have full-time PMS... I don't know how you stand it!* It's remarkable what we'll willingly go through for the chance to finally be who we authentically are—especially when we've had to live for so long with being perceived in such a fundamental way as its antithesis.

□ □ □

Resistance is Suffering

The woman I'd starting seeing for electrolysis didn't have enough time for me in her schedule, so she recommended her friend, Sue, who had a great touch with the needle, tons of compassion, and the ear of a good therapist. In fact, I came to see her as a confidante, and our sessions—painful as they were—as therapy as well.

With electrolysis, the higher a current you can take, the more likely the hair root is to be cauterized, and therefore, for the removal to be permanent. There's powerful inducement built right into the process for straddling your pain threshold. Especially if you're having it done for long periods, it's helpful to have a technician with a good rhythm to her work, so you're not just being randomly jolted. Thankfully, Sue had a good feel for that, and it made a huge difference.

I learned something very valuable about resistance and pain on that table, which I'd read about in studying Zen: *Resistance is suffering.* It's one thing to understand an idea conceptually; it's another to get it experientially, and I had plenty of opportunity for that. In the first sessions, I'd left feeling wiped out by the seemingly endless series of jolts, but I soon realized that if I didn't flinch with each impulse, it wasn't nearly as traumatic and exhausting.

I even started working with it by trying to increase the sensation of pain—figuring if I could do that, I could also lessen it. I quickly found that I was already experiencing the maximum pain, and the fear of it's being greater if I didn't try to push it back was what made me resist and flinch.

The breakthrough was remarkable: By remaining open to the impulses, I actually had options for dealing with them. Instead of trying to minimize the pain at the spot it entered, I could dissipate it by absorbing it throughout the energy field coursing through my whole body. I could also cue my body to relax instead of automatically flinching, and focus my attention on something else: perhaps an idea, something I was working on in the studio, or talking with Sue. Or I could even go into a meditative state—what is sometimes called an *alpha* state of awareness—in which one's focus is more on an expansive sense of consciousness than on one's body.

By letting go of resistance and its attendant knee-jerk reaction, the trauma was greatly reduced. And this is where the technician's skill is crucial: It's much easier, as you might imagine, surrendering to a rhythmic stream than a more staccato tempo. There were areas, though, like above the lip, which were just excruciating no matter what I tried. All I could do was try to dissipate the pain so I wouldn't be too traumatized by it, and focus on acceptance. Sometimes, it seemed nearly as hard on Sue in setting up the pain as it was for me in receiving it.

What I learned became a tremendous help in minimizing the trauma on the table. As I noted earlier, it's one thing to understand an idea conceptually, and it's another to get it experientially—which I certainly did. But I would add one caveat: it's also important to apply the understanding to the rest of one's life for full effect. *Resistance is suffering*, indeed, and while it's relatively easy now to look back and see where I might have looked out across the landscape of my life at any given moment, pinpointed the resistance of my own making, and moved toward reducing the suffering, I can also see the blinding burden of so much childhood hurt coursing through me at the time —like sediment stirred by a raging torrent of hormones.

Speaking Out

Around the time of the *Wake and Re-awakening* ritual, a friend of Caroline asked if I wanted to be on a gender panel for a local group called San Francisco Sex Information (SFSI), which gives extensive trainings to familiarize attendees with every kind of sexuality. Many attendees would go on to volunteer on the group's hotline, which was set up to give out free information on safer sex practices, sexually transmitted diseases, gender identity, sexual identity, and contact information for many other kinds of resources, etc.

These gender panels would usually include two transsexuals— one male-to-female (MTF) and one female-to-male (FTM)—and a transvestite. I was already on such panels, organized by the therapist who'd written the letter that allowed me to start on the hormones, so I was happy to do it.

There was much in the act of sharing that was therapeutically affirming. With so many questioning looks as I went about in the world, I could speak directly in these settings about my experience, and was respected—even honored—for following my calling. And, too, it's enormously empowering to simply speak one's truth per se, especially to a group gathered to hear it. It felt wonderful, as well, to be of some service in making even a little more room for others by showing up and articulating the journey.

While it took a long time to come around to embodying and living it, my eventual self-acceptance with regard to gender was truly an outgrowth of spiritual unfolding. Being able to share the journey as spiritual path—rather than an unfortunate life circumstance that needed correcting—had the potential to help others in opening to this dimension in themselves. Since many of those in the therapist's groups were graduate students in Sexuality Studies, and would go on to become therapists themselves, I hoped it would broaden their perspective, and that they'd share this sense of spiritual calling—even if just implicitly—with their future clients.

□ □ □

Homing In

While registering for a personal growth workshop, I told the staff that I was transitioning from male to female, at which they seemed perplexed about where to house me. I laughed and volunteered to pitch a tent in-between the men's and women's compounds, and move it a little closer to the women's every day. They laughed, and put me in the women's area.

□ □ □

As I've variously noted, while my relations in the human realm have been more challenging, I've found the Elements—Earth, Water, Fire, Air, and Space—to be unconditionally available. Certainly, I've been blessed along the way with having attracted at each place I've called home a small cluster of close friends who haven't seemed to know any better than to think the world of me.

But during this summer in San Francisco, amid the wash of hormones and transition, I needed—perhaps more than ever—the kind of connection with humanity that comes from profound physical embrace; and with waking up—yet again, in a long string of mornings—in the presence of an abiding lover. Though even at the time I could hardly blame anyone for avoiding getting involved with someone in such an emotionally raw state, aloneness cut right through me—especially in the hollow of night.

Go West

Given the lack of human partnership, I turned, as I often have as an artist, to my relationship with the Elements. In human relationships, we're attracted to someone in part because this person complements us—gives a fuller experience of ourselves—and with artistic media, it's no different. That summer, I was craving balance in the airy whirlwind of change, and I needed the grounding of a profound connection with the element of Earth—with form and solidity.

The transition itself was the element of Water, which is apparent in the fluidity of material, movement, and the melding of disparate things. My passion for finally coming home to myself—for years pent up and damped back—burned with the transformational element of Fire. Air—the element of causation and encompassing change— was in full form already, having blown into and through my life like a windstorm. Space, the element that contains all of the others and is yet beyond them, was spilling forth at a rate I simply couldn't absorb, for lack of grounding in form. And so I gravitated to, and embraced, Earth as if my life depended on it.

My own form was in flux; between the evolution of physical change in response to the hormonal reprogramming, the trauma of the electrolysis, and the reality of its being neither-and-both male and female, I was craving a creative medium of uncompromising solidity. It was natural at this point to gravitate to the woodworking—the furniture making—I'd started before life veered onto the gender path.

The pull toward wood seems to have arisen out the subconscious; it foreshadowed the changes to come, and the upcoming need for a medium of density. Amid the whirlwind of change, the pragmatism of its taking the form of furniture—rooted in the rhythms of daily life— made this direction all the more attractive.

Lighter Ways

If I were given the opportunity to step back in time and have one good talk with myself, this moment on the brink of the next phase would likely be at the top of a list of contenders. I'd like to think I've learned to avoid making major decisions when I'm feeling out of sorts with myself, as those choices are too readily driven by short-term needs; and all too often, those perceived needs have been underscored by motivations of which I wasn't entirely conscious. At these times, what I've needed most is awareness—but given my inclination toward action, I've tended to dive in and try to work my way through it.

One of the things I like best about living here in Bali is that things aren't so accessible, which often forces you to step back and ask yourself just how serious you are about doing something. Which isn't to say there aren't times when you just want that one impossible to get thing, or find yourself thinking dreamily about something you took completely for granted—like un-waxed dental floss or dietary supplements. Surely, you find yourself going well out of your way at times for some little thing, but here, you have much more time to deal with those intermittent inconveniences.

This is true of living in much of the third-world, of course, and you might well decide on the most un-Western response: let it go and do nothing. Or perhaps you re-approach it in a simpler, more direct manner, but either way, that knee-jerk tendency to ramp right up into action and throw some money at an issue is most often neatly sidestepped by the scarcity of resources.

In the West, it's easy to think we should be doing so many things because the materials and/or services are so accessible. We just hop in the car and run over to the store, or get online and have it sent via large brown truck. But this accessibility comes with a price: We end up chasing around after our expectations of a well-supplied lifestyle, we go around and around in our heads thinking about what we'll do, or would like to do; we spend a lot of time doing errands and arranging services; and, of course, we work, in part, to support those things. We're as busy as an ant colony, and wonder why we don't experience more freedom. So we buy other stuff that promises to give us that, and continue drowning in a sea of "convenience" and "easy payments."

Perhaps because I was raised with plenty of things, and saw firsthand their shortcomings in providing what really matters—freedom, joy, connectedness—I've been wary of trying to get those essential things at the check-out counter. But my illusion along the way was in thinking I could access those things by Doing, and plunging right into supporting the tools and working space I thought I needed. Instead of buying things as an end in themselves, I bought the means to make things, and assumed that in the process I'd create my way to what I wanted.

I've heard it said that the best way to get what you want is to know what you want, and in traveling back in time and having a good talk with myself, I'd ask me just that: *What do you* really *want, beneath this impulse to action—creative or otherwise?* And I'd tell me: *There are other ways, much lighter ways, to experience those things without making them into a burden—without causing yourself to suffer.*

3

Portrait of the Artist as
a Young Transsexual

A Difficult Labor

About nine months after starting the hormones, I leased a large warehouse-like space in a light-industrial ghetto in West Oakland and began making furniture. Considering the controlling way in which I'd been raised, working for myself meant that—although there were risks involved, and it was sure to be a lot of work—at least it'd be on my terms. This alone was extremely alluring, and that I'd worked for myself at numerous earlier times certainly made the venture less daunting. My unusually androgynous appearance and demeanor were factors, too, in choosing self-employment, as it seemed most unlikely any businessperson would want my odd presence representing their interests.

I opted for a brand new loft complex on what I later referred to as *the bad side of a hard town*, and it turned out the gates were locked at night for a reason: The area was infested with crack houses. It also turned out that those sounds that often woke me at night were not fireworks as I'd naively thought early on, but automatic weapon fire. Nice choice of landscape in which to let go into one's feminine side! It was soon obvious I'd failed miserably on the "nurturing environment" front.

It often takes us well into our twenties or thirties to shake off some of the less effective precepts with which we were raised, and to begin developing our own. From the vantage-point of hard-earned wisdom, I can see quite clearly now that while I was focused on overturning the primary precept in my life—that I was assumed to be male, and therefore *should* be a man—I'd reproduced the working conditions I chafed under growing up; my wounded Inner Child must have felt right at home. I managed to create an environment for myself that was based on obligation and duty rather than authentic expression, and I paid dearly for it. In my parents' world, being "independent" was essential, and playing out my own rendition of that illusion had a steep price for me, as well.

There was certainly some creativity in the process, but the ratio of expression to work weighed heavily toward labor, just when I needed gentleness and creative discovery. I had a lot to learn about self-love and compassion, but that opening would come later.

As if life weren't challenging enough in this world, we humans often have to take our suffering to the utmost before we acquire what we need to learn—if, indeed, we do at all. In this version of setting up the conditions for suffering, I had taken on a lot of overhead and a gritty environment in which I *had* to produce, like it or not. Many months into the venture, there was a long-dusty note I'd written in large letters hanging on the wall: *It's not a matter of whether you want to be in the studio, but rather, since you are here, how might you be happiest?*

Part of what has me shaking my head in wonder to this day is my choosing to do this while experiencing something akin to PMS full-time, and routinely undergoing an immense amount of extremely painful electrolysis. It would be more than fair to say these were not ideal conditions under which one might start a business—especially a physically challenging one.

While the world immediately outside the studio directly affronted my newfound expression, the one inside provided its own challenges. You might have observed as well as I, that just when I was starting to let go into my female expression, I took on a livelihood which drew heavily from the male side. For much of my life, I'd used tools to shape building materials in one way or another, and from that viewpoint it was a natural choice as a means of independent livelihood and creative expression.

However, with this new way of Being, my second-natured relationship with tools and materials was no longer a given. Not only did operating the power tools draw heavily from the male side, but the very familiarity of the engagement seemed to undermine the still tentative rebalancing of the male/female forces within. Later, the work would become more an opportunity for practicing that balance. Early on, though, it more often seemed—as with the environment outside—that I'd failed to provide a nurturing grounding for this emerging way of Being in the world.

At first, I despaired at being drawn back into an old way of livelihood I'd hoped to have left behind. There's nothing gentle about a radial arm saw spinning at several thousand RPM, oblivious to the difference between a tree limb and a human one. All I knew to do was call up strength inside and out, and cautiously will the process to align with my intent; gentleness and vulnerability headed for the hills.

I'd invite them back later, when the shrill motors had stopped and the dust settled. At times, it felt like one of those wretched relationships in which someone's repeatedly saying, *Sorry, baby... please come back... I promise I'll change... things'll be better...*

The situation would have been difficult enough had I been on stable ground emotionally, but thanks to the twice-daily regimen of hormones, it was—to put it mildly—a psycho-emotional nightmare. I didn't require any reason at all to feel upset; it simply welled up from a seemingly bottomless well.

Just maintaining a basic sense of equilibrium in the sea of mood swings required all the energy I had, leaving me exhausted and unable to delve into many of the issues pressing for attention. When an impetus for inner work had emerged in my former life, I'd been quite good about engaging it, dealing with it, and moving on. Now, staying on top of things was a luxury beyond reach: For the first time, I consciously let most psycho-emotional issues linger in the background, and focused almost solely on sustaining a deep sense of who I was amid the onslaught of change.

It's hard to believe I started a business of any sort in this turmoil. But there I was, doing what I felt I needed to do, and—pragmatically—I simply couldn't afford to put the tools down with every upset. So I learned to channel the emotional flux into the work, to use the physicality and motion as therapy; I just let go into the meditation of labor.

If tears flowed while sanding, they were stroked into the surface and absorbed by the wood. And since I was creating pieces that had a crafted rub of time, I didn't mind if they picked up some of the energy with which they were made; I'd grown up in a house full of antique furniture, and had often wondered what those pieces had absorbed of the many lives they'd accompanied.

The strenuous labor was fueled in part by passion for Being with creative spirit, and partly by the deep sense of alienation from childhood. Here, at least, I had all the intensity of engagement I could manage—and then some. The underlying blessing, though, was that the impetus and the wellspring from which the work and the furniture came was the core of balance and wholeness I was exploring within.

These objects flowing out of my inner and outer work would go into people's homes and become part of their lives. They felt to me rather like emissaries of that higher calling, and placing them in others' spaces lent a sense of metaphorical belonging, however tangential.

I turned to this creative landscape for connection with what seemed most essential right then: the timeless creative threshold of Being and Becoming. In the dusty landscape of the studio, the drama and difficulty of the human world fell away, and for a while at least, I became one with making.

Portrait of the Artist as a Young Transsexual

Mallet Girl Cometh

The easy sense of joy I'd known not so long before had slipped away. In its place arose a profound feeling of fulfillment. I was finally evolving homeward in the way and form of me, and in the wake of the work: beauty... objects I saw as both handsome and lovely. This confluence of feelings, emotions, presence, acceptance, and labor was the key that finally unlocked the door and allowed the female fully into the process.

It took time; I needed to know the depth and breadth of my grief, sadness, and loneliness first. I needed to *feel* the overwhelming desire for compassion; and finally, to find the resources within from which to respond. It was a sort of Catch-22: *She* wouldn't show up unless there was empathy and compassion, but it was she who ultimately brought them. So she entered shyly, waited for the willful male to yield its need for control enough to open to *her* way.

It certainly helped that her way turned out to be fairly butch. When I was most conscious of her essence, I'd find in myself a coltish boyishness—and that, I must say, felt pretty sexy. The stereotype of the "dyke with tools" found actuality in the studio, and she gradually nudged those tools out *his* hands, and kept right on going.

Redemptions

I'd always been drawn to the warmth of funky old weathered things: wood, metal, paint—anything with a patina of time on it. Picture an old, sagging, wooden barn out in a field, with huge, faded letters from some age-old advertisement, parts of which are missing because planks have been replaced over the years: That, for me, is a slice of aesthetic heaven.

It was natural, then, that the furniture I was making looked like it was discovered in an old forgotten house on the edge of the desert. Amid the inner turmoil, there was quite some satisfaction in creating objects with which I felt such resonance. I described its style at the time as *elegant primitive* because, while the construction was simple, the lines and form were more refined, and it looked like it belonged to some indistinct earlier era.

The look and feeling of time on the furniture was helped by the hand-rubbed finishes, which revealed layers of rich colors, and by the use of old wood and salvaged architectural details. I haunted the local building salvage yards, keeping an eye out for interesting things like corbels, finials, and cabinet doors that had been removed from torn-down or renovated buildings. After a trip to a paint-stripping place, they'd be set out to dry and added to the inventory—ready to inspire new pieces.

I loved giving those old things a new way of being in the world: I'd do woodworking surgery on them: transforming, reinterpreting, and reassembling them into something lovelier—rather like what was happening with my body, and my life in general.

There were quite a few boutique furniture and furnishing shops in some of the nicer neighborhoods in and around the Bay Area, and I'd keep them supplied from my inventory when pieces sold—at the same time, shifting the work around to other venues when I was making deliveries if it sat for too long in one place.

Showing up as an artist turned out to be a great lubricant for my unusual appearance; people just expect artists to be different, and I certainly didn't disappoint them in that regard. I wasn't *trying* to be anything gender-wise, and just went about my business as my androgynous self. And while I had no idea—and really didn't think about—what the owners and staff thought or said when I left, they seemed to find my self-acceptance and the ease of rapport refreshing.

Having a proper nest was essential in holding myself in the process of all this becoming and making, so I walled-off a corner of the huge, open space, and built a living area which included half of the second-story loft. True to the earthiness I needed, I made it color-rich with tones of brick, ochre, teal, and mocha. It was, naturally, wood-infused, and I lived surrounded by some of the furniture I was making. The objects of warmth and balance I was making for others served me, too, along with a deep purple claw-foot tub and a fine array of funky old weathered things of various sorts tucked around. That it made a natural showcase for the work was a most welcome bonus.

The timing happened to be right for the aesthetics, as people were hungry for the earthy feel and rich colors amid their hectic city lives. Southwestern-style furniture was in vogue, and I was fortunate in that—while my work went beautifully with that style—its uniqueness added range to the stores' offerings. Designers saw the work and sought me out for commissions; through them, and others who happened to see my space, I began using the color play and architectural forms to enliven and harmonize interiors—which offered a welcome change of pace from the furniture production.

Meanwhile, my relationship with photography had changed greatly. Growing up, it had been a way of recording what happened in my life. Later, as it became a creative medium, I largely moved away from recording happenstance and social interactions. I used it now primarily to document the process and artifacts of this other, far earthier, medium, and myself from time to time.

Looking back, having started out as a photographer was an extraordinary blessing in providing the equipment and expertise to record what came after. Without it, I wouldn't have the appreciation I do now for this earlier work, or see so clearly the entwinement of my physical transformation and the evolution of the work later on.

I realize now in delving into this phase of relentless work, that in the intervening years I've often reflexively drawn from the more difficult of its memories, and naturally found a grim picture in my mind's eye. Underlying the unpleasantness was the fact that this difficulty didn't happen *to* me; rather, I'd very much set up the conditions for my own suffering. This sense of not having taken care of myself, and the long-term experience of a heavy workload amid the stress of psycho-emotional upheaval bled over nearly everything else, coloring darkly so much that was truly wonderful. As I peel back the broad sweep of memory and the lasting impressions of hardship, though, I also see the enthusiasm, fulfillment, and far deeper joy of conscious unfoldment.

Perhaps most essential to my ability to hold it all together was a vague, but deep awareness of the rhythms of who I am. One might call it a spiritual sensibility—a sense of what I am beyond personality and circumstance. Not that I was in touch with it all the time, but there were sublime moments of exquisite satisfaction, and they most often blossomed out of a deep knowing—beyond logic or words—that I was living in the cadence of those rhythms. Simply being my female self in the world, at last, easily outweighed even the lowest moments. And when I despaired, there was in the background a profound, still spaciousness that seemed to embrace my whole Being.

Against this backdrop of timelessness and space, whatever difficulty was occurring was clearly temporary, and that realization made it much more bearable in the moment. The higher Beingness was there, whatever my psycho-emotional state, and especially as an undercurrent lending an easy sense of wonder. My relationship with my worldly identity, and with the human realm around me, was anything but stable, but the slow-motion dance of a passing cloud, the shifting angle of light with the passing season, or the shimmering delight of a flock of birds launching skyward in unison remained as an endless stream of sublime inspiration. This difficult chapter occurred one moment at a time, and there were indeed many fine ones in its arc.

In this phase of excruciatingly intense focus on physical identity, a sense of a more rarefied Beingness transcending personality, gender, time, and place, was a tremendous help in keeping it all in context. Awareness of those deeper rhythms graced me with a tendency to thrive on the inevitable change an earthly life entails, and while this period certainly held that to an extreme, it helped greatly that I'd taken it on as an adventure in unfurling. I was very much on the path of my life, and there was a profound satisfaction in finally just being myself in the world, whatever the stage of transformation at the time—and whatever the workload.

Portrait of the Artist as a Young Transsexual

I was most fortunate in having an artistic sensibility while finding my way along the gender path. All of what I made I saw as studies, with the masterwork being the unfolding of my Being in this circumstance, in this world. I was in the cadence of my deepest calling—the authentic expression of my essence—and that brought me into rhythm with the creative impulse of All That Is.

As I came to better know myself and evolved in that rhythm, so did the work. At its core, the process of art melds individual, subjective reality with the universal—the Oneness—and in the process, the content of one's earthly Being blossoms in the light of its divine context—its higher purpose. Relations with humanity aside, I could never be truly alone in the company of the Elements and natural forces amid the whirl of All That Is.

A profound blessing at the time was that I saw myself as having been born in a male body so as to have this experience of profound transformation, rather than having been "born in the wrong body." I was not a victim, but a soul adventurer on a journey that has always seemed to me to be a great honor.

In fact, the more I changed, the more deeply I understood that personality and physicality are but parts of a mask through which we present ourselves in this world. In the evolution of the mask, I've had an extraordinary opportunity to become more intimate with those aspects that have remained constant—that express the essence of who I am.

By way of deep change, I've come to see life more clearly as a field of experience, replete with options and freedom well beyond the given palette of social and cultural programming. Simply being in touch with a sense of the broader context of my process across the arc of this lifetime gave the at-times difficult details a far richer significance.

Recently, I came across some words I'd written at the time and hung on the wall of my living space. They were helpful then in keeping my bearings, and I've found them to be of value again—with slight modification—in the light of a new calling:

Sometimes it seems the vision in my Being
is bigger than I can, or want to, engage.
Yet I know
I am not given more than I am able,
that I am challenged instead to grow
and encompass that vision
in the unfoldment of my Being.

Sometimes it hurts to be that large
and feel the wounds of thinking
and doing from much smaller.

Sometimes I forgive myself for being
so much like the world around me,
and find there blessed freedom
to do this denser work,
with these hands in this breath,
in rhythm with creation.

Guy Club Goodbye

Thankfully, there were some good friends who simply enjoyed me for who I was, and this gift was a gorgeous counterpoint to the underlying sense of alienation. Nearly all those friends who remained not only close, but with whom the bonds deepened all the more because of the change, were women. They brought to my awareness the simple truth that every woman weighs—in her own way—what it means to be a woman, and they saw my emerging womanhood as an opportunity to explore it free from girlhood indoctrination into social expectations and fears. Through our conversations, I came to more fully recognize the consequences of those burdens, and to see my emergence as a creative act in revealing my own inevitably subjective version of womanhood.

Portrait of the Artist as a Young Transsexual

I was no longer in the "guy club," which meant the unspoken laws of relating male-to-male were no longer in effect, and there seemed not to be within the men I knew a willingness to re-approach our relationship. Overall, my male friends didn't have the psycho-emotional experience which allowed my female friends to delve readily into the process in the way women do with most anything going on in their lives.

Although I was quite articulate, I struggled to find common ground with the men because the language of feeling and emotion that arises out of women's more intensive psycho-emotional experience wasn't as available with them. What I was doing was not rational; only a language of feeling would suffice in expressing it. And that was the essential difference: Where the language was appreciated and understood, I could *express*—without it, all I could do was *explain*.

Sadly, my relationship with Martin lost its ease and warmth. When I chose this new life over being with Lee, he lost a great deal of respect for me. As I've said, this was not a rational process, and I suspect that instead of seeing it as a *trans*-rational—or perhaps a *meta*-rational—experience, he saw it as *irrational*, which left little room for understanding. To put it another way, instead of recognizing it as being beyond or *transcending* rationality, he only saw it as *not* rational, as falling *below* rationality—as if I'd leapt off a cliff into insanity, and was irredeemably lost to thinking souls.

Company Outside the Box

In the twenty years since I first came out as a transbeing to my friends, I've been blessed with getting to know many men who truly recognize, understand, and appreciate my journey as life path. Often, they're more spiritually inclined than most, and so have delved into their inner landscape and discovered far greater latitude in their own Being.

While I wouldn't expect anyone who isn't gender-variant

to understand innately the impetus of this path, these men have had a deep empathy with the underlying currents of humanity at play: the need to be true to oneself within, and to be oneself in the world; the honor inherent in responding to one's calling, however difficult that might be; the vulnerability of exposing one's inner process in the public sphere.

Their own journeys beyond Mind have shown them that rationality only takes one so far—that they don't need to understand the motivation intellectually. They know one's calling is a deeply personal, not necessarily rational thing, and to be passionately along one's path is its own blessing.

Those men who drifted out of my life during the transition were not so spiritually inclined—at least not at that point in their lives—and too, they had the additional challenge of having known me one way, then a radically other. We all have patterns of interaction which we reflexively apply, depending on the gender of the other person or people, and as I was venturing out across the gender divide, I suspect this brought up a lot of unconscious or barely conscious issues for them around some of those differences. Not everyone is introspective, or even curious, in those sorts of ways, and I think it was a whole lot easier for them to simply not deal with it, or me, at all.

Twenty years later, my androgyny continues to throw some people off their unconsciously standard modes of interaction. After all, if you don't know what gender someone is, what set of patterns do you apply? Sometimes, it's subtler than confusion over whether I'm a man or a woman; perhaps they see me as a woman, but one who's obviously not playing by the rules, and that's enough to set off their discomfort. In my ambiguity, I mirror a person's inner world. Some stare with delight; others with a mix of curiosity and mild resentment—as if I've stirred up their unease, and it's up to me to fix it.

I've found over the years, that in meeting me, some people are put off by the ambiguity, while others are attracted to the ranging space I inhabit. Although that immediate warmth is more often with woman-identified beings, I've been blessed with wonderful friends of various genders. I've heard it said that the more we're authentically ourselves, the better we're recognized by kindred souls—and the more readily we recognize them.

Beyond the gauntlet of stares, I know my people right off, and they know me: We're looking into each other's eyes and finding vast, familiar space to be, express, and share. These people are delighted to relate with someone whose path has taken her naturally and happily outside the box of conformity. I'm delighted to be seen in my truth, and to be in the company of people—men, women, genderqueers, or whatever the self-identity—who find themselves outside the box in their own joyful ways.

Beyond the Siren Call

Every now and then, I'd get a peripheral glimpse of myself in a store window's reflection, and be startled by the flash of objectivity. There I was doing boy-drag and girl-drag simultaneously, without even trying: My male side was exploring the feminine, while my female was busy being butch.

I'd turned out to be more butch—*soft butch* is more like it—than I'd anticipated, and some friends and family wanted to know why I'd bothered with the whole thing at all, especially since I was still attracted to women. What I shared with them gets to the essential subjectivity of gender identity and expression: Though I was fairly androgynous, and happily so, that balance only worked for me from the female side of the equation. I was not drawn to, and had no interest at all, in being an effeminate man, while being a woman with some masculine expression felt true to my essence. I suspect if I'd been born in female form, I'd likely have a similar gender expression to what I have now, but of course, my relationship with that expression would be something entirely different.

The lovely seductiveness of the feminine was the siren call beckoning me toward that side of the spectrum, but immersion in it, in lieu of the masculine, was not my way either. I found that when the seductive fetish for the feminine wore off—which it did quite quickly—it was the balance of male and female in the context of female embodiment that felt most true.

Rockets and Fireworks

Amid the studio work and gender homecoming, my late twenties was also a fertile time of exploration around my sexual identity. When I shared earlier about throwing those cards depicting who I was into the air and letting them fall into a new arrangement, some of them naturally applied to my sexuality.

That deep surrender was a kind of prayer: *Show me what I am, and I'll be it—beautifully*. Why would I want to waste time or energy fighting against what I simply am, and what makes me happy? Even when I was growing up, I was quite accepting of my sexual attraction to what I thought of as my "female side"—it was the worldly consequences of *becoming* female that terrified me. Now, I could finally explore this from the antithesis of terror.

Soon after being on the gender panel for San Francisco Sex Information, I took their extensive sexuality-training course, which also opened up many social opportunities to "find my edges" in terms of sexual attraction. While most of us grow up getting to know ourselves sexually over time, I was twenty-nine years old and suddenly opening whole aspects of myself for reappraisal.

I discovered that I hadn't changed much in my attractions and pleasures—I was just experiencing them in a form so much more attuned to my essence. I was, at this point, still in-between body-wise, which made me an interesting venue of exploration for women who had varying degrees of interest in other women. There was enough male there to be familiar, but enough female to be a departure. I called these *rocket relationships* when they could be considered relationships at all, because they passed by almost as quickly as they came.

But between the piercing sense of loneliness in the journey, the gaping childhood wounds, and the massive doses of hormones that amplified that early trauma and lent it a bottomless quality, I was an emotional

Portrait of the Artist as a Young Transsexual

mess. I still craved the affection, companionship, and heartfulness of real relationship, but at least in the meantime, this was a chance to share some touch and explore sexually without having to wait for emotion-based relationship, which had always had a habit of eluding me for long periods—even when my gender wasn't overtly in question.

One occasion which stands out as particularly delightful was with a sexuality educator and activist I'd met through SFSI. I had been through such difficulty to bring myself across the gender divide, and wanted to touch and be touched with a woman as a woman, so while we waited in line to be seated for breakfast in the Marina district one gorgeous, sunny morning, I said to Carol, *I'm in serious need of devirginizing... I'm wondering if you'd like to participate in a little ritual?* She just burst out laughing, and when she'd gathered herself, replied, *Well, I've been asked to do lots of things, but that's the first time I've ever heard it put that way! ...Sure, I'd love to!* We discussed what we'd bring to it, and arranged for our "happening."

It was such a relief and delight to put aside, for at least a short while, the emotional craving and aloneness, and just melt into pleasurable touch. Carol was an angel of sensuality, and I was welcomed home as a womanly lover of women. And that I could simply ask for what I wanted, and get such a beautiful reply was, in itself, a wonderful gift.

That memory unleashes another: I'm standing outside the loft space, leaning with a lover against her car. She has stayed the night, and we're saying goodbye after some morning sex. She looks up and around at the windows perched in the U-shaped building around the parking lot and says, *So, I'm the woman that fucks the creature...* I laugh, enjoying the stark truth of it. *Yup...* I say, *that's you: creature-fucker extraordinaire!* Rocket girl... medium-range.

In the Outskirts

At least once every week or two, I'd go for a meditative walk in Tilden Park, up in the Berkeley hills. Wandering on trails through Eucalyptus groves, I'd make my way on up to the patch of pines that offered a panoramic view of San Francisco and the Bay Area—and where, you might recall, I'd taken the first hormone pill. Those walks were absolutely essential to my equilibrium; I felt like I was plugging into my roots every time I went up there.

Oftentimes, I'd bring a favorite book of Kahlil Gibran's writings, stop in a beautiful grove of scrub oaks and read aloud. His warm words were so helpful in my feeling more a part of humanity when I was very much on the outskirts of social and cultural expectations. It was an opportunity to let my voice ring out, too, and there could hardly have been a better place to support its conscious softening.

There were fields, too, up high on the ridges where I could take my clothes off, soak up some much-needed light, and reintroduce my changing body to Sky. Most of the time back in the flatlands of West Oakland, I'd be so caught up in the productive process, it'd be hard to break away. But as soon as I entered the park, the pressures of studio output would simply dissolve, and it was hard to believe I'd had to pull myself from the work.

I felt a similar sense of liberation as I left the Bay Area every couple of months for another kind of nature getaway. Before I transitioned, I would visit a gorgeous, very earthy resort in northern California with pools fed by natural hot springs. It was "clothing optional," and nearly everyone opted-out. Later, in those tumultuous days of transition and nearly endless studio work, I'd drive a couple of hours up through wine country and stay overnight, indulging in the therapeutic waters.

Portrait of the Artist as a Young Transsexual

At the time, I had small, but womanly, breasts and a penis, and while I could have covered myself, it seemed most real and natural to be naked. It was assumed, of course, that one would show up as either a man or a woman, not both, and I ran this gauntlet of social expectation because it was an extraordinary opportunity to own my womanhood powerfully enough to encompass what was between my legs.

It presented a forum, too, in which I could take that classic nightmare of discovering you're naked in public and watch it melt in the light of presence. People would whisper and stare for a while, but they'd absorb the difference, and just go about their soaking and lounging. As usual, I carved out my own version of freedom, and let those around me just be with it.

At times, though, people would lose themselves in curiosity and/or confusion, and forget the underlying humanity we all share. One time, while I was descending a set of stairs into the warm pool, a young woman looked up at me quizzically. She turned to young man she was with, and said right out loud, *I can't tell if that's a man or a woman!* I took the last couple of steps into the chest-high water, and as I passed, whispered to her, *Well, whatever it is, it has ears...* She gasped, wide-eyed, and said nothing.

Work of Becoming

For most of my life, I've turned to the grace of creating and making for refuge. In the turbulence of so much change—so much releasing of what I'd thought of as myself—I needed to be absorbed in something beyond myself. You've likely heard of the concept of Flow, but whether you're familiar with it or not, you've almost certainly experienced it. You're in Flow when you're engaged in something to point of losing track of time, when your mind is devoted to what you're doing instead of rambling about from random thought to thought as it's normally inclined to do. Time dissolves, and so do concerns outside the process. I'd merge into Flow in the studio, and later find much work done.

I'd created a nearly insurmountable mountain of work for myself—and though I wasn't conscious of it at the time—climbed it daily as if my life depended on it. Sometimes, it was all I had for solace: I'd come home from yet another intense round of electrolysis, have a good cry, and lean right back into the making.

I needed a good, long hug, but with no one there, I threw my arms around the work instead. Bringing my attention to something absorbingly constructive kept me from spiraling into self-pity and despair.

Later, when the redness and swelling had subsided, I'd go to a local sauna and nurture myself with a good skin-healing sweat. The intense physicality of the work was my therapy, and at times, a kind of productive scream of pain and aloneness into the Void. I couldn't be in Flow and stuck in the difficult confluence of mind and emotions at the same time; it was intense connection with something, and I had a deep well of need for that in the whirl of becoming.

□ □ □

Sprouting Wings

Human beings can endure anything if there is hope—a light at the end of the proverbial tunnel. I could see and feel the changes that spurred it to the next step, and the next, and beyond that to a female form beyond the pain and becoming. I was hopeful, too, for the honor and privilege of a mutually nurturing relationship with a woman as a woman, and for richer creative expression born of the rub of my sensibility with the world across time. Perhaps most profoundly, I hoped for the presence of home inside and out—of belonging in a physical landscape where I'd simply be the woman I am, loving and being loved in a vibrant circle of sharing.

One of the heartbreakers in looking back is that I had the money for the SRS (Sex Reassignment Surgery) from selling the house, but the electrolysis and the overhead of running the shop had gradually drained it away. I was left with no apparent option but to just keep on hoping and working.

Portrait of the Artist as a Young Transsexual

For nearly three years, I kept going until I saw the treadmill for what it was: I wasn't making any money beyond the overhead, what I was creating wasn't satisfying my deeper artistic longings, and the coarseness of West Oakland was steadily wearing at my connection with soul. I craved a more natural setting for my work, wherever and whatever that might be. The electrolysis was done, I'd transitioned as far as the hormones could take me, and there was nothing left to keep me in the city.

Naturally, I was concerned about leaving the hotbed of lesbians, gays, and trans-folk of all sorts where I'd been reborn. I had no idea how I'd be received "out there," but an incident made it abundantly clear it was time to go, regardless: One day, as I was returning home in my silver Dodge van, I was zooming along a one-way, two-lane road before coming to a stop sign. A Cadillac pulled up on my right side, and a huge black man yelled through the open window, *Hey, white bitch, you want me to shoot you?* Embroiled in road rage, he started to reach over to his glove compartment, never taking his cold, angry eyes off me. I'm still astonished that I looked right back at him and casually said, *You got a problem?*

Now, it would be fair to say that would not be anywhere near the top of a sane list of recommended responses, but he just stared a moment longer and squealed off to the right. I turned left onto the main drag home, and started digesting what had just happened. The first thought which came to mind, after absorbing the fact that I could well have been shot right back there, was that it had been an appropriate time to be cautious, and it simply hadn't occurred to me to be anything of the sort. It had certainly happened too quickly for weighing options anyway, but it was utterly clear I'd become far too acclimated to the harshness of the light-industrial ghetto I'd been calling home, and it was time to start heading toward a gentler realm.

As much as I would have liked to just pack up and leave, my life wasn't so simple. There was a major interior project in the pipeline, and the breakdown of the studio setup to contend with—a huge undertaking in itself. So I spent a couple of months or so coloring that interior in the seaside town of Pacifica—just south of San Francisco—before returning to Oakland and putting most everything but the lumber inventory in storage.

Then, I was free to head off to the arid Southwest on a search mission for a new home, with a circuitous path toward Santa Fe, New Mexico.

I Am Here

Looking back over a sizable arc of lifetime, I see in my ways a strong tendency to leap into action as an alternative to sinking into fear or despair. There's a great deal of good to be said for going within and embracing the sources of suffering deeply—a fine use, indeed, of some quiet time in contemplative meditation. And there's a balancing dose of hope and healing to be found in productive interplay with the outer landscape as well. There may be at times an element of escapism in this Doing, but I'd much rather be in motion—where momentum and enthusiasm are available—than wallowing in the darker shadows of the inner landscape.

Sometimes, I've felt compelled to action which was, or just might have been, a solution of some sort to the fear or despair—as when I was afraid of not being able to pay the bills, and was soon off to the studio to make something which would, at some point at least, entice some funds my way. Other times, just getting active has been, in itself, enough to shift my attention outward—keeping the mind and energy focused expansively on the present—thereby placing myself on the path of unfolding potential. Gardening has been wonderful for this: I can be outdoors, interacting with nature, exercising some nurture—and getting some, too.

There seems to be, as well, a scale of impetus and response: In those earlier years of transition, I needed a lot of action to ground and release the apparently bottomless upset, which wasn't as much a response to the inner process of gender change itself, as to the wounds of childhood revealed and amplified by the flood of hormones. I theorized at the time that one's pain becomes engrained in the physical body, and in reprogramming mine—causing it to change right down to the cellular level—the pain was being released. Whether or not it was factually true, it certainly felt that way, and a response in physical movement felt not only natural, but necessary. Much needed releasing, and much building was done.

It's a blessing to have finally come to a place in life in which fear and despair aren't like wolves at the door. When I'm compelled to movement now, it's a much gentler thing: a calling to physical presence—to the joy of simply Being in motion. It's a response, as well, to the necessity of exercise, as I can't rely these days on the intensity of labor to keep me in shape.

Back in the days of gung ho making and building, I'd be in a check-out line or at a social event and some woman would look me over and say, *Wow, you're in great shape... you must work out!* To which I'd reply, *No, I just work!* Now, as a juggler of words, there is motion still, but much of it in far more rarefied form. And when I sculpt, it's with featherlight paper and pigments, in lieu of lumber and power tools.

The exercise is wonderful, but in recalling those earlier times, I *need* to break away and move in the landscape of the present— the better to feel the stillness from which the ongoing Now pours. One can't help but hyper-activate the program of memory in this sort of life-combing, and it loops on in the background of its own accord well after the process of writing is put aside. So I practice self-compassion along this journey of words by staying aware of my state of Being in the midst of digging up those old ghosts, and—to some intuitive rhythm—breaking away to a counter-point of blessed Now in motion.

There's a set of stone stairs lined with mossy rock walls on this sloping bit of Balinese land I call home. When I'm called to move, I do the stairs: going up them two at a time, and squeezing my butt muscles with each step down. I do them enough times to get my heart rate up, and to firmly remind me one conscious step at a time, by way of blood-coursing celebration: *I am here... I am here... I am here...*

4

Desert Home in the Sky

Alighting in Madrid

The first afternoon, I reached Lake Tahoe and headed off over the Continental Divide. Driving east along Highway 50, I soon realized that, true to form, I'd chosen the road less traveled. The official signs had the tagline *The Loneliest Highway in America* right under the 50, and I was left to wonder what, indeed, was loneliest out there. The two-lane strip of asphalt cut across a sunburned, rocky landscape that looked so barren and bombed-out, it'd be a shoo-in for a post-apocalypse movie backdrop. There was little to keep the road company, except for the dazed humans drifting through in cars every now and then.

Out there, you gas up when you can; the next station is a long ways off, and there's little but rocks and dust occupying the space between. Heading into a nighttime drive to avoid the intense sun, I stopped to fill up. I got out for a stretch as a young guy emerged from the grey-brown shop, wiping his hands with a greasy rag. *Howdy ma'm, what'll it be: regular or premium?* I'd left the womb of the Bay Area not knowing how I'd be received, and knew right then I'd be all right.

I had set up the van for camping, and felt as self-sufficient as an astronaut making my way toward Santa Fe. I van-camped at state parks, which meant setting up the camp stove, making dinner, reading awhile, and sleeping in the back of the van. There was black fabric ready to hang over the windows, so I could park on the street and sleep in there if I wanted when I reached Santa Fe, and for the first few nights, I did just that.

In the midst of stucco and stone buildings dating back to the early 1600s, there's a lovely plaza in the heart of Santa Fe. I was sitting on a shady bench there several days after my arrival, eating an ice cream cone and reading a Tom Robbins novel, when a man sat down and struck up a conversation. I shared the nature of my trip with Joe, and he said, *So, sounds like you're looking for an alternative lifestyle... You ever hear of a place called Madrid?* He seemed a little let down that I hadn't, but when he described the artist colony just south of the city, I knew I had to see it, and agreed to visit the next day.

It was love at first sight. I'd been inspired in my studio work by an affinity for things with a patina of time on them, and this little village was so filled with that sort of ambiance, I wanted to slice it up and eat it like pie. There were fabulous old rusty objects scattered in yards, accompanied by wooden things deeply grooved by sun, water, and wind. Joe and I had a great talk, and I ended up van-camping in his driveway for a while until I found a more permanent place.

Madrid, it turned out, was a haven for outlaws, misfits, and rebels of various stripes. It was a wonderfully odd and diverse group of people who had a common desire to be as far from the mainstream as they could reasonably get. One of them looked me up and down when I first got there and promptly said, *You look like you belong here!* as if it were a compliment of the highest order. Compliment or not, it was true, and I took to this village and its colorful populace like a bird to sky, and they welcomed me right in.

I hadn't been there all that long when a big, burly guy with a nose obviously broken numerous times came up to me in the tavern and said over the wailing blues band, *Hey, I don't know what your story is, but I like you, and if anyone gives you a hard time in this place, I'll beat the livin' daylights out of 'em.* He looked me straight in the eye for a moment, nodded to let me know he meant it, and walked back to his beer. I never needed his brawling assistance even a little, but damn, that was awfully sweet—in a hit-first-think-later sort of way.

I spent the Fourth of July—Independence Day—in a gravel pit with perhaps a hundred or so other people, drinking beer, yakking, and listening to a local rock band. The dry, mountain air would kick up dust devils—tiny tornado-like whirls of dust— every now and then amid the sun and rocks, and the sheer rawness of it all felt as if I'd found not just another state, but another planet to call home. Being so far in every way from the bad side of a hard town filled me with a most intense, sublime sense of freedom and possibility.

For years, I'd told friends I was figuring spirit might throw some more energy and opportunity in the direction of someone taking on the challenges of Being their true Self in the world, and doing what flowed directly out of that. I imagined Spirit looking down and saying, *Let's send some extras down to that one just to see what she does with it.* Keeping it interesting in the present seemed a good way to invite more interest down the road, and this intensely dry, wide-open realm had certainly drawn mine.

There were shops lining the main street, many of which had a small living space in back, and quite a few people made a living making and selling their wares, or just selling funky, artful stuff. With its old, wooden buildings, Madrid (pronounced MAD-rid) looked like a displaced New England town perched between sheer, rocky ridges in the high desert, and in a way, it was.

From the 1850s to the 1950s, Madrid was a coal-mining company town with a population of around three thousand—more than ten times as many people as when I was there. Most of the houses had been brought in on railcar from coalfields in Pennsylvania, which is why it looked like a Northern town. They'd been sliced in half, loaded on trains, and crudely reassembled in this dusty hamlet. To compensate for the dearth of insulation in the windy, cold winters, each was fitted with a relatively massive boiler and given—it was a company town, so it wasn't free—a hefty monthly allotment of local coal. Those old boilers were one source of the rusty artifacts ensconced in many yards and gardens.

In the early Seventies, hippies began squatting in the abandoned buildings—living there and doing what they could to scrape out a living. Not surprisingly, many turned to pottery-making. Highway 14, the scenic two-laner through the Ortiz mountain pass between Santa Fe and Albuquerque, went right through town, and some semblance of a living could be made by setting up a shop and enticing a little money from passersby with one's wares.

After Madrid's coal mining enterprise was shut down in 1954, the man who had been the manager bought the then nine thousand acre village, including over a hundred buildings, trains, trestles, and a ballpark from the coal company. Well into the Seventies, he tried to find a buyer for the whole place. I heard that at one point it was advertised in the Wall Street Journal for just two hundred and fifty thousand dollars, but there was no taker. Instead, he put out word that he'd sell off the lots individually, and whoever was renting would have first dibs. Sometime between squatting and the sale, rents had been established—from what I heard, they amounted to ten to fifteen dollars a month—and that would become the payment for the lots, which were priced between fifteen hundred and twenty five hundred dollars apiece. He set up some card tables, and the lots were sold off in one day.

By the time I arrived in 1992, it was known as an artist colony—a go-to place for unusual art, and to get a feel for what Santa Fe was like twenty years before. Madrid attracted unusual people, and with no police stationed there, it had an outlaw reputation—though certainly some of that was a holdover from its earlier days. It was a colorful mix of aging hippies, artists, gays, gender-variant folks, Vietnam vets, people "living on the land," musicians, and other assorted refugees from the mainstream.

Desert Home in the Sky

A Shack of My Own

Not one to let a little financial reality get in the way, I started poking around for a place to buy, despite the fact that I'd burnt up what equity I'd had from the last house with the furniture business and transitioning, and was even a bit in debt. Tucked up high in the peaks just over the ridge from town, there was some land with views out across a basin that must be sixty or seventy miles wide, and over to the Atalaya Mountains rising right out of Santa Fe to the north.

It was breathtaking, and heartbreaking to leave behind when—in a moment of irrepressible rationality—I realized that even if I managed to buy the land, I had no money with which to build; not to mention that it was very exposed to the natural elements up there, which would make doing anything challenging. There were, in fact, some things that the duo of shear will and creative ambition wouldn't cover, and this was one of them.

It was obvious, then, that I needed to start with a building of some sort, so I began looking closer in. Right away, I found an ideal place on the main street—that is, the one paved street, only because it happened to be part of that little two-lane highway. I started out renting it while we came up with a purchase agreement, which gave me a chance to give it an in-depth inspection.

Having grown up working on old houses, I had a really good idea of the mess I was getting into. Compared to the prices in the Bay Area, this place was a pittance, but it would obviously require a lot of work—not to mention outright tenacity—to turn into something nice.

In the back of my mind, I dreamt of a resting place with time for contemplation on a regular basis, and the space to cultivate other options for creative livelihood, but the reality of the moment suggested I settle in somewhere and get busy earning some money. In leaving California, I'd wanted to let go of furniture making and explore other avenues, but my options for livelihood were limited in New Mexico's thin economy. What jobs there were paid poorly, and working for myself did appear, once again, to be the best option; I had to live somewhere, and since I could do my work there, too, I wasn't taking on more overhead for studio space.

I was responding, in part, to the financial situation I'd created back in Oakland, but I also loved this desert place, and clearly, I wasn't yet done with the need for a direct connection with the Earth element. Here, it was the epitome of solidity—a rocky, mineral-laden landscape pushed up into a vast sky, and it was this intense feeling of Earth pressed to Sky that lent a sense of balance. In Oakland, I'd engaged Earth, but it felt disengaged from Sky, and I had to break away and go up into the hills to really connect with it. In New Mexico, Sky was an immediate presence, an entity that would not—and could not—be ignored.

Leaving the Bay Area, I'd been concerned about finding a place where I'd both feel at home, and be accepted. In Madrid, I'd not only found both, I even felt celebrated in who I was, and I was more than willing to do what it took to stay there. Beneath the creative ambition and will necessary to take on this tired old shack was a wellspring of enthusiasm for engaging this landscape and village which felt like home—and truly could be if I made it so.

When it came to a choice between comfort and life experience, I knew by then I'd choose to rough-it. In this case, I'd soon become deeply familiar with the term *indoor camping*.

Every building in town was said to have active spirits in residence, and apparently, mine was no exception. My glorified shack came complete with an aversion to anger, and was reputed to respond to it in a couple of ways— both of which I heard about from various independent sources covering a wide spectrum of dubiousness. One source—who had actually lived there some years before, and was known locally for her psychic talents—said that there was a pair of spirits: *...two old ladies who loved a party and any sort of fun*

time, but had real problems with anger and fighting of any kind. She said they responded to the latter by either opening and closing every door and window in the house at the same time, or coursing through the house as a pair of lights about eye-width apart—seemingly as a sort of warning. I'd heard about the "eyes," too, from the argument-prone couple that had rented the place the month before I took it over.

Certainly, one could go around and around with whether or not these stories held any validity, or were just part of the rich local lore, but I'd had enough occurrences of slipping through the veils between this world of form and the formless beyond, that I saw no reason not to honor what I'd heard and make some effort to engage the place energetically.

When at last the couple's month was finished, the next time I entered the house I just talked to it. I said that I was going to be making a lot of noise, and making many changes to it, but it would be done to bring in more light and joy and beauty, and I'd be doing it with good heart and intentions.

I was familiar with Native American smudging rituals, and had done them for years to cleanse the energy of places into which I was moving, so I lit the bundle of sage and sweetgrass, blessed the directions, and brought the smoke into all the rooms, especially the corners, inviting in clean, bright spirit. Also, taking a candle around to all the darker spaces, I introduced my spirit to the place. Then, it felt like it was truly mine.

There wasn't anything that didn't require replacing, including the electrical, plumbing, roof, windows, and on and on. And there were things it simply didn't have, like a water heater, flush toilet, or even insulation. By the time I took possession of the place, it was getting into September, which left little time to do much-needed repairs before the real cold came to the mountains. Too, before I could do much of anything, I needed to drive back to the Bay Area to get the tools, furniture, and supplies I'd put in storage. From the frying pan of overworked days in Oakland, I'd jumped right into the fire in New Mexico.

Writing Womb

There are times when the Western impetus to charge right out and shake a little money at a problem actually serves well. Not long ago, while I was sitting out on the veranda writing, a mosquito landed on my arm in the mid-day warm, and proceeded to feast on my blood. I do live next to a river here in Ubud, and had gotten used to their presence in the early morning and evening. Certainly by five o'clock I'd have moved inside—behind the plastic screen that hangs in lieu of a real screen door—but in the bright light of a quite dry day, the presence of this anomalous little creature felt like a wake-up call.

Suddenly, I felt finished with those limited hours of access to my favorite spot, and decided right then those little buggers would no longer chase me inside. Though at the moment I was reluctant to interrupt the flow of words, I stood up, got my helmet and motorbike keys, and headed off to a shop that makes wonderful mosquito nets. They'd made a custom one for a friend, so I knew they had canopy-style nets for large beds. I didn't need a fancy one, but I did want one large enough that I wouldn't feel hemmed-in.

With a brief exchange of broken English and halting Indonesian, we found one in stock which would create what amounted to a small room of about seven by seven feet. It was a blessing, indeed, to have the means to simply afford this solution, which cost the princely sum of about thirty dollars—likely more than half a month's salary for someone working in a store here.

Although it was originally envisioned as a pragmatic fix for a pesky problem, it's turned out to be so much more. I hung it that afternoon from bamboo canes Agung and I harvested from the yard. After attaching it to the ceiling of the veranda, I stepped back, and was immediately enchanted by its soft, draping lines. What I now call the *Writing Womb* feels like an angelic realm—enveloping my practice in gauzy white light, and offering not so much *more* space, as a unique quality of space simultaneously indoors and out.

It's the studio I haven't had for a long while, yet a delightful counterpoint to the density of metal machines and plaster walls of every studio I've previously engaged. There could hardly be a perch more befitting the lightness of calling words. And that it lets me stretch out in privacy, in the comfort of less clothing at whatever hours I choose, is a bonus most splendorous.

You may have noticed I'm more than a little attracted to things between. Not surprisingly then, this realm felt, from the moment I stepped inside, like home. It's a fabric microcosm of the sensibility that entices me here: residence that spans realms, with wafting walls as much of light as fabric and air.

□ □ □

Joyous Absurdity

Returning to the Bay Area also opened the door to reconnecting with a lover whose touch I was very much missing. A few months before leaving West Oakland, I'd met a woman at the hot springs resort north of the city. The ensuing connection was relatively uncomplicated—particularly in light of the knowledge that I would be leaving soon—but my moving to another part of the country had left it still in limbo.

The resort had a range of pools of differing temperatures, and we'd met in the warm one—the most popular place for hanging out. I was doing just that one afternoon when I felt a strong, attractive presence near me. I turned, and there was Mandy standing there quite naked as well. Without saying a word, we hugged deeply. It lasted quite some time while we both soaked up the extraordinarily warm and expansive energy.

I heard at one point—not with my ears, but very clearly as an inner voice—*I love you, I love you, I love you...* and felt it with my whole Being. When we let go, I realized we weren't the only ones who felt the charge—everyone in the pool was gazing our way with a dreamy look in their eyes.

Mandy and I shared names and talked a little, but as she'd come to the pool for a last dip before leaving, we didn't do much more than exchange phone numbers. When I went to visit her in San Jose a couple of weeks later, we got to know each other a little more. It turned out she was—not surprisingly—bisexual; she was also thirteen years older, and at the tail end of a divorce. She'd felt as if she were suffocating in the marriage, and was opening her life up to new ways of Being. As I was feeling a strong desire for a radical change of environment as well, we had a sense of ripe potential in common—although it was clearly calling us down different paths.

Since the attraction was still very much there in our visit, we naturally ended up in the same bed that night and enjoyed some really gorgeous sex. That we'd been naked when we met had neatly sidestepped the issue of having to come out to her about my gender status, and I was relieved and grateful for the unique grace of this ease.

Before we drifted off to sleep, Mandy said she'd felt for so long as if she were drowning in her marriage, and had ended up sharing a bed for longer than she'd wanted; she said that, as much as she loved the touch, she needed to sleep alone. She took me to a guest room, tucked me in, and went back to hers. I understood her needs, but I'd been feeling intensely alone in the world, and wanted to go to sleep, and wake up, next to a sweet lover. I kept this to myself, focusing instead on the lovely connection overall.

It seemed from the start, that while we were meant to be lovers, we weren't meant to fall in love. There was another role to play in each other's lives, and it was not meant to be a long-term thing. I don't quite remember if I was already talking about moving to New Mexico when we met, or if it came up soon after, but it was a factor pretty much from the start. Perhaps that other role was to provide each other with a benchmark for outstanding sex. It was simply remarkable to be with someone with whom I didn't need to explain myself, or feel incomplete in my womanly embodiment.

After an extended session of lovemaking early on in the affair, she asked, *Where's your orgasm based?... Where's it coming from?* When I thought about it, I realized it wasn't coming as much from my genitals as from the base of my spine. She laughed and nodded: *I thought it might be something like that!*

Desert Home in the Sky

What had prompted her to ask was that we were having amazingly long orgasms. From then on, I'd just reach back and touch the base of her spine, and she'd be "plugged in," too. This divine Tantric energy would just keep pouring through, until finally we'd just fall all over each other laughing with the joyous absurdity of having to decide when to stop it. Thirty, forty minutes... an hour... How much was enough?

When I arrived back in the Bay Area for my belongings, she'd moved out of the house she'd shared with her now ex-husband, and had gotten an apartment. In the couple of weeks it took to get my things in order, get a truck, and load it, we got together for a couple of dates which ended, naturally, with some delicious sex—and me sleeping on a mat on the living room floor.

Leaving her husband and home hadn't ended her sense of suffocation, and her disallowing me from sleeping in her bed was obviously not something I could take personally. Yet I couldn't ignore that what I wanted was for our sleeping arrangement to *be* more personal. In the name of good touch, I made do; I did, after all, live in another part of the country, and was getting no grief from her about leaving.

☐ ☐ ☐

Indoor Camping at Its Finest

I set out for the Southwest with the biggest truck I could rent without getting into a commercial vehicle, and pulled the van behind—making the rig as long as the long-haul trailer trucks I pulled up beside at rest areas. I woke in the cab the first morning to the sun just peeking over the desert mountains east of Bakersfield, found some reasonably palatable coffee, and just kept going. Any long-distance driving has for me at least a tinge of mission to it, but this one was especially so: It was a lot of vehicle with little room for error behind the wheel, it contained nearly everything I owned, and winter was quickly descending on my new home which was, in fact, an old shack.

Back in Madrid, I'd no sooner returned, and had to unload the truck—which was costing by the day—and get busy with house repairs. Within a week or two, I heard on the radio that snow was expected in the mountains that night, and I thought to myself, *Those poor bastards in the mountains!* I woke the next morning to find several inches of snow on the ground, and realized *I* was one those poor bastards in the mountains.

The snow melted during the day, and the house was scattered with anything capable of catching water from the dripping roof. I looked around and had a good laugh—it looked like one of those cartoon leaky-roofed houses with dozens of pots and pans placed strategically about the place.

A flush toilet would have to come later as I redesigned the house. Meanwhile, the old outhouse was filled to the brim, so I dug a new hole, and quickly built a wooden frame with old plywood on three sides. An image I'll never forget is sitting in the outhouse late at night in winter—with Fahrenheit temperatures in the single digits or low teens—and watching the burlap "door" flapping in the wind. I may have set records for efficiency in leaving "contributions" out there.

One saving grace was the house had a relatively new soapstone wood-burning stove that really put out heat—which was a good thing, because, as I've mentioned, the place had no insulation. My first thought in waking up in the morning was, *Get that stove going!* as it was the only heat source for the whole place at the beginning, and since it absorbed so much heat itself, it'd take about forty-five minutes to really get radiating.

It was indoor camping at its finest: I slept in a sleeping bag on a foam mattress, cooked on a camping stove, and relieved myself outdoors. It was invigorating, to say the least, to wake up every morning and be face-to-face with so much need for even the basic things.

At first, everything was on a makeshift basis to get the essentials in order, and get the quality of life raised—aesthetics be damned. I couldn't help but think of the interior projects I'd done—fine-tuning color and woodworking to a high degree of nuance—and here I was celebrating getting weather-stripping jammed into gaping cracks to minimize the wind blowing through the place.

Desert Home in the Sky

The first month or so was spent setting up a basic studio to facilitate working on the house, and getting the place winterized to at least a reasonable degree. I made interior walls and a door with wooden frames covered in sheet plastic between the living and working spaces. *Like Biosphere!* I'd say to friends who'd drop by to say hello and see the progress. We had to agree, though, that the walls in the other one probably didn't bow like sails every time the wind blew.

I was blessed to have some cash still from the coloring project in Pacifica, so I had the gas company come out from Santa Fe and install a propane heater in the living section; a two-burner, free-standing cooking unit on a table that stood in for a counter in the kitchen; and an on-demand water heater in the basement—all hooked up to a large, bullet-shaped tank out in the yard. With twenty-five percent down, and easy monthly payments, my standard of living took quite a leap in one day.

The only incident I knowingly had with spirits in the house happened one very cold night as I lay in the sleeping bag. I became aware of feeling the foam mat squashing down at intervals along my body, as if someone were walking on it. I was still mostly asleep, and as I tried to wake up fully, something seemed to be energetically pressing down on my chest—as if it wanted to keep me from waking. It was rather like being held under water, and a terrifying struggle ensued as I tried to reach the "surface"— in this case, wakefulness.

I have no idea how long it lasted, but by sheer force of will, I was finally able to wake up. When I did, I was covered in sweat, exhausted, and a little freaked out, but nothing strange was in the room as far as I could tell. Somehow, I fell back to sleep, and never experienced anything like it again.

While the payments on the house were a fraction of what I'd paid for the lease back in West Oakland, I did need to make some money pretty soon. The best prospects, though, were still in the Bay Area, so I put out the word there that I was still available for interior coloring projects. I don't recall how he found me, but a man whom I'd never met called and expressed interest in my coming to work with some color in his place in San Francisco, and through a friend of a friend, another party near Santa Cruz was interested as well.

The lifestyle of a freelance artisan necessarily calls for winging it, and I was doing that unabashedly. With the quality of life at the house elevated to several notches above survival mode, I began focusing on battening it down for an extended absence, and prepping for the trip back to the Bay Area. I had no idea how long I'd be gone, as the agreement with the man in San Francisco was that we'd see what had gotten done in a month, and go from there, and there was no firm arrangement for the other potential project. But there was opportunity to be had—in a lovely climate at that—and I didn't think twice about responding to the opportunity.

□ □ □

Rocky Reentry

One of the priorities in getting back to the Bay Area was a visit with the Endocrinologist, as my supply of hormones was getting low. I began spreading out the dosage as I got closer to the appointment, and the psycho-emotional backwash I'd first experienced when starting the hormones started to resurface. I'd long settled into an ongoing state of relative stability, but there they were again: upwellings of grief and sadness for little or no reason.

My appointment wasn't for another week or so after I arrived, so before I got together with Mandy, I mentioned I was in a vulnerable emotional state, and asked her to keep it in mind. We arranged to spend a weekend at a house in the country owned by a friend of hers, and stopped on the way for some healthy things to eat and some lovely wine. The place was very private, and had a pool which we took advantage of in the mid-day heat.

Of course, we made love, and I remember thinking as I turned my head to the side and saw in my mind's eye the earth going by in molten waves, that if I were to die soon, or just not have sex again for whatever reason, I could die knowing I'd really "gotten it"—had touched and been touched with exquisite grace.

Later, we lay around the pool reading and napping. Then, as if a switch had been flipped, she suddenly started criticizing me relentlessly over really small things as if she wanted to break up the simple, easy thing we had together. My request that she be easy on my vulnerable state was not only thrown out the window, it seemed like she was taking particular advantage of it. I turned to an old pattern from childhood of retracting in self-protection, and within a very short while we left. That sweet connection dissolved about as quickly as it had appeared in the warm pool at the hot springs, and I never saw her again.

Artist in Residences

The studio work sidestepped much of the complexity of workaday human affairs, and resolved the dilemma of being my unusual self and making a living in a world that condones conformity. I could just let go into the creative, energetic flow of it, and not worry about fitting into an employer's program—or pretty much any program at all, for that matter.

The on-the-road projects were, however, a world apart from the beloved, solitary studio life. I became an artist-in-residence—quite literally—in people's homes, and with this came the rub of family life in myriad forms. I showed up with a portable studio, and personal gear as one might for an extended vacation—though most of the wardrobe was composed of studio-stained shirts and pants. The things I brought lent some semblance of familiarity to being temporarily immersed full-time in other people's spaces and daily lives. It helped, too, that as I transformed one room after another, the place evoked a more balanced sense of home, for both me and the clients.

That I was compelled to work with so much Earth element—through the woodworking and completely rebuilding my own home—gives a sense of what my needs were at the time. Yet, there I was, like a gypsy, plying my creativity far away from my chosen place of grounding, in other people's homes, living in their worlds.

Most people are unaware of the psycho-emotional exchange of energy that's constantly going on as we interact: We "feed" on each other subconsciously—not recognizing the energy consumed in the process. In part from growing up in my mother's house, I knew how to make myself pretty much disappear energetically, which allowed me to float later like a ghost in other people's homes. I don't mean this in a negative sense, as if I felt like I *had* to disappear. I saw it as part of my service: I could bring an aesthetic sense of aliveness and balance to a space with little spewing my own energy, or drawing on others' in the process.

Certainly my awareness of this was an outgrowth of having spent so much time alone, but it was clearly a reason, as well, that I'd been drawn to solitude all along. One client put it nicely when she said, with considerable delight, *I usually really hate having people around the house, but with you here, I have no problem just going about my day as if I had the place to myself.* Considering that at the time I'd taken over a substantial portion of her house with my ladders and tarps and so on, I took this as quite fine feedback.

It was essential I stay aware of my own process and refrain from entangling it with these projects, as I needed to hold the focus on the vision I had for the place, and to deal with others' responses to it as it unfolded. Not only did I have to avoid being deterred by my clients' fears of not getting what they wanted, as the project evolved, there was sometimes an undercurrent of discomfort with getting more than they knew to ask for. I specialized in using color to evoke a sense of balance and harmony, and of being held in a supportive surround. As the project evolved to a critical mass of rooms working together, they'd sometimes feel a little disoriented because they weren't used to having this in their chaotic, busy lives. At those times especially, it seemed as though I should add *Space Therapist* to my business card.

I often felt like a tightrope walker, with my inner process on one side, the relationship with the clients on the other, and the vision for the space, lean and taut, right down the middle into a haze that obscured its final destination.

On the surface, it may seem odd that I, the quintessential outsider, was being called upon to create intensively-tuned interiors. But then, I'd extensively remodeled myself inside and out, had done an enormous amount of inner work in the process, and had learned to hold myself at the meeting place of inner and outer landscapes. And because I was intensely aware of the benefits of such nurturing surrounds, I could transform their space with color into something that worked far better as a place of inspiration and balance: one that would hold them like a nest in the broader landscape they called home.

The first—and at the time, only—project was well up on Corona Heights in San Francisco, a steep walk up from the heart of the Castro district. Bob turned out to be a pretty conservative lawyer, and one of, at most, a few straight men for many blocks around. It was quite extraordinary—and surreal—to shift so quickly from being alone and renovating the shack of a place in Madrid, to being in the city, in someone's highly polished home, and living with someone whose outlook was pretty much the antithesis of mine. Adding to the oddity of the moment, I landed there still experiencing the backwash of being short on hormones, and the upset of Mandy's sudden conversion from casual lover to Queen of Unpleasantness.

In the confluence of all that, it was a relief to just unload and set up the tools, dive into the work, and engage the familiar rhythms. One of the first things I'd do in color design projects was a contemplation of the palette I'd introduce, and for that, I'd do a good deal of observing. My approach was to support the people's sensibilities and create a feeling of really belonging in their home, so the palette of colors would integrate them, their belongings, the architecture, and the surrounding landscape.

This was one of the more creative aspects, along with orchestrating a sort of conversation among those colors throughout the space. To engage a vision that holds all those elements, one has to surrender one's own concerns and open to What Is in *this place*, in *this* moment—and I was plenty happy to just let go into that. I was out of the mountain cold, in a great part of a favorite city, being creative, and making some much-needed cash.

It was creative, to be sure, but not in an open, discovery-oriented way, so with this sort of project I thought of myself as a *Creative Mercenary*—which I sometimes joked about putting on my business card, as well. It wasn't artistically ideal, but it was a blessing to have the ability, and an honor to make a living adding beauty to the world while having a real impact on people's quality of life—and to exercise so much freedom in the process. It was freedom with a price, however, in that I periodically experienced anxiety from not knowing how I'd pay the bills just down the road—a lifestyle rather like a tightrope act, as well.

Lorraine—the woman with whom I'd been talking about doing another project while I was on the West Coast—brought her family up from Santa Cruz to see this project in San Francisco. We hit it off immediately, as often happened with people attracted to my work. She and her husband appreciated the quality of the finishing and the vision that pulled it all together, but she wasn't afraid to say she wanted more vibrant color in her place.

The palette at Bob's was pretty muted—understated and elegant, with eggshell tones of yellows, greens, blues, and purples—which worked very nicely in the context of his place and personality, but Lorraine was definitely a high-energy person with a rambunctious bunch of boys. Her project felt like a fine counterpoint to the one at hand, and given that I could sense what was needed in any space, I assured her they'd be very happy with what I came up with for them.

In about six week's time, I'd finished roughly half the space at Bob's place, and we spoke of my coming back, perhaps about the same time the next year. I repacked the studio gear, and headed south toward Santa Cruz, keenly aware of the double-edged quality of sensitivity which comes into play with this kind of lifestyle: The work required a good deal of empathy, but it also meant being prone to overwhelm from so much newness and none of my own Earth for grounding—with the faint exception of the deeply familiar tools.

While the impetus at Bob's had been to soften and warm the experience of the dense urban setting and create a backdrop for his art collection, the scene in the hills near Santa Cruz could hardly have been more different. Set on a hilltop with expansive views of the lowlands and out over the bay, the house had ceilings that soared to over fifteen feet and a feeling of being thrust into the sky. In this regard, it resembled being in the hills of New Mexico, except here on the coast, the land was much softer and the sky not nearly as imposing. In fact, the coastal fog that often drifted through in the evening usually hung around until it was burned off in the mid-morning sun.

One advantage of being an artist-in-residence was that I could regularly experience the space in all its phases: from dawn to mid-day sun to dusk, and by electric light at night. Here, the palette would need to work well in light sometimes subdued and diffused, and at others, almost overwhelmingly bright and sheer.

With a good set of colors at hand, I proceeded organically, never trying to lay out the whole scheme up front. Observing from the rhythms of the day, I'd gather little bits of insight into what a space needed, so when the time came to apply the finish there, I already pretty much knew what to do. I'd most often fine-tune the original colors to account for the actuality of the setting: the neighboring hues, the qualities of daylight entering the space, the subtle colors cast by reflected light from the outdoors and among the surfaces around the rooms.

Once again, the contrast with my interrupted new life in Madrid bordered on the surreal. I could hardly have felt further from the wood burning stove, frigid outhouse, billowing plastic walls, and long stretch of mud that passed for a driveway. I'd arrived in the wet season, so the cool, foggy mornings sometimes tapered into rain, but usually evolved into warm, sunny afternoons. Massive bushes of datura trumpets had plenty of company in their blooming, the grass was absurdly green, and the trees were a well-leaved far cry from the skeletal ones I'd left behind.

Though I was working about ten hours a day, seven days a week—as I had in San Francisco—I didn't mind. I'd take off part of a day here and there, and it was less time than I'd been putting in on the house in New Mexico and during the studio days back in Oakland. It was such a blessing to be amid the green and warm, it even felt at times like a quasi-vacation.

Perched on a hilltop overlooking the coast, and on stepladders transforming the blank canvas of white walls, I was in my medium: in motion between realms. The study of color theory, which had been integral to the awakening of my creative spirit so many years before, had turned out to be the headwaters of a passionate affair with light, and I was deeply grateful for this powerful undercurrent in my life.

In all the social interactions amidst these projects, my gender never overtly came up—not that my being unusual went noticed. I was blessed in being most interested in showing up as the *person* I was, rather than looking for affirmation of my being a woman. I was self-accepting, and people just went along with me. I mentioned earlier the mutual, unconscious "siphoning" of energy as humans interact, and in this regard, I wasn't trying to draw a certain reaction from them; in fact, I was offering a sense of spaciousness—of self-license to Be—in the process of my being at ease with myself.

Desert Home in the Sky

With a natural ending place for the project in sight, I was getting antsy to return home to Madrid. As I had at Bob's, I worked for about six weeks at Lorraine's, and we spoke as well about coloring the other half the following year.

With the gear stowed once more in back, I made my way down through central California, and across the bottom of the Sierra Nevada Range at the Tehachapi Pass. (I don't know exactly why it was, but every time I'd see those clusters of massive windmills on those dry hills, I'd cry—there was just something so graceful and hopeful about them.) Then, I joined the road out across the rocky, dry scrublands, and over the alpine mountains through Flagstaff. With a hard left to the north at Albuquerque, the gear and I were soon up into the Ortiz Mountains on Highway 14—which passed right by my own home sweet shack.

Back to Basics

There were signs of early spring everywhere when I woke once again on my own futon. The night was still quite cold, but the sun rose earlier and higher, the trees were budding nicely, and the birds flitted about with anticipation. The shift in focus was quite dramatic: From the fine-tuning of colors to support nuanced plays of harmony and flow, I was suddenly back to the most rudimentary stages of remodeling an old building in desperate need of everything. But whereas before I'd left the light had been descending into the cold, dark north, now it was rising into warmer, longer days—and with it came a sense of stretching out into possibility and renewal.

Returning with enough cash to pay the overhead for a good while, buy piles of materials, and have time once again to devote myself fully to working on the property, certainly underscored the optimism. I'd spent three months—with a total of three days off—being a creative mercenary and housemate in two radically different environments; it was time at last to settle into my own space and rhythms, and focus on getting the setting for this new life in New Mexico beyond the rudimentary foothold I'd established in the fall. At this point, the impetus was to develop the basic functionality of the house as a home, and for working both *in* and *on* it.

I spent the first two months stripping back the layers of "hippie remodeling" the place had been subjected to since the early Seventies. I'd heard that for many of the intervening years, the local currency was primarily marijuana, and I was often curious if this had anything to do with the wonders of improvisation I unearthed in the process. Having grown up working on old houses, I had a pretty good idea of what one might find inside walls and ceilings, but this place really stood out for its unabashed make-do resourcefulness.

No place to put the old materials? No problem, just build right over them. No more room for wires in an electrical junction box? Well, just keep jamming them in and let them spill out the front so it resembles an octopus, and then wall it over. No small finishing nails to tack down the particleboard under the linoleum on the bathroom floor? Then go right ahead and use massive three-inch framing nails so it can only be taken up in pieces the size of postage stamps. And on it went, until finally I had a place that was workable—skeletal, but workable.

Some interior walls were removed in the process, which allowed for more open space—most of which was taken up by the studio. I slept on a futon on a platform in what had been the rudimentary bathroom just off the kitchen, which in turn became the living room as well. What I called the sunroom—because it faced south and had wonderful solar exposure in winter—became the finishing room.

Previous owners had opened up the attic space and used it as a loft; I cut out about a third of its floor to make more headspace in the front of the house. This gave it a more open, spacious feeling, and—since it was being used as the main studio space—also accommodated the handling of long pieces of lumber. The remainder of the loft became a storage area for wood and other studio materials—and inevitably, thick layers of fine wood dust.

The Choice Between

Down a long alley, just off a busy, well-touristed street, my home among the mango and hibiscus trees is tucked away behind walls, of which the Balinese just can't seem to get enough. The sounds of buses and motorbikes zooming along Monkey Forest Road fade well before you enter, and everyone who visits beams as the perfunctory concrete path and walls suddenly give way to lush, tropical plants and ornate Balinese architecture.

That alley-long transition from rollicking rub with humanity to quiet solitude suits me well; I'm happiest with a choice between them, and ready access to both. I enjoy solitude, and I'd certainly go so far as to say I *need* solitude to be in touch with who I am in this world, but that doesn't mean I'm inclined toward seclusion as a way of life.

Though they have aloneness in common, for me, the emphasis with *solitude* is on the choosing of companionship outside the human, while with *seclusion*, it's on renouncing human contact. There may not seem to be much of a difference on the surface, but the ramifications are profound: I see solitude as a state of turning temporarily toward something else—perhaps nature, or a meditative or creative practice— which may well happen with other people relatively nearby, and it implies turning back toward, and reuniting with, one's fellow humans. The intention with seclusion, however, is to be apart from other people, and connotes more a lifestyle of withdrawal.

I've found both to be enormously rewarding, but I've been far more drawn to modes of living and working that allow me to readily break away from my solitary rhythms and enjoy the company of humankind—for a while. Then I return happily to the more subtle realms: creative process, nature, spirit, the inner landscape, or simply a gentle sense of still, silent, spaciousness. What I enjoy most is a mix of companionship, and the freedom to waft amongst the range of forms it might take.

There were many years in which solitude wasn't as much a choice as a necessary form of refuge and self-care from the wounds of early circumstance—years in which it was tinged with feelings of isolation. The blessing—the joy—now is in the spaciousness pervading whatever form companionship takes.

It seems the birds and I share more than a love of sky: We flit from our nests, tend to the things of the outer world, and flit right back home to the trees.

Nature *and* Nurture

While I thrive on change—especially in larger, life-altering respects—underneath the shifting surface, I also enjoy the rhythms weaving through it all a thread of familiarity. In Madrid, I'd get the studio work or a house project up and going in the morning, then head down the jumbled stone steps to the road and head left to the coffee shop. Along the way, I'd stop in at friends' shops and yak with them briefly, and with folks along the street. It would take a good hour or so to get back; I'd return with my social quota filled to overflowing, and dive right back into the flow of work.

Sporadically during the day, I'd put down the tools, walk out into the yard, and merge with the growing things. I wrote at the time:

> *I know these gardens well;*
> *I have grown here.*
> *And though this body*
> *comes and goes at will,*
> *my spirit dwells here*
> *amongst the green and moist.*

On the way out the door, I'd grab the pruning shears and put them in my pocket in case there were some bits of branch in need of nipping—which there usually were. It always felt like an exercise in mutual nurture: I took care of this slice of nature, and it cushioned and fed my Being in the world. Though it wasn't nearly as satisfying, even in winter I'd slide into a jacket and go out to visit the dormant trees, vines, and grasses. Coming back into the radiant warmth of the wood stove, I'd feel refilled with Sky, and grateful for the robust heat.

Desert Home in the Sky

Later, when the work evolved dramatically, I would put together a portfolio incorporating some reflections on the process of making. In it, I wrote:

> *I turn to the gardens surrounding the house and studio constantly for inspiration, grounding, and connection with the natural world. The gardens form a buffer in which I find sanctuary; they mediate between my space and the larger world, nestling nature around so we're safe and grown together. I'm nurtured creatively because I can refresh my connection with the land, and with the rooted, winged, and legged ones there. By glancing through the window, or walking several paces, I can enter another world busy with life and ready to embrace the senses.*

This deep confluence with nature was an antidote to the soul-draining studio setting I'd had back in Oakland, and to the unmoored periods when I'd venture out to do far away projects. The ongoing relationship with the natural world also helped in taking the edge off the still-primitive living conditions, and the haunting desire for a partner-in-love.

□ □ □

Falling Into Void

There was one especially difficult moment that's hard to place precisely—perhaps it was in the second year in Madrid. The season, though, is crystal clear, as it was getting dark in the late afternoon; the sky and everything under it was soft gray with a lavender-orange cast reserved for the late phase of autumn's surrender to the Solstice. I gazed out the small north window of the studio, past the ballpark and the opening in the ridge that revealed the Cerrillos Hills reaching up over 9,000 feet—resembling a mini mountain range right out of a fairy-tale. As the sun set behind the ridge, the soft western light shone on those peaks

149

most radiantly, lending them the air of a Promised Land floating in a landscape cold to the bone.

A wave of loneliness swept through, ushering in an overwhelming sense of voidness. The sense of potential I normally rode like a wave had vanished, and I felt as if I'd washed up exhausted on a gray shore. I could have turned away and done something to break the dark spell, but it didn't occur to me to do anything but simply stand there and feel it.

That distant Promised Land was fading as I stood in the gathering dusk, in a building in need of everything, and it seemed I had little but longing for partnership in the world. I remember thinking after a while that I understood how someone could decide not to go on living; here I was with so much creativity, passion, and potential, yet the bleakness had descended like a fog, banishing all this vitality to the most remote abstractness. It seemed essential in that grim span, though, to just accept this layer of human Being, and recognize the blessing of its usual keeping to the deepest shadows.

In my life in general, and my creative practice in particular, I'd so often turned to stillness as an opening to the realm of potential. I'd describe it briefly as a deep, non-thinking state of Being in which one is aware of nothingness and everything-ness in the same breath. Like the yin-yang symbol, it includes the dark and the light. In that late afternoon, I'd fallen into the Void, in which the shadow side obscured the light—the everything-ness aspect that is the essence of life—leaving only the nothingness at an emotionally trying moment.

Yet staying open to this experience of darkness, and feeling the bedrock of despair—utterly outside the realm of hope—was one of the finest gifts I've ever given myself. It was a profound opportunity to explore the landscape of that abyss: to know it as part of Being, to feel the topography of a shadowed corner of emptiness, and recognize more clearly and deeply the counterpoint of what normally provided a sense of vitality and joy in living in this world.

It was, most essentially, a chance to witness this landscape from the core of my Being—which simply Is—and to recognize it as just a facet in the spectrum of human Being, rather than something that defines me. If I had pulled myself right out of this intense sense of void at the start, it would have set up the conditions for fearing it in the future. I felt in the moment instead, that this embrace of the shadow supplanted a barely conscious fear of what *might* exist there. The gift of facing it was more inner space. And space is, indeed, blessed freedom.

I've learned in the intervening years, that the light offsetting the dark of the Void is love, and it's the open heart that makes the difference between emptiness in the inner landscape, and a vast sense of spaciousness that invites expansion. I'd always been drawn to the Way of Consciousness, but now its partner in revealing divinity, the Way of the Heart, was beginning to emerge.

Hello, New Mexico

In leaving West Oakland, I'd wanted to open up to a new way of earning a living, but given the anemic economy in New Mexico, my propensity for flexibility and independence, and the fact that I'd taken on a property requiring quite some investment of time and money, the best option seemed to be to continue plying the furniture craft and see where it took me. And while the coloring work back in the Bay Area was a blessing, it was clear I needed to get some local interest going.

Those earlier years as a photographer came in handy in recording the work, and since I'd made a habit of shooting each piece before it left the studio, I had plenty of high-quality images to work with when it came time to put together some portfolios to leave with interior designers.

I began scouting around Santa Fe, meeting them, and putting the word out. From the years in the Bay Area, I knew that even one designer who really liked and used one's work could pretty well keep one busy, so I kept my eye out for the more personal connection that makes for a warm working relationship. It was soon evident I had this kind of rapport with the first designer I'd visited.

While she didn't keep me busy full-time, she had a knack for phoning me with a prospect just when I needed something to happen. Or I could call her and let her I know I was available for more basic sorts of interior work—like painting—if I needed the money. A couple of friends who had shops in Madrid also showed the work, and though not a lot of sales came out those venues, every sale helped, and having my work available locally provided a feeling of momentum with the work, and wonderful connection in the village.

If I had a commission, it got top priority; things especially needing to get done on the house were next in line; and thirdly, I needed to keep making pieces to evolve the work and have some available for showing. There was never "nothing to do"—just an endless stream of projects. I loved the variation—the constantly unfolding potential—but I also felt held at times to a treadmill of my own making with no end in sight.

By early fall, I needed to get working on insulating the place. Fortunately, I'd already stripped back the layers of thick cardboard and paneling of various sorts so I could readily blow insulation into the walls—most of which were lined on the inside with horizontal pine boards from floor to ceiling. For the ceilings and some of the other walls, I stapled up fiberglass insulation. It made a world of difference thermally, though aesthetically, it left a lot to be desired: I lived for years with walls and ceilings emblazoned with "Manville" up and down and across.

If I didn't get out dancing at least once a week, I felt like something essential was missing in my life. Sometimes it was at the Mineshaft Tavern in Madrid—nicknamed the *Mindshaft* by some of the locals—where touring Blues bands or other sorts of local bands would play for appreciative crowds eager to boogy. Other times, I went into Santa Fe to the mixed gay clubs, or to a dance studio with alcohol- and shoe-free events like the one I'd gone to with Vulker when I'd first arrived in the Bay Area.

Desert Home in the Sky

I so loved flying in my body, and it was the only thing I did with other people that was about moving in rhythm together. All those communities were so different, but an underlying joy of sharing movement cut right across them all. Getting myself out there to dance offered ongoing hope of meeting someone special, as well, and broke up the daily focus on production.

Oddly Enough

Among our crew of outlaws, misfits, and rebels in the village was an old-timer of Irish heritage named Tina, who had a twinkle in her eyes, and far more heart than teeth. I don't know what she got by on in the way of money, but having next to nothing didn't impede her generous spirit. That summer, she was talking up a fundraiser she wanted to put together for an AIDS support organization based in Santa Fe—to be held in the theater up behind the tavern in Madrid. Normally used for staging old-fashioned melodrama plays, it would serve nicely for what she had in mind.

Eventually, it became clear to a group of us that her passion for the project was not going to translate into a happening solely under her guidance, so we organized a committee and divvied-up the work: arranging use of the theater, and the tavern for an after-party; getting food to sell at intermission; putting out word for people to create acts; designing, making, and putting up posters, and so on.

Oddly enough, her idea was to put on a gender-twisting variety show, and invite the audience to dress up, too. She called it the *He/She Bang*, and it was just crazy enough to be intriguing, especially in a village of perhaps three hundred people up at 6,000 feet in the mountain desert.

There remained one last position to be filled in bringing it together: We needed an MC for the show. Looking around, I quickly realized no else was going to step forward and put themselves on the front line of this unproven, quite shaky production, so I shrugged and said, *I'll do it!* I was, after all, the most overtly gender-variant person around. From the years in and near San Francisco, I'd pretty much seen it all, and could certainly help push the envelope and make more space for people to take some chances. And who better to front the *He/She Bang* than the woman whose pickup truck had license plates that spelled out: TRANS.

We enticed people to come up with acts, slotted them to create what would hopefully be a good rhythm to the show, and decided on a stage background resembling a cafe—in part so we could have some locals sitting around up there for moral support. We were winging it all the way through the preparations, and hoping it would come together on the night of the show.

Maybe it was mostly out of curiosity, but we had a really good turnout—filling the theater seating on the main floor, and the balcony, too. I stepped onto the stage in a style I thought of as "Androgyne Semiformal"—which included some of the funkier wardrobe I'd not worn since those wilder San Francisco days—and introduced the show: *Ladies and gentlemen! Boys and girls! And everyone else! Welcome to the first Annual He/She Bang!* I looked out over an audience rife with anticipation, and could see big, burly men in dresses and wigs smiling right back. Their showing up in such splendid form really spurred us on.

During one of the earlier acts, I slid out of the MC costume and into the outfit for mine. I'd chosen a track by Enigma for its combination of sacred timbre and driving rhythm, and when the curtain was down, I stood ready, wearing a long black cape and curving black hat, gently swinging a tea-steeping ball burning incense—much like I'd seen in church growing up.

When the curtain went up, I stepped forward with a serious tone and blessed the audience with priestly gestures to a chorus of male voices sounding as though it were wafting down from the rafters of a cathedral. I turned toward the back of the stage, and handed off the incense burner to Lily, who was sitting in the "cafe." She had no idea I was going to hand it off to her, so at first she just looked at me not knowing what to do. I whispered to her, *Take it, dammit!* and she reached out and accepted it reverently—like we'd planned it all along.

When the rhythm kicked in and joined the voices, my back was still to the audience; my arms were outstretched, holding the cape open and slightly away. I dropped it on the first beat, and heard the audience gasp: I was wearing a black bustier, black fishnet stockings, and a black scarf hanging loosely from front to back between my legs from a thin belt.

From there, I just let the empowered female spill out from the staid, controlled male entrance, and I was in my medium. In a way, it was an introduction of the essence of my trans-beingness to the community, and they appreciated me all the more for it.

There was an undercurrent of Catholicism in the area, and for a long time after, I'd meet people every now and then who said they'd seen the performance and thought it was a little naughty; but they said so with a big grin—and a look in their eyes that said they appreciated the inherent sacredness, too.

Everyone performed as if we'd rehearsed. Near the end of the show, as I came out to introduce a local band, the whole place felt splendidly charged, and with the stage lights cutting through the smoke, it looked like a club tucked away off some alley in New York City. We'd managed to pull together a pretty radical show, gather the community—locally, and up into Santa Fe—to watch and participate, and raise some money for a great cause.

Afterward, the audience created its own "act" as the He/She Bang moved down to the tavern and we danced and drank until late. Over a beer, I told a friend I'd been a little worried gender-wise about leaving the Bay Area; we looked around and back at each other, and just started laughing. On the way home, I said to myself—to the part of me that as a child had wondered if I'd ever be able to speak fluently: *Hey, sweetie, look at that—it turned out all right after all.*

I saw Tina the next day, and she was beaming like a proud mom.

Rocky Horror Redux

Months ago, I stepped onto a jet that ushered me out of one kind of life and into another. I'd had a tendency to keep pretty much to myself and focus on whatever medium was calling, but in the moving about that travel entails, there was no opportunity for retreating into a zone of my own making. In the midst of opening myself up to the world and having more people in my vicinity day-to-day, I surprised myself by finding it quite enjoyable.

Three months and dozens of temporary rooms and cafes later, I found my refuge. It's a blessing to have arrived at a place that reflects the rich sense of sanctuary I feel within, and to have the space to freely choose once again to engage others—or not. The course of this life has been a quite dramatic slaloming between phases of more or less engagement with the human realm, but in this combing-through of those far corners of my past, and herding the joys, difficulties, and longings onto page, I'm not surprised to find the familiar modes of creative process reemerging—prompting me toward the gentle, unconditional embrace of solitude. In the midst of this intense introspection and contemplation, I feel the energy required to interact with others more acutely.

There are occasions that call me out on a regular basis, though—like the Monday night dinner and movie event held every other week at the Yoga Barn. The gorgeous buffet is a nice break from my own cooking, and since there's no theater in town and I don't have a television, it's a fine opportunity to mix it up socially, then lie back on pillows, eat popcorn, and watch whatever happens to be showing. That usually means, as Charley likes to say in introducing the films, *documentaries of the social issues of the day*, or perhaps a nature-oriented program of the National Geographic sort.

This week's showing struck me as a particularly odd choice, then, when it turned out to be *The Rocky Horror Picture Show*. Without the autumnal cooling-off and increasingly slanting sunlight to set the stage for it, I'd completely forgotten about Halloween. So the movie turned out to be quite sensible after all—at least to a transplanted American—and in perfect synchronicity with this reaching into the past, as it reminded me of the *He/She Bang*, just when I was delving into that period in Madrid.

For those who have somehow missed it in its thirty-plus years of showings, *The Rocky Horror Picture Show* is a campy, romping musical unabashedly loosely based on *Frankenstein*. Tim Curry, fabulously outlandish in resplendent drag, plays the lead as Dr. Frank N. Furter. He makes a grand entrance, belting out: *I'm a transvestite transsexual from Transylvania!* and never lets up his passion for being just that the entire show. It's wild, cheesy, and driven by an infectious musical score.

The last—and only—time I'd seen it was back in college with my brother and a couple of his friends. I was amazed in watching this time how much of it I'd forgotten—until I realized twenty-eight years have passed in the meantime. But the source of haziness was more than the passage of time: The film had cut way too close to what was going on inside, and suppressing it likely pushed parts of the movie, too, into the recesses.

This time, the experience could hardly have been more different— and it sketches the near end of the arc that started with the young man dressing up as an androgyne for Halloween back in college and lands right here in Bali. As I lay back, popcorn in hand, I was delighted to hear the word *trans* thrown around with abandon, and it was wonderful to see someone just reveling in what they are, and their being appreciated for it —even if that trans depiction was completely overblown.

This was a rare opportunity to feel well within the outer edges gender-wise, instead of defining them, as I often do as I go about my daily life. For a little while, I was on the inside curve, enjoying the spacious license of someone else holding the edge—and doing so with panache.

☐ ☐ ☐

Déjà Vu

That fall, Lorraine commissioned several large pieces of furniture for her house near Santa Cruz, and I got busy on those so they'd be ready to be brought out for the second round of color design and painting back in the Bay Area. As they neared completion, I started focusing on pulling together the gear for the trip, and prepping the house for abandonment for the winter.

With more than a hint of déjà vu in the air, and gobs of clay mud on the ground, I loaded the rented trailer in the early morning and headed out as snow flurries foreshadowed a coming storm. The southern end of the village ramped right up into the highest passes through the Ortiz Mountains, so once I cleared those and descended into Albuquerque, I could relax into the vast, nearly featureless landscape out to the mountains around Flagstaff. A half-hour or so of winter driving later, it was smooth going again all the way to northern California.

With the furniture dropped off at Lorraine's home, I headed to Bob's for round two of coloring before returning to Santa Cruz. On this second trip, I came out to Lorraine as a transwoman, and she was wonderfully understanding and supportive. She'd had gay friends for many years, and recognized without hesitation the beauty and necessity of simply Being oneself in the world. Between Bob's place and hers, I was gone again for about three months, and returned in March to Madrid—to another early spring unfurling.

☐ ☐ ☐

Tooling Toward Liberation

Funds in hand, I poured my energy into the house again, and began smoothing some of its rougher edges. A friend who had a shop-cum-home down the street was refinancing his place to get some cash to put into it, and I was thunderstruck with the idea that I could do this as well. At the time, I had a simple loan directly with the folks from whom I'd bought the place.

Refinancing with a corporate lender normally requires the property to have the basic amenities one expects to find in a sound house, but my friend knew one which was, shall we say, *flexible* when it came to these old places. When I'd first arrived, county inspectors were afraid to go to Madrid, and banks overtly red-lined—refused to provide—loans, even though the practice was illegal. Now that real estate values were on the rise, they'd softened their tone considerably. County inspectors were reluctant to go there because of old rumors, and the sometimes-brusque receptions from some die-hard old-timers, but loans could apparently be gotten.

Over the almost two years of sporadic, but intensive, projects, I'd managed to make the place somewhat presentable, though I still found it hard to believe any lender would provide a traditional loan on the place. I had a really good laugh, though, when I read the appraiser's report, which described the house as having a *rustic interior common to the area*"—in other words, it looked like a shack inside, like lots of others in the village.

It lacked a flush toilet, but I explained that as the reason I wanted to borrow the money. I did indeed plan to add a bathroom addition, but since I'd be doing the work myself, there would actually be money for something else, which I had put out my mind because for so long it had seemed financially unfeasible.

You couldn't just Google things back then, but fortunately I knew I could call the folks at San Francisco Sex Information to track down the surgeon I vaguely remembered being mentioned in a television program many years before. From what they told me, the famous Dr. Stanley Biber— one of the pioneers of male-to-female Sex Reassignment Surgery (SRS)— was a mere four hours away, just across the northern New Mexico border, in Trinidad, Colorado.

I'd put so much time, effort, and resources into other forms— the furniture, my house, and others' homes—and it was clearly time to focus on my own physicality. With no idea what SRS would cost, I spoke with his staff, and was pleasantly surprised to find it was indeed within reach. He would do the operation in two stages— the second being more of a cosmetic fine-tuning—and so now, I needed to focus only on the first.

I scheduled a surgery date with them for mid-October, still not sure how I'd pay for it. Soon after the phone call, I went out into the desert, declared my intentions to the universe, and asked for the refinancing to come through—if it served the higher good.

Between the rising real estate values, and the work I'd put into the place, there turned out to be a nice bit of equity in the property, so the loan was readily funded. The news let loose a flood of desire for the homecoming which had been sidetracked for the nearly six years since I'd taken the first hormone pill up in the Temple of the Pines, high in the Berkeley Hills. It had washed me into the outskirts of the feminine, and while in the meantime I'd squatted in the thick of the sprawling neighborhood, soon, I was finally going home in physicality.

The cash from the coloring projects would get me by for some months to come, and with the loan, I could get the bathroom addition underway. I wasn't about to take on the recovery hobbling out to the outhouse in whatever seasonal circumstance, and absolutely not in the late-fall cold and ice. Too, I wanted to give my physically more womanly self-to-be the gift of a proper bathroom. Even if I didn't get it completely done, I wanted it to be at least functionally a place of healing: to shower, soak—and, yes, to simply flush—surrounded by warmth.

Some local help with the foundation and framing got the addition off to a good—but erratic—start, as hiring them turned out to be rather like herding cats. It was crucial to get the room closed-in from the highly variant weather as soon as possible, as I'd been offered a coloring project up in Boulder, Colorado. I'd have preferred to focus solely on the addition and the upcoming change, but the opportunity sounded intriguing, and seemed like something I really should do for the business. If I could get the bathroom closed-in, it would be feasible to come back after the fall cold had arrived, and work on the interior before the surgery.

The trip to Boulder also allowed for a preliminary appointment with Dr. Biber, and a chance to get at least a little familiar with the local layout. Driving into Trinidad, I felt like I'd been tossed back about twenty years to the kind of northern town in which I'd grown up. A blue-collar, brick-making locale, it hardly seemed like the Capital of SRS Surgery that it was. Dr. Biber was also the town's General Practitioner, and his waiting room reflected the everyday medical needs of the local community; if I stood out as "one of those," no one let on.

Dr. Biber looked and acted every bit the country doctor he was, and wouldn't have seemed at all out of place at the wheel of tractor. With his office dating back several decades at least, it was all quite surreal—to the point that I wouldn't have been surprised to have woken up and discovered it was just the unlikely setting of a strange dream. He was quite old at this point, and I found myself feeling a little anxious from time to time, between then and the surgery date, that he might pass away in the meantime.

At lunch in a local diner, I felt oddly suspended in time and place: The transformation for which I'd waited so long was palpable, but still a month and half, and two projects away. It was, quite naturally, akin to the Salvador Dali-esque landscape of melting time that preceded the start of the hormones six years earlier. I stayed the night, and headed up to Boulder in the new light of the next day.

The directions took the truckload of gear and me out into farmland tucked along the Rocky Mountain Range. The first time I saw the barn—or what was once a barn—I thought to myself, *Now, that's a place I could happily live!* The owners had cleaned out a one-hundred year-old livestock and hay barn, and transformed it into a soaring home. They'd built a master-suite loft into half the main space, and left the other half to rise twenty-five feet to the peak. Carefully insulating and sheetrocking around the structural timbers instead of covering them, they'd preserved the barn's rustic-cathedral ambience while taming its rougher edges. They'd had to dig out five or more feet of manure from the lower floor—discovering numerous skeletal animal remains in the process—and dump it on the surrounding fields before they could transform that area into living space as well.

I was there to finish the floors with layers of oil glazes made from plant-based oils and earth pigments built up to create a rich patina. The idea was to allow the beauty of the cherry wood to show through the translucent coloration that subtly defined the various areas of the open space, and to give them a look of having been around for a long time. It was essentially a fifteen hundred square foot oil painting, plus another seven hundred square feet for the master-suite upstairs. I was also there to develop a palette for the walls, and get as many of those painted as I reasonably could.

They put me up in an Airstream trailer a short walk away, which I loved because it allowed me to get away from the worksite and have my own space. Between the blocks of intensive work time, I'd go out into the fields, past the hay barns and massive stacks of bales, to the woods on the far side. These were opportunities to observe the nuanced hues of the landscape for the palette, get away from the trance of productivity, and revel in rhythms of my own. There, I couldn't help but be reminded of childhood forays of discovery and sanctuary, and wept more than a few times for the joy of being so close to what I'd thought impossible all those years ago.

I did what I could in a month's time; though they were disappointed I was leaving in the midst of wall-finishing, I had to return and get my own bathroom in at least functional form before heading back up to Trinidad. In a way, all of this busy-ness was a blessing, as it was a first-rate diversion from the natural eagerness to push the calendar along.

Angels, and a Nest That Flushes

Dr. Biber's instructions were to stop the hormones two weeks ahead of the surgery, so after the first week back home from the Boulder project, I went into psycho-emotional backwash mode—underscoring the upcoming event with added intensity. I remember walking with a

Desert Home in the Sky

friend in the woods up in the Ski Basin above Santa Fe, talking about the changes to come, doing my best to see through, and past, the layers of upwelling emotionality, and stay grounded in my body. Yet there was refuge in this only to a point: Being more consciously in my body inevitably sparked thoughts of the looming personal remodeling, which launched yet another rush of time-warping longing.

Over dinner one night at my house, I came out to a lesbian couple with whom I'd really connected. It seems odd now they hadn't heard from others that I was trans, but they lived "on the land" outside of town, and spent a lot of their off-work time building a straw-bale home out there, so perhaps they just weren't in the loop of in-town gossip.

When I told them that I'd soon be heading out for the surgery, Mary shook her head, grinning, and said, *You must really love yourself!* This was perhaps the best response I'd ever gotten, and it just warmed my heart to be seen so clearly. *Oh, I do... I really do,* I said, feeling my eyes glow and well up with such beautiful recognition of the essence of it all.

We talked some more, and I thought to ask them to accompany me to Trinidad. I wanted to wake up from the surgery to familiar faces and perhaps have my hand held awhile—and who better than these two women who loved each other as I hoped to share love one day. They looked at each other briefly, and both turned back to me and said at the same time, *Yes, of course!*

With about two weeks to get the bathroom functional, I had a pile of work in front of me—which, as I've said, was a welcome distraction. After scheduling a plumber and buying the fixtures, I ran the wiring, installed the insulation, sheetrocked the walls, and laid the oak floor. For a tub, I went to a feed store and got a galvanized steel water container normally used for putting out water for livestock. Its oval shape was ideal, but the bottom was flat, so

I made a contoured redwood floor and an angled backrest for each end, and put it up on shaped wooden blocks. When the plumber and I got it hooked up, we stood back and had a good laugh at this funky "Cowboy Claw-foot" tub that worked so nicely, despite its humble origins.

The guy I'd hired to do the tiling in the shower turned the deposit I'd given him into alcohol and drank it the night before he was to start—leaving him apologetic, but incapacitated. So I got to work myself, and lined the corner in redwood planks saturated in natural oils, which gave it a feeling of warmth that I enjoyed for the rest of the time I was there.

Before leaving for Trinidad, I looked around and saw a room that made up for its lack of wall finishing and wood trim with beautiful light pouring in through a long skylight and huge windows facing east and south. I laid out some towels, candles, incense, and special soaps to welcome my wounded, but more womanly, body home.

☐ ☐ ☐

Toward Airy Pants

Debbie and Mary, the lesbian couple I'd asked to accompany me, came by in the early morning with their van, and we began the four-hour journey through northern New Mexico, up through the steep mountain passes, and just across the Colorado border into Trinidad. We needed to arrive in the early afternoon for an appointment with Dr. Biber, in preparation for surgery the next day.

After the visit, we took a scenic drive through the gorgeous highland countryside. The whole time, though, I was having a parallel experience filled with anticipation amid a backdrop of concern that some terrible thing would happen that would preclude my transformation.

That evening after dinner, they dropped me off at the hospital, and I was readied for the operation starting early the next morning.

I wondered what was going through her mind as the young Hispanic woman quietly shaved my genital area: Did she have any sense of this operation as a gender homecoming, or were a person's motivations in doing this radical thing just a vast mystery utterly beyond just doing this odd task in the course of her job? I was too wound up in the impending change to inquire; in what seemed like moments, it was time for the last shower I'd have with male genitalia, and for the first eleven days of my new form.

There was a sound system in the operating room, and Dr. Biber had invited me to bring some music I'd like to having playing during the operation. I brought a favorite cassette tape of Vivaldi's *Four Seasons* violin concertos and another of Gregorian chant with a rich, layered, sacred tone. I'd be unconscious in terms of ordinary consciousness, of course, but I was sure that I'd also be aware in higher ways of those comforting sounds. I did wake up, though, at one point during the operation: I vaguely remember the haunting Gregorian strain, and the upside down anesthetist looking over me and whispering, *It's going very well...* at which point, he must have turned a knob.

I woke foggily to Debbie and Mary smiling down at me, and smiled weakly back. It was essentially hello and goodbye, as they needed to head back to Madrid, and I was drifting right back into unconsciousness. However brief, I felt blessed to the core to have woken to those angels in physical form.

Over the next nine days, I got to know that bed intimately. Amazingly, I was off the injected painkillers in two days, and only needed the pain pills for a couple of days more. The hospital stay was more annoying and uncomfortable than painful, except for the second night, when a nurse who clearly had some unresolved issues injected me as if she were harpooning a whale—leaving me traumatized and unable to lay in any position comfortably for the rest of the night. I told my absolutely wonderful primary nurse that the night nurse should not be looking after trans patients, and thankfully, I never saw her again.

In the last couple of days, I could walk nimbly around the ward, and tried to build up a little strength. Finally, the hospital's liaison dropped me off at the hotel where I was meeting another angelic friend, Adrienne, who was coming up with my truck and her toddler. All I could do was lie back in that 1970s era room and watch really awful cartoons for distraction until they arrived later in the afternoon.

The next morning, we headed back to Madrid—a very long four hours to be sitting up away—but it felt good, nonetheless, to be liberated from the whir of the hospital and small rooms of various sorts. We stopped at a favorite health food store in Santa Fe, and I clung to the cart, hobbling down the aisles pale as a ghost. Back in the truck and down to Madrid, Adrienne dropped me at the house, brought in the groceries, and left soon after—her little *Monster Man* in tow.

Sunshine On My Stitches

I was alone at home: grateful to be there, but weak to the bone. I'd been used to being highly active and physically effective, and had never felt so physically vulnerable. Within twenty hours, I'd gone from the support of a hospital staff to being on my own, and all I could do was focus on each moment. Having the new bathroom waiting was a huge boost, as it was nearly November, and the hard-core cold temperatures had arrived in my absence in full force.

I'd always disliked getting up in the middle of the night for anything, but with the tightening and cramping of the muscles that had been spread apart to make room for the new cavity, I needed to stretch every few hours. This nightmarish round of gentle exercise simply had to be done, so I shook off the sleepiness enough to slide carefully out of bed, and with slow squatting motions chased off some of the dull, throbbing soreness for a while. It must have lent some perspective, though, because ever since, I've never really minded getting up in the night.

In those rare moments when I've shared with friends about the operation, I've usually gotten a wincing look—often followed by something like: *Oh, that must've hurt!* My memory of the recovery, though, doesn't revolve around pain, but rather, a deep soreness gradually subsiding with the bruising and swelling.

However, in the first months, and sporadically for years thereafter, I'd get a brief, sharp pain in the same place to one side where the surgery was. At first, all I had to do was simply look at a sharp knife to set off the surge of high, thin pain. Later, it occurred only when I was preparing food with a sharp knife—not when I used sharp chisels or other tools. It seems my body remembered the scalpel, and held the trauma in its own way. Eventually, the pain stopped being called by knives.

Time did indeed heal this wound—with some assistance. The bathroom became my locus of recovery in a way I hadn't expected: I moved a favorite antique chair padded with pillows to a spot across from the tub, and with my feet nicely apart on the edge of the tub, I could read or write, or just sit there, and get some of the low Southern sunlight that flooded into the room right down there where I needed it most. The light served not only the physical healing—it fueled, as well, my soul. And that my own intention-guided hands had provided this sacred place made it all the sweeter.

About two weeks after the operation, voting day arrived. I wasn't about to abdicate my duty as a responsible citizen, so I bundled up in warm layers, inched my way out to the truck, and drove over to Cerrillos to cast my votes. Every time I shifted, I had to press the clutch in, so I rode there pretty much in second-gear. The excursion certainly offered some insight into the care with which the elderly watch for surfaces that might make them slip and fall. What I remember most, though, was the cool, airy space in the front of my pants.

Needing some sky and open landscape, I took the truck out again about a week later and explored some back roads south of town. I don't know if I've ever driven so carefully in my life; one patch of black ice could send me off the road, and I was obviously in no position to deal with getting out of a ditch, or worse. But I was gradually getting a little more sure-footed, and feeling increasingly antsy to get active again.

Dr. Biber had advised against any heavy lifting for four to six weeks, but he hadn't said anything about dancing, so I put the stereo to good use and grooved gingerly around the house to build up my range of motion. Later, when I sat down from a round of full-tilt boogying at the tavern, I could hardly believe it had been just five weeks since the operation. By this time, I was already working on the house again, and had put in place the floor joists to raise the level of the sunroom to match the new bathroom. I was back to the mountain of work, but it felt so good to be nearly in full motion again—and in much sleeker form!

I'd spent six years owning my womanhood while being physically both male and female. Now, without the caveat between my legs, my body was finally a womanly home. There would still be the second operation to contend with later, so it was at this point rather like the house: extensively remodeled, but still waiting to be fleshed out in finished form.

Freak

At another Monday night dinner and movie event, I encountered a young Austrian man I'd recently met at a cafe. We'd had a lovely talk about spiritual pilgrimage, in which he said he'd tried a great number of approaches to the divine, in so many corners of the world, and had found a teacher here in Ubud with whom he seemed to resonate most deeply. Alexander had the look in his eyes one often sees in a seeker, which could be mistaken for gazing at something distant, but is more accurately an attentiveness to the space encompassing the far away and the far within.

His plate heaped with healthy food from the buffet, he set it down on the wooden table next to me, and we picked right up on our earlier conversation. He was glowing even more than before, and confided in accented English that he'd been writing quite a lot about his journey; his eyes widened knowingly when I shared that I'd been doing the same. We delighted in the synchronicity, went on to share some impressions of writing from one's path, and of writing as a path in itself.

The joy of discovering what shows up on the page when you don't know what you'll write spilled into the deeper learning and growing we experience in simply trying to articulate what we really mean, and we hoped in unison it might have some value for others. There was great worth, we agreed, in the process of getting outside of ourselves that which we know, as it made more room for other, more peripheral, things to shift from obscurity into knowing.

We seemed to recognize simultaneously that we'd both been spending substantial amounts of time in solitude, and yet we'd stepped away from it only to run right into someone else on a remarkably similar course. Alexander said that being more open than ever to the possibility of the moment had prompted him to sit by me—that in his earlier life he'd never have chosen to sit down, as he put it, *by a freak!*

It took me a moment to realize he meant me, as he'd said it with a big, bright smile and obviously not an ounce of intended offense. I laughed, enjoying the sheer truthfulness of it, and wondering if he realized the word in English would have negative connotations for most people.

Yet his exclamation reverberates through me even days later, and when I reach down inside and ask myself why, the answer is that this person with a wide-open spirit and the innocence of a puppy spoke right to my anomalous presence, and that's a more honest appraisal than I'm used to. In a nutshell, it sums up much of my social reception in the last twenty years: that while I have many fruitful exchanges, I have often been seen the whole time as an outsider, and remain so, despite the connection—I'm the strangely interesting person they interacted with that day.

Those people who simply enjoy my spirit beyond this anomalous form are likely to have discovered within themselves more license to be who they are, and it's in this pool I find my true friends. We have this self-sanctioned space in common—though for me, it's written on my body, and unless I've come out to them, it usually remains unspoken.

Though I'd prefer a less-charged word than *freak*, it's not as if what he said were untrue; indeed, it's because what he said *was* true that it rings through me still. It's the course of my life laid bare: that in a world fixated on being this *or* that, my being what I authentically am—this *and* that—lands me here, in the outskirts: not just in this highlighted moment, but as a regular occurrence in the unfolding of time. There's the truth of it, delightedly underscored and served in a lovely bowl.

I went for a nice dinner and a movie, and got for dessert a full course of my way in the world. For this clarity, I'm grateful—and for the balm that is the simplicity of solitude.

5

The Treebone Garden

Life in the 'hood

My neighbor Keith was hardly a neighbor at all. I wouldn't see him for weeks at a time, and when I did, he was just barely there. He seemed to have been a sensitive soul that had gotten pulled into drugs so deeply and early in life, they'd become a way of life, livelihood, and Being. Decades of hardcore use had left its toll, and what remained of Keith was a pasty shell of humanity that emitted only the faintest flickers of what I imagined to be his younger self.

Most of the time, he was secluded in his house behind the tall, pieced-together wooden fences around his yard, protected by his large dog, and laying low—more because of other druggies he was sure wanted his stash or cash than fear of the law. He wasn't just paranoid: I'd heard he'd been involved with the really ugly, toxic stuff—beyond just using—and it certainly wasn't unreasonable to think that desperate druggies could show up anytime.

I rarely saw anyone go to his well-obscured place. Every now and then in the winter, though, some of the old-timers would throw split wood into his yard to help feed his wood-burning stove.

Once, he shared across the ancient wood leaning precariously into my yard that I was a good neighbor, and he liked having my energy next door. It warmed my heart that this person, whose world had shrunk to roughly the size of his house, found solace nearby. He mentioned, too, a pair of lights like eyes hovering in various spots up in the rafters of his house, and wondered if I'd seen anything like them in mine.

One day not long after, there was a ruckus next door; I soon heard Keith had passed away, and had been found several days later in his house. The guys sent by the County to get his remains said they'd never seen a body so decomposed in such a short time. I wasn't surprised—the process appeared to have started long before he took his last breath.

On a plateau over the ridge on the northwest edge of the village, there's a sun- and wind-burned cemetery: A fittingly odd collection of traditional stone statues and headstones from much earlier days, and handmade and found-object remembrances more suited to the artist colony of more recent times. We buried Keith up there one brilliant afternoon, and a good swath of locals—especially the old-timers—showed up to see him off.

As the ceremony was ending, I suddenly realized I'd forgotten a pot of rice cooking on the stove at home, and by then, it was certainly well past done. I hopped into the truck and raced home to minimize the damage—a long trail of road dust spewing behind. Dashing up the stairs to the front door of the house, I reached out to put the key in the lock.

Just then, I looked up and saw a huge black snake hanging off the front door, inches from my face. The Christmas before, I'd put up a coil of rusty barbed wire as a wreath of sorts, and this snake was curled around it—head lifted in my direction at eye-level and flicking its tongue. I leapt back in that seemingly slow-motion speed reserved for implosions of ordinary reality.

For several days, I'd spot the snake here and there in the garden in front of the house near Keith's—then it was gone for good. It was clearly a visitation of some sort, and with its leaving, I suddenly had a powerful feeling Keith had said goodbye.

The Treebone Garden

That summer, in the oscillations between working *in* the house and *on* it, I was in the midst of an intense round of remodeling, when one day I went out to the driveway to put some things in the back of the truck and head off to Santa Fe to do some errands. As I opened the window at the rear of the camper shell and looked up to the front of the truck, it seemed odd that there was gray material hanging from the ceiling of the cab.

I ran around to the front door, opened it, and stood back: the inside of the cab had been burned. There was a fast-food cup on the seat, so I knew it was intentional—probably used to carry the fuel that set the fire. The irony wasn't lost on me: I'd spent three years in an area replete with crack-houses and automatic weapon-fire back in Oakland with no harm done, and here in this rural village, my truck was burned.

I immediately called a friend to see if I could borrow his truck, and went to Santa Fe with one more errand. Not knowing what might come next, it seemed like a good idea to protect myself, so I stopped at a gun store, bought a shotgun, and practiced on their range. I chose a 20-gauge, five-shot, pump-action model with the shortest legal barrel length, in case someone got in the house and I needed to maneuver in a tight space. I also adjusted the choke wide open, so I could shoot from the hip if necessary, and not have to aim precisely. It could be argued that a pistol would have made more sense, but I figured the sound of a shotgun being pumped would be enough to stop most anyone in their tracks, and preclude the need for shooting.

All this was a profound counter-point to the feminine energy flowing into the studio work, to say the least, and laden with moral conundrums. Would I actually shoot someone who entered my house threateningly? ...I believed I would if I had to.

My intense reaction came from the realization that I'd unintentionally left the truck unlocked that evening, and if it had been locked when someone had a cup of fuel, a lighter, and bad intentions, the next available target would have been the rack of wood mounted to the outside of the house toward the driveway—which would have burned the place to the ground in no time. Given this scenario, it may well have been a blessing it was unlocked. In the meantime, I had no idea as to what else they might try, or how personal it really was.

The sheriff arrived the next day, and it was clear from the start that my situation was just a tiny speck in the astonishingly large territory he covered. When I asked if he'd be doing an investigation, he smirked, kicked the ground with the toe of his dusty boot, and looked down for a moment. Then he looked up and said, *Lady, what I suggest you do is go out and buy yourself a gun...* In other words, beyond his making an official report for insurance purposes, I was on my own. The gun was already loaded and ready by my bed.

There was soon little doubt in my mind who'd done it: The village next door had some really dysfunctional families that had spawned some profoundly unhappy, disaffected kids. There had been a rash of fires, and they seemed to target anything new—which the truck relatively was. I heard later from Tina that there was an anti-gay thread to it as well. Someone else said they'd done it because I supposedly had yelled at them late one night to stop shooting their pistol in the old ballpark across the street from the house—which, of course, I hadn't done. Really now, how much sense would it make to go yelling at someone who has a gun and is shooting it—in the dark, no less?

At first I was quite angry, and had more than a few unpleasant thoughts toward those young guys. That all changed in a moment, though, when I realized they'd get their way if their actions dragged me down into their darkness. I could see where their actions were coming from and their likely future for which they were setting up the conditions. They were just playing out their karma, and I didn't want to be bound up in it. At this point, I just let it go, and felt a wave of relief in not having to carry the burden of anger around.

The whole village was horrified by the act, and they rallied around—telling me as I ran into them how much they supported my being there, and doing what they could to help. One tough little lesbian who'd been an Army drill sergeant offered to come stay over and watch the place

The Treebone Garden

the first couple of nights after it happened—though I didn't take her up on it. The repairs took about a month, and meanwhile folks lent me vehicles to go into town to get supplies.

One friend—a really good-hearted guy who'd earned a great deal of respect in that nearby village—told those young guys that I was his friend, and that if they harmed me again, he'd take it personally and come after them. It was a sort of NATO-on-a-small-scale-in-the-desert approach that may well have gotten through to them—at least in regard to staying away from me.

In winter, I'd put out seeds in feeders in the front and back of the house, which made my little slice of land very popular with the feathered community. I'd wake up to a swooping cacophony of birdcalls as they feasted on sunflower seeds and other delights, and during the day there was an endless supply of chatter and entertaining jockeying for prime feeding spots. To my chagrin, the little birds weren't the only ones feeding there: They'd attracted a Sparrow Hawk that was interested in feasting on *them*.

In wild, zigzagging flights around the yard—reminiscent of World War I dogfights—they'd fly for their lives with the hawk in close pursuit. While I do respect nature's food chain, and recognize the necessity and inevitability of bigger creatures eating smaller ones, this was in *my* garden, and I was queen of that domain. It was, after all, the wee bit of nature in which I had some say, and I felt like a protective mother. I also felt a little responsible in having attracted the birds with scrumptious treats, thereby making them convenient targets.

One day, as I was about to step out of the studio toward the driveway, I saw the hawk sitting in a small tree about fifty feet away. It hadn't seen me, so I stood still and watched it for a few moments before I knew what I wanted to do. I did, indeed, feel like a protective mother just then, and from the sense of being the only thing standing between my little friends and That Which Would Eat Them, I pulled my energy into a tight ball in my belly, focused intensely, and hurled it at the bird of prey—not that I expected it to actually have any effect. Just before it hit, however, the hawk turned and looked right at me, but it was too late: It fell sideways from the tree, and swooped away just before its head hit the ground. I never saw it again.

While I'd like to report that a resounding birdie cheer rang through the neighborhood, the feathered ones simply returned in ones, twos, and small groups, and continued with their joyous, but always cautious feeding.

⬚ ⬚ ⬚

Breakthrough

It's said that the years reveal what the days don't show, which would explain why I never made the connection before between the curves that started showing up in the work, and the preceding surgery. I'd relied on the salvaged architectural bits to add gestural qualities to the furniture, but the overall lines had been quite traditionally straight.

When I started the furniture work in Oakland, I was more of a carpenter, but gradually, I'd evolved into a woodworker. It seems now that the urge to introduce far more sweeping curvature came directly out of the deeper resonance with female physicality after the surgery. And there to meet this passion were the skills, experience, and tools to begin its unfurling.

The woodworking had arisen out of a powerful need to ground the changes in my life, and especially in my body. With the calling to curve some of the lines of the pieces, the element of Water was flowing in, and with it, a greater fluidity, inter-mixing, and melding of many aspects. There was more opportunity to bring nature into the form of the work, which was coinciding with the natural finishes that had recently made their way to the studio. Claiming more of my

The Treebone Garden

own female physically opened the door for the female more generally to pour into the work, and it gave license for the Feminine and the Mother to come into the studio, as well.

The petroleum distillate-based paints I'd started out using back in Oakland were quite unhealthy, both for the planet and me, and I'd been thrilled to find gorgeous, far more expressive alternatives. These plant-based oil finishes enticed my senses, suggesting new possibilities for deep, rich layers of earth pigments which would still allow the beauty of the wood to show through. Instead of feeling repelled by the finishing materials, whole new levels of relationship were being revealed. In choosing the natural materials, I invited more nurturance of myself, the things I was making, and nature itself into the studio. And better yet, they were the most buttery, exquisite oils I'd ever used.

Soon after the introduction of plant-based oils, the furniture began to be shown at a gallery on Canyon Road in Santa Fe—assuring it, at the very least, some good exposure in a fine location. They didn't end up selling much work, but a friend of the owner had a gallery in Aspen, Colorado, and a few months later, this connection had huge ramifications. When Bette called and said she'd like to commission some pieces for her gallery, I saw an unprecedented opportunity to shift the style radically and create a set of seminal pieces that could start a new portfolio.

Bette wanted a representative body of work that would be for sale, but would also generate commissions. I'd always left my work on consignment at galleries, hoping that what I'd already created would sell, and that it would also spawn commissions in the meantime; this time, the showpieces themselves were being commissioned. I'd be paid for the work up front, which allowed me to invest a substantial span of time and energy.

The surgery had released me more fully into woman-ness, and it showed up now unabashedly in the lines and forms of the work. When the curves first appeared, they were slight departures from a largely traditional aesthetic based on the straight lines of the milled lumber from which it was made. With this new work, the aesthetic was based on relationships among arcing and serpentine lines, and rounded, softly bulging forms inspired by those found growing in nature.

In the months of creating those first five pieces for the gallery, the *Treebone Garden* style came into Being. Nearly seven years before, I'd sat high in the Berkeley Hills and swallowed a pill that felt like a dam bursting—releasing a flood of passion for connection with the feminine. The *Treebone Garden* was the artistic equivalent of that moment, spread out over many months.

Following quickly on the heels of the element of Water coming into the work, Space followed suit. In breaking with traditional furniture aesthetics, potential was revealed for inviting in whole other realms—for celebrating the essence and confluence of the myriad forms in existence all around.

The next year, I would put together a portfolio of the new *Treebone Garden* work in which I offered some written background on the work in general, the landscape from which it arose, and the person making it. By including more than just images, I could give a deeper sense of the work—not the same as my sharing it with them personally, of course, but a feeling at least of the sensuality behind them. I made several copies for my own use, and one for each gallery that showed the work. It began with an Artist's Statement:

> *The Treebone Garden series is an ongoing exploration of relationship between land, plant, animal, and architectural forms. With this series, the work shifts in a more sculptural, organic direction, away from traditional approaches to furniture design. I find myself at times torn between a passion for creating interactive objects accessible through their functionality, and flying away from those parameters with free-form sculpture. This evolving body of work describes a series of romps along the paths between.*

After many years of studio work, I am very much enjoying the grace with which forms, materials, techniques, and finishes flow into and through the process: some entering for a particular piece, others lingering, then fading like a comet's tail. Underlying this constant movement in approach is an intense desire to reveal the sensual gesture of each piece.

After those five pieces were delivered late in the fall, I focused on making new ones in the *Treebone Garden* vein—as both creative exploration, and to have work to show that would hopefully elicit further commissions. The work was much more personal—yet more universal—than before, and as it unfolded, my passion for the creative process grew, too.

I didn't see it in these terms at the time, but this is where the element of Fire entered the studio. With this rebirth, the work reflected quite beautifully my own shape-shifting transformation. The creative process had become more than sanctuary—it was passionately expressive of my own essence, as well as of the forms I was integrating. I wrote later in that portfolio:

Over the years, the work has became more fluid and alive, and less architectural. It has become, in part, an exploration of asymmetrical, gestural balance. Creating a sense of movement is not enough; it must also have grounding—a sense of place from which it moves.

The exploration continued into the spring, thanks to the funding from the initial series. At this point, I was thinking of the advice sometimes given to artists: *Show what you want to make.* I wanted to devote my studio work to the *Treebone Garden,* and for that, I needed more pieces to show in galleries, and to build up the portfolio.

Mercenary With Mallet

Later that spring, a lean, long-haired man I'd recently seen a bit around the village came to my house with some rolled-up drawings and a proposition. A Japanese-inspired spa up in the Ski Basin above Santa Fe was undertaking major building and remodeling, and it turned out that David was both the designer and the person in charge of making it happen on the ground. Looking over the architectural drawings, I was impressed with his vision and the scale of the project. He clearly had a good eye for design, as well as a keen sense of detail. I'd always loved Japanese architecture—especially Shinto shrines and rural folkhouses—so I was immediately attracted to the aesthetic, as well.

He said he needed woodworkers who could do high-end custom work on a freelance basis, and wondered if I were interested. It certainly seemed to be a good way to have a flexible income stream and keep the *Treebone Garden* work progressing at the same time. I had developed a broad range of woodworking skills and a fine kit of tools by this time, and it would be a good opportunity to take both for a spin. My passion was clearly with the furniture making, but to be called to, and productively employed in, what one would care to do beautifully is a blessing in itself. So I agreed to go to site and look at the project.

When I arrived for the initial visit, I'd been to the spa numerous times already as a customer, and so was familiar with the setting at over 8,000 feet in the gorgeous Atalaya Mountains. From the public parking area below, you climb many stairs up to the buildings and soaking tubs perched above. It was clear from the outset that the sheer terrain was going to be a challenge. About halfway up a service road to the top, there was a small on-site woodworking shop tucked into a slope off to the side, with stacks of beautiful hardwood lumber of various species ready for use. I could see doing some site work—and was glad I was used to breathing thin air for that—but I'd also want to do as much as possible in my own studio.

The Treebone Garden

While I took the project on as a creative mercenary, there turned out to be considerable value beyond the money earned: In terms of materials, it introduced me to a far broader range of hardwoods than I'd been working with, and a chance to get a good feel for the qualities of each. We also worked with a lot of branches and whole trunks of smaller trees, chosen especially for their undulating, gestural forms. And the project developed my shaping techniques, as we were aggressively modifying the linear lumber—in response to the patterns of the wood grain—to take it in the direction of the natural trees and limbs. All of this seeped nicely into my furniture making.

I'd go to the spa, look over the drawings with David, take measurements, load some wood, and go back to the studio to make parts that could be reassembled and installed back on site. Some of these were quite challenging: I made a railing assembly from walnut, aspen, and bamboo that was quite sculptural—requiring not just precise measurement, but envisioning where irregular materials would land. Its posts were from unmilled aspen tree trunks, and one wended all the way to the building's ridge beam, about twenty feet above.

The most dramatic project was a massive double-door frame assembly, with a huge mahogany threshold and a joined window frame to one side—all mortised and tenoned together. It was so large that I had to assemble it on sawhorses out in the yard, as there simply wasn't enough space in the studio. When it came time to install it, the pressure was on: I was the only woman on the woodworking and construction crews, and the latter were primarily made up of macho Hispanic guys. Getting this right would be a feather in the cap of womankind, and blowing it would be, quite simply, unthinkable.

On the day of the installation, it began pouring rain as soon as I got the parts inside, and because the roof wasn't complete, water was splashing through the place. After laying out and assembling the parts in a reasonably dry area, I took some final measurements of heights and roof angles now that the building was actually constructed, and made custom cuts to fine-tune the door frame to the opening. The plan was to lift the sill supporting the roof on that side of the building, insert the frame, and set it back down.

When I was ready, they gathered every guy from the crews to lift, just as it began to rain yet more torrentially. Right outside of where the door would go, the dirt had turned to thick mud, and the timing could hardly have been worse—but it wasn't my call. Everyone looked at me for the thumbs-up on the frame's readiness, then we stood it up and pulled it over to the wall.

With Herculean pushing, a lot of grunting, and some thoroughly muddy boots, they lifted the roof just enough to slide the frame in— and it fit... perfectly. Everyone nodded their approval, but said nothing. I stood back and said, *Lovely!* just to underscore that a woman had finessed this. They smirked, and went back to what they'd been doing.

The staff at the spa thought it was great to have a woman doing this high-end work, and to back that up, they wouldn't let me pay when I'd come for a sauna and soak long after I'd finished the work there. This was the best tip I'd ever received, and a fine tribute to juxtaposed realities: They were celebrating my being a woman doing fine work in a male-dominated realm, while I celebrated leaving behind identity with the male realm, and being a woman just doing her work.

□ □ □

Double-edged Passion

In the midst of the months-long work for the spa, I'd managed to make a few new *Treebone Garden* pieces and get them into another gallery on Canyon Road—one much better situated than the first— and soon there was more interest in the work. As commissions began trickling in, it was clearly time to refocus solely on the furniture.

With each piece, the new style was revealing itself— both in the initial drawings, and how they were fleshed out in their making. The forms were evolving—as were the finishes—and every piece seemed like a teacher. Usually within days of finishing a piece it would be gone, which lent the making a feeling at times of being a series of intense, short-term affairs.

The Treebone Garden

All the while, it was physically demanding, extremely dangerous work—in an environment laden with fine dust, which required wearing a dust mask far more than I'd have preferred. There were times I went out to the gardens to enjoy them, and other moments when I just needed to break away from the dust, the intensity of the tools, and the necessity of being absolutely attentive to avoid injury; then, it was more about re-grounding in nature.

It was a double-edged existence to be sure: On one side was the sense of passion, connection, and creative satisfaction; on the other, was the constant risk of serious injury, the non-stop work, and the energy required to maintain the physical reality of the creative vision for the studio work and the property.

When a gallery commissioned a piece, I occasionally didn't meet the client, but most often, I had contact of some sort. If they were local, I'd go to their home to get a feel of the setting, and/or they'd come for a studio visit. I enjoyed the rapport, and felt like what I was doing made a difference in people's lives—at least in a quality of life sense.

Often, in the midst of my showing some drawings or a piece in progress, a client would gaze around at the wood and tools, and at the walls still bare to the underlying wood or insulation, and turn to me, asking, *Do you know how fortunate you are to be in touch with your passion?* I assured them that I knew very well; it was, after all, the glue holding it all together.

Certainly, the connection with passion was not accidental or just fortunate. The primary reason I was in touch with it was that I'd made space in my life for its presence. I'd nurtured it, and practiced with it daily. It wouldn't be a stretch to say that creative passion was my primary relationship. And most crucially, I had let go of things inside and out along the way that would have dampened or blocked it.

A Man or a Woman?

A man I've often bumped into around Ubud, and spoken to numerous times at the cafe, said to my friend Abi in hushed tones the other day, *So...is Shannon a man or a woman?* She's one of only two people here with whom I've shared my gender origins, and she's quick as a whip when put on the spot. Without batting an eye, she suggested he just come right out and ask me, adding that she's sure I wouldn't be offended, and I'd probably have a good laugh if he did. *Good answer!* I told her, and wondered aloud what I'd say if he actually followed through, since I didn't know him all that well.

It does help to have an answer in mind, if only to avoid the awkwardness of coming up with something in the rare incidence of being put on the spot. For years I've held in reserve a simple *Yes!* to the question of my being a man or a woman, but have had few opportunities to use it. Nearly everyone has gone with a visual rather than verbal directness in the matter, resulting in a lot of curious stares and little chance for such "cleverness" on my part.

Most everyone who has come right out and asked has been under the age of about twelve. Looking around to make sure there aren't any adults around to scold them, they'll sidle up and ask, *So... are you a boy or a girl?* I might mock surprise, throw my hands up in the air and ask, *Do I really have to pick just one?* They inevitably look around a moment, searching their data bank of enculturation, and turn back my way laughing... *Well, yes! You're supposed to!* I do my very best disappointed look, then brighten up and say something like, *Well, then, I'll be a girl who sort of looks like a boy,* or *Maybe I'll pick one later*. Something in their Being prompts them to be bold and ask— to investigate the supposed boundary that's being overtly crossed. I do enjoy planting little seeds that suggest there's more than they're being told, and seeing the light of wonder in their smiling eyes.

Early on in my gender journey I was quite open: In San Francisco, I saw myself as an activist of sorts, speaking on panels and giving talks in various educational settings. I found it wonderfully affirming, and it felt good to be of some service in making even a little more room for others. In New Mexico, I was so out of the closet I actually had—as I've mentioned—license plates that proclaimed "TRANS." Before I had SRS (sex reassignment surgery), I just wore baggy pants, and never tried to hide my "extras." Since then, though, I've generally chosen not to tell people. I've tended to share my gender journey with close friends in the natural course of sharing, but usually only after I've known them awhile.

There's something gained and something lost in coming out to someone, and if it's not common knowledge, I get to weigh the value of that trade-off on a case-by-case basis. What I gain in sharing my gender process is the ability to really open up about one of the most formative aspects of my life, and to be myself overtly as a transperson; what I lose is the simplicity of being experienced by others as the woman I am per se. With friends, it's an unencumbered choice, and for the most part inessential to share at all; until I feel particularly moved to do so—and the feeling sticks with me for a while—I just go about being my womanly androgynous self with them.

On the other hand, new relationships that might evolve into something more intimate were for many years a much more complex matter, fraught with concerns that if I came out too soon I would lose—we *both* would lose—the simplicity of my just being this male-ish woman, and a person with so many other dimensions. And if I waited too long, she may have felt cheated of something she "should" have been told.

This was a conundrum, indeed, added to the usual dance of getting to know someone: where her edges were, and if the trust was there in the many ways that arise in any emerging intimate relationship. Regardless of the timing of the sharing, there was usually only a short period before she'd succumb to the whir of mind amid the pressure of social expectation, and run right into a wall of her own fears. Soon thereafter she was backpedaling away—the word *friends* lubricating her departure.

Surgery didn't "fix" that dynamic, though it certainly reduced the intensity of it. I am, and will continue to be, a transwoman, and that calls for a partner of fierce openness and compassion. The realization I arrived at many years ago is that her simply seeing and loving my essence regardless of gender is the fertile ground—the necessary, *only* ground—from which something exquisitely intimate can grow. Certainly, even this, in itself, is no guarantee that issues won't surface along the way. But absent that sublime sort of connection, I'd much rather simply be what is commonly called *alone*, but which I know includes the deep, intimate companionship of All That Is, replete with the shimmering embrace of divine love.

Outside the call and response of the social realm, the truth of this Beingness is as nuanced as Essence itself, and it percolates through layers of human expression from a singularity without form. You see, I, like you, at the most essential level, simply *Am*. That is, who—or rather, *what*—I truly am is Being, which is vastly beyond mere physical form. As I move about as an entity in this physical world, I exist as a person—a unique human being who has some relatively consistent traits across time. Out of the confluence of those traits—many of which are karmic—spills this personality.

I find it more natural to exist in the world *from* Self and *through* personhood, rather than operating within the cultural expectations of a certain gender. This personhood—the worldly gesture of my humanity—despite having arrived in a male body, resonates far more with the female; it is, for me, the nearest approximation of my essence. And in that affinity, my womanhood expresses itself in a spectrum of maleness and femaleness, often leaning more toward the male than is the culturally sanctioned norm for women.

In this world, we are expected to operate decidedly from one of two commonly recognized genders: One is supposed to identify as either male or female, and behave accordingly. Yet my compass points toward the non-duality of Essence, which is oblivious to the meaning of *or*. I didn't set out to transcend the duality of gender; it's simply the broader landscape into which my path of gender authenticity has opened.

The man who asked Abi if I'm a man or a woman likes to use his mind, so I'd thought that if he brought it up with me, I'd perhaps ask him where he sees more value: in having an interesting answer floating around in his head, or in having a living, breathing mystery with which to interact.

But as it turned out, we met yesterday on a sidewalk on Monkey Forest Road, launched into a far-ranging yak about spiritual path and surrendering to one's unfolding, and segued right into gender-as-path most gracefully. As it turned out, he'd wanted for many years to know his spirit more intimately beyond male or female; he placed his hands prayer-like to his heart and bowed slightly in recognition of my homecoming. I returned the gesture, in recognition of the journey of another awakened soul. An honor and a blessing all around, to be truly seen in the light of one's heartfelt way.

With Child

My friend Brianna and I were sitting in the well-worn wooden bleachers at the ballpark in Madrid when she turned to me and said, *Every time I look into your eyes, I see a deep sadness back there. You know, you don't have to drag around that sack of crap if you don't want to.* I must have been ready to hear those words, because I knew what she said was true, and that it was time to do something about it.

On the surface, I was saddened by not having a partner-in-love, but the roots went much deeper: My Inner Child had been gravely wounded since I was in fact a child, and was crying out for love and attention. Perhaps the part of me that could really hear Brianna's words understood that I was finally capable of mothering, and could offer what my own mother couldn't: unconditional love, understanding, and embrace.

I'd been so driven in my life, all the while pretty much unconscious of this essential part from which joy, passion, and the feminine flow. The adult side of me had kicked into gear at a very early age as a way of taking care of myself, and while I'd done a pretty good job of doing that in relation to the outer world, I had a relationship with my Inner Child that was not so different in some ways from the one I'd had with my parents growing up.

It was clear I needed to get to the root of this relationship, so I found a therapist specializing in working with the child within. A couple of sessions was enough to initiate my own process of learning to recognize, communicate with, and hold this part of me that had fled to the farthest corner under my mother's harsh rule.

Over the years, I'd experienced a good deal of passion and joy in my life, but it was based much more in creative doings and in relationship with the natural forces, than in the source within. When I turned my attention to the child side, I discovered the clear upwelling of a spring that had been muddied by early-life circumstance.

I found, too, a part of my Being in need of love—as is any child—as well as a Beingness blazing *with* love. I discovered such acceptance and forgiveness that I finally got to experience what *unconditional* really means: As I walked by a mirror in the house one day, I caught a glimpse of myself. Something told me to go back and take a good look, and when I did, she said right out loud, *I love you, even if you can't pay the bills.* This was my Inner Child telling me that I was loved even if I failed as a provider, and I knew right then the power and meaning of forgiveness. The message was loud and clear:

Just love... not if, or when... just love.

I stopped waiting to get to some condition that would qualify me for this depth of self-love; whenever my mind conjured an image of self-love at some point when I was different down the road, I simply stopped thinking and went straight into unabashed acceptance in the moment. And I stopped waiting for someone to come along and show me that I'm loved. I took whatever I felt I had waiting in the wings to give to someone else to aid in their healing, and I gave it to myself. That sadness behind my eyes was a deep hole of longing waiting to be filled, and I found that I fit in there just perfectly.

This turning point was the beginning of a newfound relationship, and like all relationships, it took work and practice to weave it into my life. It was the start of a conversation without end, and part of the work was to be aware of her presence, listen when she spoke up, and to check in if she didn't. Sometimes, I'd be working in the studio, and she'd say right out loud, *This isn't fun, you know... We're working too hard.* I'd take a garden break, go make a special snack, or tell her that if we worked for a while longer, we'd do something fun later—which we always did.

The Treebone Garden

I realized along the way that what she really wanted was loving attention, acknowledgement of her gifts, and appreciation of her presence—like any child does. All this may sound rather silly on the surface, but it's enriched my life immeasurably by bringing, and keeping, me more in touch with the wellspring of joy, passion, and nurturance at the core of my Being.

I didn't give up hope of finding a partner-in-love, but I did stop waiting to be fulfilled by someone outside of me. And I felt better able to recognize my potential partner: She's already loved—self-loved—and already happy. She's enthusiastically open to someone of my ilk, ready to celebrate mutual joy—in stillness and in motion, through loving presence and touch, across time.

In getting in touch with my Inner Child—and thereby my Inner Mother—I looked out across the landscape of my birth mother's upbringing and saw the unaffectionate way in which she had been raised. Second oldest of nine children, she'd been handed responsibility for them at a young age, and received at best very poor modeling for what it means to be a nurturing parent. Born and raised during the Great Depression by a pious Catholic mother and a pull-yourself-up-by-your-bootstraps father, she'd grown up in a time underscored by a sensibility of survival, in a household in which personal feelings were considered an unwarranted extravagance.

From this field of honest appraisal, it would have taken considerable effort to sidestep the impression that she'd done the best she could with a limited set of inner tools. I've heard it said that forgiveness is not something you do for someone else; it's a gift you give yourself—an opportunity to let go of the dead weight of resentment and anger, and move forward lightened of the burden.

In discovering my Inner Mother, I found the opening to understanding my birth mother, and left the offense of those early years behind. It seems that while understanding in itself can very well blossom into forgiveness, at least some degree of willingness to forgive is necessary to open the way to understanding. And it may be that with deep understanding, one realizes that ultimately there is nothing—no separate other—to forgive.

In contemplating my mother's harsh ways of child rearing, I could see she wasn't acting out of malice, but rather out of her limitations: Out of touch with her own feelings, she had no empathy with ours. Light and space replaced resentment, and this opening became the doorway—the invitation—to find my balance of Mother and Child within.

Sometimes forgiveness is a kind of lubricant that shifts the dynamic and ushers in greater mutual understanding and sense of connection. I wish I could say that in the process she found an opening, too, but it seems that in forgiveness all we can do is extend ourselves more wholly, and that the acceptance of the gift of this spaciousness by some supposed "other" is beyond our reach.

□ □ □

Span

Toward the end of the day, I often went across the street, through the old ballpark, and down the trail into the arroyo that sliced the hills on its way north to lower ground. *Arroyo* means "dry river bed," and most of time it was just that. But when it ran—as it did sometimes during the summer monsoon when the surrounding ground was saturated—it sounded like a ghost of the trains that once ran coal to distant cities and towns. As it flowed through the village, it was shallow and wide, but as it channeled down through the hills it picked up more run-off.

Over countless years, a gorge had been carved into the soft stone. In the middle of that gash arose two prominent features: massive piles of tailings—the burnt, terra-cotta-like leftovers from long-ago coal processing—and a yet-more massive protrusion of solid rock and boulders the size of cars.

The Treebone Garden

Up high on the rock there was a cave facing west with a view out over the valley floor and up the side of a pinion- and juniper-stubbled ridge. Sunsets were stunning from there—especially during the monsoon, when astonishingly tall and massive cloud formations sailed the sky.

But I went there for something subtler: Birds of prey would launch from just above the cave on thermals rising from the valley floor, and I could hear air rake across their wings against a background of near silence. They'd lift out onto unseen currents, wings taut, piercing eyes sweeping below, and part of me floated right out with them. In this span, my soul was free—released beyond time to Sky.

That refueling dwarfed the labored concerns of the day, and set me right with the world. I'd walk home—dry, gritty ground crunching under my shoes—and work into the far end of evening.

□ □ □

Why Aren't You Famous?

A new friend I've met at the cafe looks over a portfolio from my years as a furniture maker. *So, why aren't you famous?* she asks. I tell her I had other priorities, and leave it at that. We don't know each other well enough yet, but I want to tell her the truth: that at the time, I was busy changing my sex and dealing with old ghosts—that I'd had my hands full just living in solitude, and sticking my head out just far and long enough to attract more projects.

And what good would fame have done me, except perhaps in adding to the monetary value of the work? While the money would surely have helped, I simply didn't have the need or desire for being well known. I didn't need the distraction, either. What I needed was found quite simply in Being with the work: the grounding physicality of it, certainly—and more essentially, the blessed vocation of gender shape-shifter as shifter of other physical forms.

Fame would have required that I take on helpers, and this was a solo journey of discovery and self-therapy. And perhaps other artists will understand this best: While they came through me, and when they were finished, the wooden creatures that showed up in the studio by my hands taught me a great deal about integration, balance, beauty, sensuality, space, rhythm, and so much more—and the nuance of this relationship required quietude.

My hands were full, too, of tools and grief, wood and bandages, and looking back it seems like I was trying to work my way to transcendent redemption, as if I could conjure it in the studio and climb inside to another kind of life where solitude was less a necessity and more a cherished option.

It was a difficult confluence of deep creative satisfaction and frequent anxiety over keeping up with the overhead of a shop, a house and its renovation, and the associated costs of life in modern America—all the while investing sums large and small in the evolving landscape of my physical form. So I worked long days in the dust for years, self-indentured to the love of birthing what was in my heart and spirit to make, to the mooring of soul to malleable earth, and to the inbred illusion that I could rest, finally, at some point down the road if I just worked hard enough in the present.

From this equatorial warmth, surrounded by lush growth and the shimmering light of the Writing Womb, it's easy to recount the intense output of those desert years—accomplished somehow under the duress of hormones, stress, periods of ill-health, and seemingly insatiable aloneness in the realm of human intimacy—and be astonished at the relentless drive willing it all to resolution.

Like a whirling dervish, I kept spinning, spiraling with feet in this world and eyes on the Divine, toward stillness: sweet, blessed, eternal Space.

Beast of the Belly

The initial phase of building a new piece was mostly brute labor: rough-milling lumber to required dimensions, joining planks edge-to-edge to make large plates, cutting and honing the basic forms and joinery. It was a dramatic shift from the nuanced fine-tuning of the finish of the previous one—energetically and physically. At first, I'd feed the piece with my effort and energy; it was pure labor, and, as it was the initiation of the piece that would emerge into full form later, it drew heavily from the male side.

Eventually, though, it would be ready to stand on its own; then it would come into being as an entity—a rather preadolescent one, but an object unto itself nonetheless. At this point, my relationship with it would change: It had arisen like an embryo out of the realm of the possible, and become a child-like creation in need of nurturing to bring out its full potential.

As the piece became more fleshed out and detailed, its forms began to interact visually; the energetic table turned as the piece became a source of energy, and I began to get sustenance from *its* presence. This would be emphasized as the finish was applied—as the colors and depth of surface activated the forms and amplified their interaction.

My appetite would shift to the energy radiating from the birthing process itself, and from the sense of movement erupting from stillness. The creative process was still a great deal of work requiring calories, so in those phases, I had to watch my diet to be sure I was eating plenty to fuel me physically.

The *He/She Bang* had continued as an annual event, and I noticed as it came around again that fall I'd been ill in one way or another for most of the previous year. I was only performing this time, and as I put my costume together, the mirror revealed an unhealthily thin me. I'd been eating plenty of food, but I had a strange feeling something else was getting much of the benefit of it.

It may seem odd to come to such a sudden realization of long-term ill-health, but the gradual decline was masked by the energetic ebb and flow of the making, my tendency to focus willfully on being productive each day, and the fact that we all get a range of symptoms and ailments from time to time in the normal course of life. Underlying all that, though, was the reality of the intense process over the years—that I'd long been used to waves of discomfort and difficult states.

But looking back over the year, the allergy symptoms had been stronger and lasted longer, the "summer cold" lingered but never quite blossomed into a full-blown cold, a low-grade "flu" came and went, and I often felt nauseous and fatigued. What really brought it all into perspective—ironically enough— was that my mind had become foggy.

I'd managed to produce prolifically and to beautiful effect, but it was taking every bit of will I could muster. I'd go through phases in which I'd work for a couple of hours, then lie down for a half-hour, and back and forth like that to get through the day. And I'd simply adapted to working with a background of more or less nausea.

Having tried every avenue I could think of to get to the bottom of the problem—from Western medicine to Naturopathy—with little success beyond a little pacifying of some symptoms, I was feeling frustrated on top of it all. So when someone suggested a woman doctor in Santa Fe with whom a number of local women had success in dealing with difficult health issues, I figured I had nothing to lose in seeing her.

Dr. Cindy—as I called her—turned out to be a Naturopath, a Medical Doctor, and an oracle. She had an extraordinary ability to "read" below the surface of the symptoms and see the underlying causes—whether they were physical, psychological, or emotional. On my first visit, she looked me over and said, *I think you have a serious case of Candida*. While we all have *Candida Albicans*—a form of yeast—in our gastro-intestinal (G-I) tracts, she was suggesting that I was suffering from an overgrowth—an imbalance between it and the healthy bacteria essential to proper digestion.

My Candida had gone well beyond the G-I tract—migrating almost certainly to the blood—and she suspected the overgrowth arose from a combination of surgical trauma and having taken antibiotics without replenishing the friendly bacteria with probiotics afterward. If ever there were a candidate for the "I Wish I Knew Then What I Know Now" file, this would be a shoo-in. It's simply impossible to convey the extent of the difficulty which may well have been avoided with a single bottle of *l. bifidus* and its bacterial cohorts.

Besides some Western medicine to kill off at least some portion of the yeast right away, and probiotics and supplements to give it some competition over time, she advised a sweeping change in my diet. So, for the next three years, I ate no grain but quinoa, no sugar, no sweets, and drank no alcohol. I ate a quarter-pound of buffalo a day, and lots of vegetables, nuts, and beans.

When I told friends about my radically changed diet, some of them shook their heads and said, *I could never do that!* I assured them that if they'd had an acute, debilitating condition for long enough, and a radically new diet made them feel better, they most certainly could—and would.

For the first three weeks I felt hungry, even if I'd just eaten a full meal, and that's when I knew I was dealing with an insidious intrusion. That invasive yeast colony was prompting my body to request the kinds of food *it* wanted; it seemed, and acted, like an alien entity a la the X-files. As most would, I found this rather alarming, and took it as a rallying call to do everything I could to fight it. The intense feeling of fending off a foreign intruder made being disciplined about the diet much easier. When I was tempted to cheat, all I had to do was think about that disgusting colony in residence in my body—refusing to feed it was an act of defiance.

The nausea gradually dissipated as the yeast overgrowth died off, and my strength and stamina slowly returned. For a long time, it was hard not to assume that every little hint of an ailment was related to it, since at first, so much was.

Of all the creative accomplishments over those intensely difficult years, the fact that I made beautiful, graceful things at all in grip of that debilitation, is easily one of the most satisfying.

Rebounding

Nearly four years since the initial surgery, I remained unfinished down there—rather like a prepubescent girl. Perhaps the layers of serpentine lines and clefts showing up in the furniture in the meantime were, in part, an unconscious reflection of a growing pull toward completion, but those difficult health issues had sidetracked any thoughts of responding. With good health regained, it was time to honor and address the further evolution of my own form.

I'd started the hormones in October ten years before, had the initial surgery in October four years before, and it just so happened the final SRS would be in that month, too. This time, however, it wasn't nearly as psycho-emotionally charged—I saw it as more of a cosmetic fine-tuning. And the recovery wouldn't be as difficult: just two nights in the hospital, maybe a week or so of real healing, and another of taking it easy.

A month or so before the surgery, I met a woman at a party who had perhaps the most unusual presence I'd ever experienced; it was also deeply familiar, and we ended talking the rest of the time there. We agreed to get together and visit some more, and soon after, we did. She was quite lovely, but for some reason I wasn't physically attracted to her; when I searched a little deeper, there was a feeling that she was only partly of this world, and that our connection was about something more rarefied.

When I first met Sylvia, I wasn't surprised at all to learn that she was a healer. She shared that when she was young—maybe four or five—her mother would discover her in odd places around the house, sitting in a lotus position, leaning all the way forward so that her forehead neared the ground and her arms stretched further out in front of her. When her mother asked what she was doing, she said, *Waiting*. Now, she was in nursing school en route to becoming a hospice nurse, and I couldn't imagine a finer presence to see one off from this world

We ran into each other a few of weeks before the surgery at a health food store in Santa Fe, and sat down at a table to chat. I hadn't thought of it before, but it just seemed right to ask her to accompany me to

Trinidad. Without hesitating, she delightedly agreed. I'd gone for groceries and found that I'd been sent another angel to see me through a physically challenging time. With her and Dr. Cindy's support, I felt ready for the surgery and a graceful recovery.

Sylvia wanted to watch the operation, and while the hospital had strict rules about having only staff in the operating room, Dr. Biber saw no harm—she was a nursing student, after all. With his help, she got to see an operation that I'm sure very few nursing students get introduced to, while I got to have her witnessing presence. We never discussed what she saw, not because we avoided it—the subject just never came up.

After a one-night stay in the hospital, we headed back to Madrid— very slowly. Sylvia was so mellow behind the wheel, the usual four-hour trip took five, which was a long time to be sitting up just twenty-four hours after the operation. But I wasn't complaining: I'd been so blessed with extraordinary companionship and support, and was closer by the moment to my own sweet place of healing.

As soon as the incisions stabilized, I padded myself with cloth and carefully headed back into the studio work. Knowing I'd be anxious to get productive again, I'd left some less physically challenging things to work on, like fine sanding and oil finishing. There was a deep sense of healing balance as the pendulum swung back into the world of form outside my own.

In the months that followed, thoughts that had been submerged— by the need to stay productive to keep that life going, by ill-health, and by the fact that the house was still far from finished—began to surface and press for attention. I'd be working in the studio or walking in the garden, and what had been in the periphery would show up front and center. It was clear in those moments that I'd felt mired in this place and way of working for some time; I wanted more room to freely explore sculpturally, as well as more intellectual stimulation.

Doing relatively well financially with the furniture was wonderful, but I was feeling close to completion with expressing myself through the positive tension of form and function, and wanted to leave the functional aspect behind. My livelihood, though, was still very much tied to that balance: it was the combination of artfulness and practicality that prompted the sales of what I made.

With the completion of the surgery, I was experiencing an unexpectedly surging sense of freedom and potential, which may well have made room for those thoughts to surface. It seems that the transformational element of Fire had drawn forth Air: Movement and change were blowing into my life, and were eager to show up in the creative work. There was a new sense that I could move on, though it wasn't clear to where, or what. One thing which was clear, however, was that the house had to get finished, and it was going to be another marathon undertaking.

The furniture making continued, but with a renewed focus on the house, as well. When I thought about how else I might make a living, teaching seemed like a distinct possibility—if not right away, then perhaps later, when I wasn't so geared toward making.

What I wanted most was freedom, so the idea then was to sell the house, and experience some unfettered room for a while: perhaps traveling around the country, spending my time writing and doing a little making for the joy of it.

Many years later, I'd attend a retreat for transwomen, and one of them would say, *I didn't have the surgery so I could run around excitedly with a vagina... I did it so I could have what is normal for me, and go on with other things in my life*. I'd naturally think back to this period of personal renaissance, and how finishing that project between my legs did indeed make room for other things in my life.

The Treebone Garden

Fork in the Freedom Road

One morning, I told my brother, Christopher, that I was fantasizing about a small, vintage Airstream trailer behind my truck, with time to go wherever I wanted to be. A half-hour later, the phone rang, and it was him saying he'd just met a friend of a friend who happened to have a small, 1962 Airstream trailer for sale, and that I'd probably enjoy knowing this woman as well. He gave me Ellen's phone number at her home in Massachusetts, and we did, in fact, have a nice rapport. We discussed the trailer, and she agreed to send some pictures.

Christopher had mentioned that Ellen was a professor at a university in Massachusetts, and besides the fact that she had a trailer for sale and was married, I knew little else about her. When I spoke to her again, though, I got the feeling I was supposed to send her a furniture portfolio, though I didn't know why. She just said, *Ok, then...* and gave me her address. I sent it off, and dove back into the work.

About a week later, I got an email from her: She'd passed the portfolio along to the professor who headed up the Furniture Design Program in the Artisanry Department at the university where she taught, and he'd asked her to give me his contact numbers at the school and his home. I took this to mean he really enjoyed the work. I'd never even heard of such a program, or known that you could get a Master's Degree in artisanry, but it did explain why I'd intuitively sent the portfolio to Ellen.

When I spoke with the professor, I knew immediately he was someone with whom I'd like to study and work. At one point in our talk, I said, *I think I may be done with furniture... would that be a problem?* We were talking about the possibility of my entering the Furniture Design Program, after all. He just chuckled and said, *No, you're obviously a mature artist. You can come and do whatever you want... You can even invite a professor from the Sculpture Department to sit on your committee.* This was music to my ears, as I'd really wanted to move in the direction of pure sculpture anyway.

Quite quickly, my vision of a more open-ended freedom in the world at large was being funneled into a more open-ended artistic freedom in a structured setting. I couldn't ignore the serendipity with which it came together; in fact, the way it unfolded—as if part of a larger plan—was part of the allure. It seemed my path wended its way, not as I'd fantasized, but quite naturally—and more directly—toward what I'd really wanted all along: room to explore creatively, intellectual stimulation, and a solid background for the option of teaching if I chose to do so later on.

□ □ □

Portraits in Wood, Oils, and Power Tools

The house remodeling needed to be done long enough before I was to leave so there would be time to sell the place. With a departure date of August 1st, a mountain of work to do, and a few months in which to get it done, I settled into a marathon run of longer than usual workdays. Though my normal work-life of oscillating between the remodeling and furniture making drew heavily from the male side, at times like these— when the intensity redoubled and I reached yet further in for reserves of will and stamina—I needed to own my womanhood yet more deeply.

In a way, it was like those times when I'd go naked at the hotsprings back in California, and was called to own my womanhood more powerfully because I still had a penis. But with the remodeling, this experience of womanhood encompassing male presence went on for many months. Though I was expressing a lot of male energy through the tools, I was consciously doing so from my female, and from that perspective, it often felt truly rewarding to be so physically effective.

But there were times in the thick of this productive marathon when I just wanted to relax into a gentler life, and all I could do was have a good cry, throw my arms around me and say, *Soon, Soon... It may not seem like it, but there is, in fact, a finite amount of work to be done here.*

□ □ □

The Treebone Garden

Well before I got near the end of the renovation and started putting things into storage in Santa Fe, I'd taken on the last of the *Treebone Garden* commissions—a pair of small, very curvaceous tables and a long, low dresser. Ending the series doing my best work and still learning from each piece was deeply satisfying; it would have been heartbreaking to carry on with the work after the passion for it had dwindled. I'd expressed my highest aspirations in the marriage of form and function, and it was essential—to the ushering in of whatever was next—to finish on a high note.

I've heard it said that everything an artist makes is a form of self-portrait; when the series was done, I could look around at the pieces I still had, or flip through the portfolio, and delightedly say, *There I am: as a table, as a bench, as an altar, as a cabinet, as a bed...*

When the house was done, I looked around and remembered what I'd said seven years before when the house was finally mine, and I entered it as such for the first time: *...that I'd bring in more light and joy and beauty.* Sun streaked through skylights and small windows set high in the upper walls, across oiled oak floors renewed with matching patches quietly revealing the wash of its eighty-six years. It wasn't large, but it felt spacious inside and connected with the natural world outside. It was open to the light and beauty of the landscape, but protected from the extremes of wet and dry, hot and cold. It basked in its new form, and there I was, all around me.

Winging It Toward the Horizon

As the date for leaving approached, there were two imposing complications, the more immediate and overarching of which was that the house hadn't sold. The real estate market in Madrid wasn't strong, and between what I owed and what I had put into the place, it wasn't simply a matter of reducing the price to entice a buyer. The next best option seemed to be to rent it, and fortunately, shortly before leaving, a friend offered to help oversee that process. While it was a relief to have a backup plan, it was also deeply disappointing to be unable to make a clean break with it energetically, and feel resolved after so much devotion and work.

The other complication was that I hadn't been assured of getting a Teaching Assistant position at the university, which was the only way the program was going to be affordable, even with a school loan. But the serendipity with which it had come together suggested it would somehow turn out all right—if only because it *had* to. Still, having the distinct possibility of showing up in Massachusetts and facing a serious dilemma with even being able to enter the program, on top of leaving with the house unsold and unrented, set up a background of anxiety.

It certainly wasn't the grounded, resolved exit I would have chosen, and all I could do to stay in the flow of change was let go into the sense of potential. I'd been winging it for a long while at this point, so it wasn't unusual to have major factors in my life up in the air, but even by that standard, this was still a lot of floating unknown.

With many pickup truck loads of tools, materials, household goods, and furniture in storage in Santa Fe, all that remained were the things that would go with me to school: clothes, tools, and a few pieces of *Treebone Garden* furniture. Shortly before leaving, I went up on the ridge overlooking the property to say goodbye. A storage unit twenty-five miles away held the things that made this house a home and studio; I wanted to do the same for the intangibles, so that energetic parts of me weren't marooned and entangled with the next nesters. I did this for my own wellbeing, and for theirs—to give them a clean start in what would be their new home.

Closing my eyes, I became still and let the seven years of living there wash through me. I sensed as deeply as I could my aspirations for this house when I arrived; the Herculean effort in making it the lovely dwelling it had come to be; the sacrifices, celebrations, disappointments, and difficulties; the fulfillment of having turned an old house much in need of loving vision and work into an inevitably older house glowing with warmth, light, and embrace. I didn't try to make everything that happened all right—just felt the gesture of it.

I brought my awareness to the remaining attachments to this place of transformation, and with a deep breath called back those bits of my Being still lingering there—envisioned it returning as I inhaled. I took it in as fully as I could, and let this three-quarters of an acre in Madrid, New Mexico be what it was without me.

Naturally, I wished it were a final goodbye, but I looked out over the property and the whole village with a sublime sense of neutrality, thankful for the opening to go on now to exploring in other realms. Entering the Artisanry Program meant not having the degree of solitude I'd had in creating here—and I was more than ready for the creative interaction as I made way down the rock-strewn ridge.

Longing... Belonging

The realm of humans can be wonderful in myriad ways, of course, but as everyone knows uniquely, it can also be experienced as harsh, stressful, bewildering, and heartbreaking in ways subtle and profound. I find that, besides being inspired to make from a vision I want to translate into form, I'm still drawn to phases of picking up tools and materials in part for the sense they offer of refuge from the human realm. Whatever the impetus, I want at times to just share essence with natural materials, and focus on the simple presence that comes with hands-on creative practice.

There were often times, though, in West Oakland, and Madrid, too, when being in the studio wasn't just a creative nicety; I thoroughly *needed* a grounding sanctum of materials and touch. In this realm, I could devote myself to concerns that were finer, more integrating and uplifting, than those of the world outside: inner and outer balance, aesthetics, design, the nature of physical form, and artisanry. This was the most natural way for me of melding craft and art—as well as livelihood and exploration—in that time and place.

From this contemplative life in Ubud, ten years and half a planet down the road, it's easy to feel the contrast, and appreciate the degree to which that studio in the mountains of New Mexico was my retreat. And retreat I did: into forms from nature, into entities of lush, quiet complexity and layers of translucent color. At a time when my identity was re-forming, and later, when my way of Being in the world was still visibly not "with the program," it was empowering and affirming to simply bring my attention and passion to an artistically ambitious task and see it through.

On the surface, I was making furniture which I hoped would evoke in whomever was using it a feeling of presence and uplift in everyday life. But more essentially, it was deeply grounding to work toward a gorgeous, asymmetrically balanced marriage of form and function, structure and sculpture, and I needed all the grounding I could get. I look back with unabashed delight at the sensual forms that arose amongst the wood chips and dust in those emotion-charged days. It was a therapeutically creative union of landscape, plant, animal, and female forms with a male underpinning of structure and functionality: a unity of forms, essence, and the arc of my odd existence. Each piece was a universe unto itself, and I was delighted to be sucked into its gravitational pull; it whirled around me, and I around it.

The sense of belonging and intimacy that I wasn't finding in my more worldly life was diffused and suffused by the forms that came into Being simply because I showed up to make them. When I was asked how I came up with these things, I would shrug and say, *I go to the studio each day and stay busy there, and these things appear.* It was deeply satisfying in part because, as long as I showed up, so did the relationship.

In the studio, I could just be who I was unselfconsciously, and extend myself without fear of becoming too attached or complicated or needy or emotional, or any of the other things that were regular disconnects in my attempts at love and touch in the outer world. Beyond the entanglement of human fickleness, I was free to have direct, far-ranging relationships: with nature, creativity, physical form, essence, the Divine—things as uncomplicated and available as the dog that doesn't know any better than to greet you eagerly when you come home feeling bruised by the human world.

If there was fickleness present, it was clearly mine. Whatever my capacity for presence in this relationship, there was only unconditional acceptance of my sensibility, and thereby of me as maker—as shape-shifter.

One of the finest compliments I received at the time was from a choral composer who owned a gallery and showed my work for a while. He said that his musical life revolved around point and counterpoint, and that he immediately saw that in my work, in the way every gesture had a physical response, or created one implicitly. I hadn't thought of it this way, but it offered new insight into how the relationship I was experiencing in the process of making, was showing up in the objects themselves:

Point...Counterpoint.
Call...Response.
Longing...Art.

Longing for female form to love and touch, I worked with what I had in the studio in a sped-up version of what was taking so many years with my own physicality. Sumptuous forms in wood—stroked thousands of times in the process of sanding and finishing—stood in for the warm flesh and skin I was missing, that seemed always just out of reach. I could touch these undulations, and lavish on them some part of the reservoir of nurturance and heartful attention that had waited far too long for a lover of the human sort.

It seems that the course of this lifetime is an ongoing, invitational lesson in the broadest kind of interrelatedness, and that it underscores what spiritual teachers have said for millennia: that one chooses to live from suffering or joy, and the difference is not found *out there* in worldly circumstance, but in our willingness to look within and see past our programs of beliefs, thoughts, and emotions. Beyond those limiting patterns, acceptance of What Is reveals a far more spacious view—awareness of, and *from*, the higher Self.

Spaciousness is Joy.

I could have framed this sweep of aloneness as rejection, and thereby fed the beast of suffering with heaps of victimhood. Fortunately, I was beginning to see in the ebb and flow of my own life what I'd read about from various—often Buddhist—sources: that the degree to which one insists on a stance of separation, one suffers. I was blessed with seeing this circumstance as a nudging toward going deeper, and opening to union in myriad other ways that feed the light of joy, love, peace, and freedom.

What I really wanted, and what, it seems, we all *truly* want, was connection at the level of essence; by that measure, the world of form alone would always fall short. I might have retracted into misery and despair for lack of intimate human partnership, but by the grace of that broader view, I looked to creative spirit for soul-nourishing connection, and found vastly more.

We're socialized toward playing out our desire for connection through human relationship, but if one peels back the surface of desire of any sort, there's the deepest pool that ripples outward through consciousness, from the center of one's present awareness to the ultimate belonging: the Oneness. I've found that simply Being in touch with the gesture of my Being in this arc of unfoldment toward the light far surpasses any particular form of connection, and that recognizing and embracing this exquisite passage is the very root of love, peace, and joy.

> *There is no love greater than love with no object.*
> *For then you, yourself, have become love itself.*
> > *-Rumi*

When we love someone or some thing, there's a tendency to be blinded by illusion: that the source of love is *out there*, and without it, we suffer a loss; or that we need that object to release the love within. To love unbidden by anything in the world is to simply love... without reason, without condition. In the boundless light, the open heart knows that love is not a feeling, but a state of Being—not something one gets or gives, but one's true nature.

Ultimately, there is nothing outside of the Self—nothing to belong *to*. One simply *is*, and that which exists cannot be outside of All That Is—the Oneness. Wholeness waits beyond time for us to shed the habits of our limitations.

6

Lumenhorse

With the Program

When I crossed the Massachusetts state line, I burst into tears. More precisely, my body burst into tears: The bones knew they were home after seventeen years in the West. I felt enveloped in the lush green of early August's summer prime, and the dense growth of woods along the freeway looked like a rain forest after years of living in the arid Southwest. Between the humidity and sea-level density, I seemed to be swimming in air. My lungs were used to working harder in the thinner air at 6,000 or more feet, and now even shallow breaths seemed more than full.

Arriving in the coastal town of New Bedford I was exhausted, but had to get to the school and unload the trailer before the janitor left for the weekend. Along the way, and in the following days as I began looking for a place to live, I found that so much of what I'd held fondly about the region was still there: in the canopies of broadleaf trees arching over streets, the white wooden buildings with deep porches, the roll of the well-hilled land.

I felt the deep roots of birthing in this part of the planet, and reveled in the countless intangible rhythms I likely wouldn't have noticed but for having lived for so long in other regions. Sensing the worldliness that informed me I was no longer of this place, I felt, too, the wending path that would surely lead me away once again in a few year's time.

I arrived a few weeks early to be on the pulse of the potential of a teaching position, and to set up the studio space to be in motion for the beginning of the school year—if, in fact, the position opened up; there was no backup plan for making ends meet if it didn't. But as I've said, the way the program had come into my life—and at just the time I was ready to shift gears in my creative process—suggested there was more to it beyond the surface of circumstance.

As it turned out, a professor in another department had passed away shortly before I arrived, and in the ensuing shuffling of positions, a Teaching Assistantship opened up. As those were normally awarded to second- and third-year students in the three-year program, I felt doubly blessed when I got a phone call with the news that it had been given to me. It seemed the professor heading the Wood and Furniture Program had been busy in the background rooting for me.

The Artisanry Program was housed well away from the main campus in an old, three-story, former factory building, and the first thing I did in setting up the studio was build some makeshift walls in the cavernous space for a modicum of privacy, and to keep my tools more secured. I was the only grad student I was aware of who'd had a career in artisanry; many others had come from undergraduate arts programs, and so were used to working in community studios.

Obviously, my experience—both in creative process and output — could hardly have been more different; and as the Queen of Solitude, I felt most centered with some semblance of at least visual boundaries for my creative realm. I wanted to see where my creativity would take me if freed from the constraints of livelihood, but I didn't want to sacrifice my bearings in exploring this new mode of making.

Lumenhorse

Since the first SRS operation, I'd been less inclined to share my trans status, if only because I was no longer as in-between physically and in identity; and certainly after the second one, I felt that much more settled in my womanhood. While I was very much a transwoman, and would always be one, the emphasis had shifted to the *woman* aspect. If I felt a deep connection with someone, and it seemed natural and mutually beneficial to share my path with them, I went ahead and shared—cognizant that it would shift the dynamics of the relationship to some degree.

Before heading back to Massachusetts, I'd made a conscious decision to keep my gender path to myself if possible, though naturally, I had no idea if it would come up anyway. In New Mexico, I was nearly always seen as a woman, but once in a while, someone who was familiar with trans people would recognize me as such, and I knew the spectrum of possible response could make such revelations unpredictable, to say the least. What I actually experienced at school was an odd "don't ask, don't tell" situation in that it didn't come up, and I didn't bring it up.

I told only one close friend because it just didn't seem like a good idea to tell anyone else with the endless flow of gossip through the place. I was rather amazed from time to time that there wasn't chatter going on in that regard—at least that I knew of; but then, I was purposefully out of the loop of gossip. My friend would have told me if there were such talk, however, and I never got any weird vibe that things were being said behind my back—at least about my gender. Looking back, it really is extraordinary that in the three years I was there, my being trans didn't surface as general knowledge at some point.

I had assumed there would be other gay grad students among the forty-five of us in the various media—this was an arts program, after all—but if there were, I never knew. Maybe the other students just assumed that I was a lesbian—and a dyke at that—and felt uncomfortable in bringing even that up. I remember telling the friend to whom I'd come out how lonely I was feeling for lack of community; it seemed as though I'd dropped back fifteen or twenty years in the advancement of gay—let alone gender-variant—people's relationship with the mainstream, as compared to the West Coast and Southwest.

Of course, it was wonderful that I wasn't harassed—overtly or even subtly. Yet who I was as a gay woman and a transwoman was not on the radar at all in terms of connection or community, either. I was so starved for company of at least somewhat my ilk, I drove one morning to Provincetown—at the tip of Cape Cod—to have breakfast with gay people: a two-hour trip each way, not to meet anyone in particular, but just to share an environment with other gays.

But while I lacked any semblance of community in being gay or trans, it was also a relief to have gender issues on the back burner, making more room up front for open-ended creative exploration. I was making objects that seemed to me very androgynous, but gender never entered overtly into the discussion, or exploration, of the work. It wasn't as if I were hiding it—my own gender balance just flowed out through the work, and didn't need to be remarked upon.

Much as the energetic relationship would shift as I made a piece of furniture—from my feeding it, to it feeding me—the relationship between gender and art switched at this point, too: Whereas I had earlier sacrificed artistic exploration to support my focus on gender, in my new life at school, gender went into the background and served as a quiet wellspring for the artistic exploration. The poet in me saw that the gender path had led out onto a gentle, simple landscape, opening the inner space to follow the Way of Art into the mountains.

Lumenhorse

There were other trade-offs, as well: In relation to the art world, I'd been working like a monk in a cave up there in the mountains of New Mexico—not at all concerned about what was happening in the realms of furniture art and design, or sculpture. What I was making there poured out of my soul, reflecting the focus on personal integration, and love of nature and the natural forces. As I've said, it was refuge and an active sort of therapy that provided a sense of connection amid the longing and solitude. In opening myself to the community of the program, I was also opening my creative process to include an awareness of its relationship with the world of art.

The riches of my beloved gardens and the New Mexico landscape shifted into a lushness of mediums: Suddenly, I had at my fingertips access to tools, materials, and expertise in metals, fibers, and clay. Wood was no longer a given as I explored attractions to copper, hand-made paper, and waxed-linen thread. New, more skeletal forms were possible, and with them, there was more room for the encompassing movement of Air, the melding of Water, and the expansive essence of Space to flow into the work.

And while I still lived alone, a portion of my creative solitude was happily replaced with interactions with others who were passionate makers, too, and had expertise in fine metalworking and papermaking—who in turn looked to me for guidance in working with wood.

Discovery

Upon finishing the undergraduate work seventeen years earlier, I'd wanted—as I wrote at the end of the first chapter—*to grow and mature so I'd have layers of living to create with, and from.* Entering this graduate arts program at the age of thirty-nine to explore and engage new mediums, I did, indeed, have layers aplenty. I was in the upper end of the age range—though I wasn't the oldest grad student there—and having really lived and gotten to know myself on so many levels made a world of difference. There was a similar depth and confidence in the work of some of the other more mature grad students: We weren't striving for profundity, and there was an undercurrent of ease in having a richer life palette from which to work.

As I started to gain some momentum in the program, I couldn't help but recall one afternoon in New Mexico when I was driving the truck down to Albuquerque, surfing the radio waves trying to find something worth listening to amid the long stretches of dry hills. I happened on an interview with an author who was saying that, although it's suggested that writers write about what they know, she'd modify this to suggest they write what they *don't know* about what they know.

She was making the point that *discovery* is an essential factor in creating an evocative work. I was struck at the time with how well what she'd said applied to any medium, and with how much more passionate I was about the studio work as the *Treebone Garden* series was developing amid waves of delicious discovery.

As many artists have, I'd found that opening the familiar to the unknown invited in freshness, passion, and the possibility of transformation; and that without such discovery, a process couldn't be transformative—whether it's art or life in general. I saw the earlier furniture from West Oakland and the first few years in Madrid as rich in color play and somewhat interesting in design, but not very explorative—I simply didn't have the energy for more discovery in that realm with all the personal transformation going on inside and out.

Later in Madrid—as my body came into truer alignment with my sense of Being—discovery really entered the work and flourished with the *Treebone Garden* pieces. But even there it was limited by their functionality, and in that they were mostly commissions needing to be aesthetically effective in the given settings.

Finally, in this new, open-ended phase of creativity, I could unplug the work from having a pragmatic purpose of holding things, or being something on which someone could sit or sleep, and let its purpose be the sculptural expression of something more rarefied: perhaps a dance between Air and Water, or an overlapping of animal body structure and leaf-like skin that evokes a sense of intimacy.

Lumenhorse

I knew as an artist, and from the years of walking the gender path, that personal discovery melds seamlessly with universal discovery; or, to put it another way: that the deeply personal *is* universal. In getting to the essence underneath the circumstance of my life, the rhythms, patterns, and feelings that were revealed were simply, innately human.

I felt no need to address gender directly in my creative work because the underpinnings of my experience with it boiled down to things like balance, gesture, rhythm, call-and-response, integration, and so on— and these were the core elements in my art. My artwork didn't need to be *about* gender because they flowed from the same source, and were essentially the same thing:

**Gender is an art of my Being,
and transgender-ness is a font of discovery.**

Back in Madrid, I had wanted to break away from the grind of studio output and remodeling, and exercise more intellectual stimulation— especially in relation to my creative inclinations. In grad school, I found it in droves; it was a wonderful opening to what was going on in the art world, not just in terms of what was being created, but what was being discussed and debated. More important, though, was that it got me writing regularly about my own work—looking more deeply at the motivations and effectiveness of what I was making, and its evolution along the exploratory path.

I'd written poems and mini-essays over the years and promptly filed them away in folders with names like *Thoughts* or *Ideas*. Often, they were fragments jotted down during times of emotional stress or creative epiphany, and they served the purpose of integrating what was going on—after which they were pretty much forgotten. When it came time to present the *Treebone Garden* work to the world, I found it wonderfully satisfying to write about the work, and place those words alongside the images. And I do use the word *about* purposefully: The words stood outside the process of making and the objects that came forth from it, and peered in reflectively.

In school, however, the studio work and the objects that arose from it grounded the writing and called it to bring Air, Water, and Space to the process. Language was as much a tool as were hammers and cutters: It opened up the subtleties and unearthed the connections—integrating the experience and making it far richer than if I'd just been making objects and observing them more casually.

Finally, after years of focusing on earthier matters, my creative spirit was free to soar, and I was blessed with operating in a vacuum that challenged me to take the work to the next level and the next, and to articulate—with as much depth and precision as possible—what was occurring along the way.

□ □ □

Being the Practice

Early in the program, I wrote about the creative process which had evolved over the years, and which was continuing to ripen and unfurl. With concerns of livelihood aside, there was space to contemplate its role as the core of my spiritual practice:

> *Eastern philosophy has been one of the most important influences in my life: Buddhist thought has shown me the value of awareness, presence, and being; of bearing witness to the nature of what is; of stillness. Out of that spaciousness, I recognize that my creativity is not a compartment of my life in general—it is my life, with the blessing of the somewhat arranged circumstance of the studio. The Oneness spills, falls into this living: fragments into idea, material, making. I gather some of these shards, and call it my work.*
>
> *I have learned that I don't have to be "in the mood" to create: The work itself is satisfying, therapeutic. Often, I just go to the studio and stay busy there. By busy, I don't mean to imply that I'm constantly physically active.*

Rather, I'm focused on the work, whether in making or contemplation. When I am the process—when the materials, the creative energy, and I are no longer distinct—the physical outcome feels like a bonus.

Sometimes I enter the studio with very specific ideas—a strong sense of direction and purpose. At these times, I have to be careful: of pushing the process; of scumbling the interactivity of vision, material, and spirit with the wash of me. I'm cautious, because driving the process separates me from the joy of being an intermediary between the way of this place and something extra-ordinary—of being a facilitator between the dense circumstance of this reality and the vast pool of potential.

I try to stay out of the way of the flow of potential.

I keep engaging the creative process because I am most myself in the midst of it; I experience the best of me there. The studio is more than a place: It is a placeholder for a heightened state of Being. The physicality of the walls and work grounds that flight, holds the senses to this world.

Yet, I also experience the least of me there: The personality that lubricates my way in the world fades as I merge with matter and spirit, light and shadow. This Zen practice of transcending the physical through the physical feeds my spirit, and nourishes my life outside the sanctuary of making.

Because I want to avoid limiting what I'm creating to what I think it is, or might be, I let go of who I think I am, revealing more of my potential. When I see past my own limitations, distinction and separation fade, and matter becomes in my mind's eye energized—in a sense, "liquid." In this seeing, matter and Mind meld, and images shift fluidly with vision-inspired thought.

The essence of my role as an artist is to bear witness to the nature of What Is, knowing that behind the appearance of every thing is every other form it might take. If I am silent and still, the materials reveal themselves in their relationships with other elements, showing more of their potential.

I try to stay out of the way of the flow of potential.

□ □ □

Life as Art

I've come to see my life more clearly as transformative art—that underneath the mediums of the studio there's a deeper one more than worthy of the quality of creative attention I've brought to making objects. In many respects, I was operating from this approach already—diving headlong into the unknown of my unfolding internally, physically, and even geographically—but bringing this more fully into awareness as a practice has invited in more expansiveness, peace, fulfillment and joy. It did, in fact, lead me here to Bali, where my understanding of what it means to practice life as art continues to evolve.

As an artist, I know the importance of responding to the nature of the materials, rather than wishing they were different, or trying to force them to be what they aren't. In the practice of life as art, I'm seeing that the quality of what I create is directly related to my response to the material of my life—to simply What Is—within and without.

As with materials in the studio, it's the element of discovery that opens What Is beyond the obvious—the surface appearance—and ushers in glimpses of the unknown. And as with a studio practice, I must show up: Active, ongoing engagement with discovery is the essence of creative practice of whatever sort, and that calls for an attitude of expansiveness, along with gratitude for what is revealed.

Sitting in contemplation, overlooking the wildly-colored fishing boats dragged ashore in the seaside village of Candidasa, I'm reminded that an image I've often found useful for thinking about engaging the unknown in life is that of waves pounding against the shore. I ask myself which I would rather be doing: trying to stand in the water, but getting tumbled around as the waves crash into me, or riding on top of them on a surfboard. The waves are the same, yet they're transfigured in the light of the awareness that I'm not a victim of the unknown, but an active participant in its revelation.

I've observed that when we focus on knowing ourselves more fully, the familiarity provides a sense of fluidity by which we can better ride the inevitable unknown—whether it appears on its own, or we seek it out. I'm not suggesting that this magically glides us past the difficulties, but rather, that it avails us of greater awareness and thereby a broader range of choices: We can more often anticipate, and even choose, the waves we ride, and we have more options in how we ride them—anticipated or not. This means that what might otherwise have swamped us has far greater potential for opening us to richer self-understanding, and being a transformative experience.

Gender is an art of my Being, and transgender-ness is a font of discovery.

One could hardly have a more charged impetus for self-discovery than a calling to radically change one's apparent gender—which one might well be tempted to place under the heading of *Uninvited Unknowns*. Yet, we can also perceive the calling to that, or any, realignment as a tremendously creative, spiritually transformative opportunity.

I feel thoroughly blessed that, as an artist, I've seen this gender path in terms of formlessness meeting form—essence pouring through physicality—and this encompassing perspective has given it a powerful sacredness. I see my body as an evolving reflection of who I am—rather than it defining my Beingness—and this inner sense of identity that transcends the physical has lent a great deal of latitude in being myself in the world... in Being Self.

Because the consciousness of the world at large is fixated on physicality, one is generally seen as *being* one's body, rather than as a *Being in* one's body. I've focused on my essence—which naturally expresses itself as female energy aligned with an unabashed male presence—and the resultant comfort with myself has created space for most people to just enjoy who I am, despite their sometimes not knowing precisely what that is gender-wise. I've shown up as an unknown who knows itself, and that's allowed me to surf the waves of unknown generated by my betweenness; I bring with me the spaciousness that makes this possible.

Whenever I bask in the presence of someone who is continually opening to their inner calling—practicing the art of who they are—I'm reminded that the finest gift we can bring to those around us is our own awakening to our true Selves. This is the finest gift... and the finest art.

I see no difference between this kind of personal unfolding, and the sacred role of the artist—which is to stand at the threshold and introduce the unknown to form, and form to the unknown.

These artful meetings are homecomings of the most elemental, essential kind: The unknown is not just out there, nor simply within; it *is* us, and from behind the masks that lend us definition in this physical world, we peer out at essence in form, inspired and transfixed.

⬜ ⬜ ⬜

Light into Matter

Given that any journey of discovery begins with familiar surroundings and ventures out from there, I started the program with what I knew, and only a vague sense of where I wanted the work to go. As the passion for making functional objects was waning in New Mexico, I'd made a couple of large sculptures in the aesthetic of the *Treebone Garden* furniture—incorporating the curves and serpentine lines, and finished with layers of translucent, pigmented oils.

When I landed in Massachusetts, they were fresh in my mind, but I knew I wanted to break away from starting with lumber—what I thought of as *sliced tree bones*. The landlady of the old Victorian house-turned-apartment building in which I lived had some woods behind her home, and she welcomed me to take whatever branches I wanted, especially since I was looking for dead ones. To my delight, there were mature elm trees back there with gorgeous, well-seasoned limbs seemingly waiting for a higher purpose.

Over the first semester, I worked those branches into abstract figures with carved, bone-like "joints" wherever they shifted direction. Yet, after a second piece in that mode, I felt limited by the given forms of the branches, and turned to copper for more flexibility and gestural expression. The copper wire quickly turned into graceful, skeletal armatures, which called for some sort of overlaid "skin" to create undulating surfaces.

When we shared our work in one of the classes that brought together grad students working in all media, a woman from the Fibers department shared her love of the process of hand-making paper. My heart was pounding as she passed around some gorgeously textured sheets: I'd found my new—or at least *a* new—medium, and an enthusiastic teacher and soon-to-be colleague in the intricacies of working with various kinds of pulp.

The gestural and rhythmical qualities I'd explored in the furniture and more recent sculptural work in New Mexico were still very much part of the new direction. Moving away from both functionality and the density of wood opened the work to much more expression of rhythm and sequence. With the copper, I could make hollow, rib-like "skeletons," and let high-shrinkage pulp dry over them, creating gaunt, pronounced sequences of curved surfaces that echoed the overall gesture. The work had opened up to real free-form possibilities.

I'd always felt drawn to the interior spaces of the furniture, and had finished the insides of my pieces with the same care as the outer surfaces. Too, I'd often incorporated vertical, altar-like elements into the tops of the furniture to create a sense of space being "held," of belonging with essence—of intimacy. I'd often thought of this area as being rather like a field embraced by a larger landscape.

With these new lean, curvaceous cavities, interior and exterior spaces could intermingle, revealing ambiguous zones that were neither and both. It's hardly surprising I was attracted to these, or that spaces that generated a sense of holding and intimacy would draw my passionate interest.

As I began contemplating the roles of light and shadow with this new work, it was natural to consider bringing light *into* them as well. With the furniture, the relationship with light was based on its reflection from the surfaces, thereby making their qualities apparent: color, luster, form, texture, and so on. Shadow—areas of diminished light—described the form and depth of recesses and areas underneath. For the new sculptures, light from outside had a similar effect, except that where the surface was translucent, it allowed light to pass through to the inside, softening the quality of shadow.

With light from inside the form, however, the translucence opened up the surface visually, allowing the fibers and backlit framework to be revealed. The piece "shaped" the light outwardly, as well, spilling it into the surrounding area, creating myriad relationships with other surfaces.

In the flow of this exploration, I didn't need to know *why* it was terrain abounding with delicious possibility; it was quite enough that I was working in form with elements that seemed essential to my Being—that coalesced in objects that were new to this world, yet to me, were gorgeously familiar. And by a stroke of pure pragmatism, new materials were about to enter the studio, which furthered this vein of investigation considerably.

The following summer, I proposed making several sets of low-voltage lighting systems for Lorraine's house in Santa Cruz, and she loved the idea. She knew by then she could trust me to just show up with something that would work beautifully, so I didn't send drawings or give any details of what I was considering. Not providing visual ideas up front left the creative potential wide open, and that in itself was tremendously inspiring. I did give some sense, though, of what I envisioned: they would help connect the gardens, which were so visible through the windows, to the interior of her house, and they'd be vine-like with hanging insect- or sea creature-like fixtures.

As a starting point, I had in mind the organic forms and cavities the new work had already revealed. The difficulty in moving from this concept to the actual objects, however, was that the forms I was working with were made of paper, and the bulbs would be quite hot. The challenge would be to translate the fluidity of the paper "skins" to metal. Leafing through an industrial supply catalog, I found some intriguing materials: wire-cloth and very thin sheet metal—both in copper and brass.

When the materials arrived, I had to start from scratch and figure out how to manipulate these to create convex and concave forms. I kept pushing the envelope, trying various tools and approaches, until I had a way of working with them that lent a feeling of fluidity and organic form.

I landed in California with a ready-to-install kit: ten each of four fixture designs; specially twisted copper wire to create the vines and conduct electricity; and hand-made copper mounts to hold the units to the ceilings. Since the arrangement of the copper "vines" was free-form, I custom-made the tendrils that supported them out in the garage with a hammer and torch. It was such a joy to bring this play of matter and light (which I called *Anomalons*) to a space I'd colored years before, and to re-approach it now as the sculptor that I knew—even then—was waiting in the wings.

Although I was busy working with earthy materials, and the attention in the program was very much on the resultant objects, my primary focus was on what I was beginning to call the *Threshold*—the less tangible creative landscape where form and formlessness intersect. What drew my attention was the meeting and melding of the inner and outer, and the encompassing Beingness that remained unchanged.

In the spring of the second year, we were to give a presentation of the sources from which our work arose. Wanting to acknowledge the formless aspect as well, I shared this piece of writing that reminds me of the skeletal forms with which I was working:

Maker

Were you to ask,
I would reply:
I am a maker.
But really,
I am just breathing
and all that forming
is circumstance.
I am just breathing
and the rest is motion.
I am breathing
in motion and circumstance.
I am the ride
for these draft horse hands.
I am working
in rhythm with creation.
I, maker,
shape-shifter.

□ □ □

Lumenhorse

Early in the second year of the program, the professor who headed the department had mentioned that he saw me as someone who could do the program effectively in two years, and asked if I wanted to do it that way or take the full three years. After a good deal of thought, I decided that after all those years of studio work in which artistic discovery had been limited by the demands of livelihood, and by the web of myriad other choices, it was time to stretch out and explore.

I'd done plenty of marathon runs of work, and didn't want to rush through this valuable phase. It would have meant going right into writing the thesis, and there was so much more I wanted to discover before narrowing the creative exploration and delving into intense analysis.

□ □ □

Matter into Light

The work was developing at a galloping pace: The wire-cloth and hammered copper materials used for the *Anomalons* lights bled right into the studio work in general, and I found myself turning to them even when heat wasn't as much a concern. They were ideal for further exploration of those skeletal cavities I'd worked with in copper and paper. Having a light source within allowed for numerous layers of wire cloth—and with this, there was opportunity for exploring more subtle aspects of intimacy.

I discovered that, by arranging layers of translucent materials to partially block the view of the inside, a sense of mystery was maintained. And allowing only degrees of visual access into this alluring space created a lovely tension that set up the conditions for evoking intimacy.

Having an obscured light source within provided a focal point that pulled one's attention through the layers, and I loved how the various areas inside those layered cavities wafted between qualities of interior and exterior amid the play of light and shadow. And all of this was occurring amid the larger play of gesture and rhythm, and the interplay of biomorphic forms. At the time I wrote:

With the introduction of illumination within the more recent work, the inner space has developed a force of its own. It is no longer an area held apart, but a portal for the emergence of stillness—an activated space that leads out beyond itself. The simple modulation of interior and exterior in Alight has developed into varied layers through which the illumination finds expression. Each translucent layer and reflective surface develops the qualities of the light as it moves through the piece and outward, into space, and across nearby surfaces.

I called this work *Lumenhorse* because it combined light, matter, and a sense of energetic movement. *Lumenhorse* is an alteration of *windhorse*, a term used collectively for a variety of Tibetan devices—such as prayer wheels and flags—inscribed with prayers or incantations. Through intention and movement, these words and thoughts are released beyond the physical world. I saw my work doing essentially the same thing, but with light instead of wind.

□ □ □

Later in the second year, I mentioned to the professor that I had quite a number of pieces of my earlier furniture sitting in a storage unit in Santa Fe. He suggested a gallery in Malibu, California, which would likely be interested in selling them if I had any interest in letting them go. I did, indeed, and a short time later, the response I got to the packet of pictures I'd sent off to the gallery was most enthusiastic.

We agreed to meet in Santa Fe, look over the inventory, and decide what pieces to send out to the West Coast. When I opened the unit, Bob's face lit right up: There were nearly thirty cabinets and tables, and numerous smaller items like mirrors—considerably more than I'd remembered tucking away in my energetic run-up to leaving for school. We hit it off immediately, and had a great time picking out twelve or thirteen pieces for the first shipment—the start of a very warm connection that went on for years.

Lumenhorse

Bringing light into the new work had certainly activated it and added tremendous depth, but it also raised questions about its function. I'd moved away from the furniture making to explore free-form sculpture, but as it turned into lighting, the functionality was creeping back in:

> *A major focus in the last few months has been the introduction of light sources within the work. While sculptural considerations predominate, this addition has called for an assessment of my motivations with respect to the function of each piece. Am I creating sculpture that incorporates some light play as an expressive element, or is this sculpture that is meant to interact with architecture by acting as a light source, or both? What is its balance of sculpture and functionality?*
>
> *Is this a sculpture that happens to emit light, a sculpture that also performs a lighting function, or a lighting fixture that has sculptural qualities? Clarity on these issues is particularly critical at those choice points that affect the qualities of the light produced. In the give-and-take of aesthetics and light production, there are huge creative differences between sculptures that incorporate light, expressive lighting pieces that add visual interest to an environment, and producing light for specific, task-oriented activities.*

With the deeply familiar tension of form and function resonating through the work, I created a leaf-inspired lamp base in clay, made a plaster mould of it, and had it cast in bronze. With a dozen of these available, I embarked on a series of lamps that erupted stem-like out of the base and "blossomed" into a light-emitting top made of hand-made paper or hammered copper, and called them *Floriform Variations*. I wrapped the undulating, hollow copper stems in raffia—grassy fiber—

to give a fleshy quality, and wrapped this in various colors of waxed linen thread to play with sequence amid the rhythm of the undulation. Given the progression of the work, I was feeling inclined at the time to set up a sculptural lighting studio after graduation.

From an open exploration of fluid, skeletal forms, I'd made my way unintentionally back to an intense affair with Earth. While the *Lumenhorse* work in general wasn't by any means as heavy as the bronze-based *Floriform Variations* lamps, they did epitomize an aspect that had me concerned: Between the density of the metals and the compression of the waxed linen binding, this evolutionary direction was feeling too earth-bound.

I'd left the wood behind in part because it felt that way as well, and yet I was apparently not quite done with density as an essential element of the work. Not only were those bases more dense than wood, but even the form that arose out of it was bound tightly all the way to the tips that held the shade. I can see now that as more expansive elements flowed into the work, I needed to engage Earth more intensely than ever in the studio. I didn't know it at the time, but the pendulum was set to find its counterpoint.

DuneWorks

In the midst of hammering copper and intense binding, I'd applied for a much sought after two-week artist residency on Cape Cod, which housed participants in historic painters' shacks set out in the dunes. A couple of months later, a letter arrived announcing that I'd been awarded a stay that included the 4th of July, and I couldn't think of a better way to celebrate freedom.

Lumenhorse

Much like the point back in Madrid when I was invited to craft a set of pieces for the gallery—and took advantage of that to re-approach the work—this would be an extraordinary chance to interact with an intense landscape, create impermanent pieces, and let that ripple through its evolution.

The impermanence was especially welcome, as I'd focused for so long on objects which would last for as long as possible with everyday use, then sculptural works which would hopefully be long-lived, too. The dune projects would last for perhaps a few days—or at least long enough to record them with film and video—then simply disappear. There was enormous license in this, and fine opportunity to experience new facets of presence in the making.

In setting out on this creative journey, I was acutely aware that, while the art was in the explorative process of making and Being with the work, in the long-term, the arti*facts* of the process wouldn't be the objects as usual, but recordings of them. Photography would be more than documentation out in the dunes: It had resurfaced as a medium unto itself—this time accompanied by video.

It's quite a challenge to pack for an extended creative outing when you don't know for certain what you'll be making—rather like packing for a vacation in which you don't know what climate you'll be in. In a way, there being no electricity at the shack simplified things in that respect: Whatever I made would be done by hand. There would be no standing structure out there—besides the shack—so I added some coils of copper wire of various thicknesses to the pile, along with some wire-working hand tools.

For a surface material, I found a couple of long, wide pieces of off-white gauze cloth, and added some waxed-linen thread of the same color for tying. Some watercolors and paper seemed appropriate, but no radio—too distracting. The recording gear was crucial, and sizeable: 35mm, medium-format, and video.

In late morning, I met the driver who would take me out to the shack. We transferred my stuff to his pickup truck, and left mine parked by the road. As we entered the dunes, he got out to unlock the gate and let some air out of the tires. Then we floated out on those soft wheels as if in a boat, and followed the nearest approximation of a road winding through the wind-swept hills of sand. A short while later, we pulled up to a weather-beaten shack perched up on a massive slope overlooking one of the most serious stretches of ocean I'd ever felt.

We hopped out and unloaded the gear before he showed me around. There was a fresh water well with a hand-pump down below, a nicely functioning outhouse, a propane refrigerator, and kerosene lamps in lieu of electric light.

He was due back in town, so he said over his shoulder on the way back to the truck that he'd be back in a week to check on me, and the propane supply. And then I was alone in h-e-a-v-e-n. If there had been a set of controls hanging down from the stratosphere—allowing one to adjust the blueness of sky, or intensity of sun, or air temperature, or amount of breeze—I'd have left them all just as they were.

At first I just looked around the place and took in the vast landscape washed in spectral light, grinning like a six-year-old with the blessing of having landed in such a gorgeous realm. I had a good laugh when I thought back to my place in Madrid, and how its bare-bones simplicity hadn't been so different—except, of course, that it was nearly winter when I'd arrived, even the bare bones weren't in place, and the only ocean around was made of air.

Living close to my needs suited me, and I'd have taken pumping my own water and using the outhouse over "luxury accommodation" in a heartbeat. I swear the water tastes sweeter when you've hauled it up the slope yourself. Not that I'd necessarily want to be doing that long-term, but for these two weeks, it was a pleasure. And with an explicit agenda of immersing myself in this place, a good rub with it all was essential.

Lumenhorse

Fortunately, I'd brought everything in big plastic bins with covers, because—as if to compensate for the lack of electricity and running water—there were plenty of mice. It seems the woman who'd stayed here before me hadn't the heart to kick them out, but had the heart to pass them on in growing numbers. So my first project was to pull everything away from the rough-hewn planks that constituted walls, and shoo those cute little critters out. They in turn spent the next two weeks trying to scratch their way back in at night.

Having settled in, I stood in the doorway looking out over the sweep of sea grass that stretched out toward the water and cupped slightly before dropping off twenty-five feet to the narrow beach below. From the shack, you couldn't see the beach, so it looked as if the water came right up to the grass—which may not have seemed especially odd, except that the ocean was massively dark. The Continental Shelf drops off precipitously into the Atlantic right there, and this fierce body of water seemed to be held back by those slender grasses.

The wind-swept dunes—some, hundreds of feet high—were evidence aplenty that the sky was not always so gentle. Yet land had its way with both: For the sea it was a solid buttress; and for the sky like butter, ready to be whipped into whimsical forms.

I realized that I'd stepped into a drama that had been unfolding for eons, and that this intensity of land, sea, and sky wasn't just the backdrop; these were to be the major drivers of the work. I knew then that I'd make three pieces—one to honor the essence of each pairing: Earth and Sky, Water and Earth, Sky and Water.

Another focus for these two weeks was to get the basis of my thesis together, so I'd come prepared for some writing. What I didn't expect, however, was that it would become so integral to the creative process. The joyous wafting between language and physicality that suffused those two weeks stands out as one of the most sublime creative experiences of my life, and among the happiest of times, as well.

I'd be working on a copper armature, and suddenly open to an inspiration or insight that was too rarefied to express in form, and the writing would take over. Then, when it had run its course and what called for expression could only be found in form, I'd turn back to the materials, feeling freshly reconnected. At school, I'd been writing *from* the work; here, the writing was an integral part *of* it.

An intense sense of *meeting* surfaced very quickly. I, of course, was meeting this place, but there was a much deeper gathering—as I've mentioned—of land, sea, and sky. The ongoing explorations with paper and light in the studio had suggested that materials which were translucent and/or fragmented could interact with light in a way that made it seem almost physical: They could be a meeting place between matter and light. The gauze cloth—supported and shaped by the copper wire—seemed, then, an ideal conduit for bringing the essence of those pairings of forces to form.

But to approach this ongoing dynamic and invite its essence into my process, I needed to do more than just show up with some materials. A proper introduction was in order, and it was the writing that opened it out beyond the physical world, and introduced it as ritual:

The Meeting

Down to the well-pump river
to rinse with the wet of here
this whispery cloth of its old ways.

Then to hold it to wind
and let these ivory fibers and the breath
of these whiskered grasses know one another.

Down to the salt waters
with coils of copper raw and bare
to baptize in tidal cadence this buttery ore
to the thundered rhythm of this land.
Then to lay it to ground
to let these sinewy strands
and the unremitting motion
of these liquid sands know one another.

Gather then this gossamer flesh,
this pliant bone now wed to this place

and make of here.

For many years, I'd been making objects that often required weeks of time and effort, and when they were done, they stood as little universes unto themselves. Here, I could make something in a few hours, or perhaps a day or so, and bring it directly into collaboration with the forces of nature. And I could move it about if I wanted, changing the dynamics with the landscape.

Starting with Earth and Sky—perhaps because it's the meeting I found most immediately resonant—I began sketching, and soon found that sea anemone-like form taking shape. It seemed like a sort of portal where Earth extended into Sky, or Sky might channel down into Earth. Several hours later, I had a freestanding, spiraling armature over seven feet tall ready to be wrapped in gauze the next morning.

I woke and set about my morning routine—or at least a version thereof converted to more primitive conditions—all the while eyeing the skeletal form waiting for its skin. Echoing the spiraling copper, I wound the gauze from top to bottom. With this completed, I moved it around to various sites as my prior life as a photographer came to the fore.

I named it *Terra Flitten*, and for several days rejoiced at seeing this portal between Earth and Sky here and there—especially from the shack. Waking up to it perched down below in the sea grass in the early morning light, or seeing up on a dune as I went to the pump for water, placed a kind of marker of my spirit firmly and deliciously where it belongs: between realms in a landscape of form, with access to both.

There was enough material for the second piece, so *Terra Flitten* both *was* some company and *had* some company for a few days more. For this next piece, I focused on the meeting of Earth and Water. I'd been drawn to the wave-like forms of the wind-blown dunes, and it seemed natural to create a piece that melded dune and wave.

This was the most complex armature, and it insisted on settling in one place: as an extension of a small, rising bit of ground. The photographer in me loved the way light passed through it from behind in the morning light, showing its skeletal frame, then glanced off its surface past noon, making it seem much more solid. *Dune Waven* sat there on its sandy throne, celebrating between-ness for the rest of the stay.

The final piece, a meeting of Water and Sky, took advantage of the prevailing north-to-south wind. As with my own metamorphosis, the materials in *Terra Flitten* were transformed into *Agua Wingen*—the simplest of the three, structurally speaking, but also the most experientially profound. It funneled the wind under and across fourteen feet of gauze cloth, billowing it in constantly changing ripples and waves. *Agua Wingen* was the only one of the three pieces which didn't include Earth, and it was a blessing that in the intuitive flow of making, it was the last.

As it neared completion, it seemed as if the wind was teaching me how to "fly" it. With the final tweaking, it suddenly took on a life of its own—it became a *windhorse*. I immediately felt a deep sense of completion: I knew that even if I never made anything again, I could leave this world feeling resolved in making.

In this moment, I was unplugged from my *need* to work with Earth—with form—as a grounding force. It would always be there if I chose to work with it, but this culminated the necessity of creative relationship with it. And, as if to bring the point home in imagery I couldn't ignore, the form of a bird showed up in the shadows of the folds—its wings flapping as my soul was released.

The explorative journey in the studio had evolved from curving line through space and light, in rhythm and sequence, through shadow and intimacy, to the density of bronze and intensive binding with gestural release. It led, finally, to this opening, and *Agua Wingen*—on the heels of *Terra Flitten* and *Dune Waven*—became a portal that took me directly to the ultimate space between: the heart. I stood beside it weeping, saying out loud over and over again: *I'm in love... I'm in love... I'm in love...*

Reflecting on it weeks later, I wrote:

> *I made a sculpture of copper, gauze, and wind*
> *in celebration of Water and Sky at the dunes.*
> *Called it Agua Wingen.*
> *I say I made this, but it made itself with my help,*
> *and taught me to fly it,*
> *took me on matter turned liquid to Sky.*
> *Like the swallows—*
> *no, with the swallows—sailing on air.*

▢ ▢ ▢

Bali Stillness

As natural as it is to attribute the stillness I'm feeling these days to this exotic surround, I know I'm not experiencing it because of this place, or even the mellow lifestyle here. Rather, the stillness rests in me, and this place—and its way—is home because it reflects so beautifully my inner landscape. As jagged peeks are worn with wind and water into smoother forms, so too, time has curbed my more physically ambitious impulses. Yet the passion that fueled those challenging—sometimes years-long—projects hasn't diminished; thankfully, it has with age changed form and blossomed anew.

The get-up-and-go drive I once had fell off the wagon some miles back, and I've no inclination to go back and find it. In my twenties, I learned in studying Zen about the difference between Being and Doing—between consciously living one's essence and immersion in one's actions—and too, that effortlessness emerges naturally from a balanced melding of the two. I brought as much presence—sense of Being—as I could to the projects at hand, but nonetheless often found myself suffering from the overload of Doing.

I'm thinking of the furniture making, too, but the house rebuilding epitomizes the abrasiveness of a great deal of the work. For so long, I wanted to decouple my sensitivity from the sensory assault of the building process, but the tools and the mess were also the means by which I engaged creative livelihood, and thereby, to exercise more sensitivity on a daily basis. As with so much of life and relationship in this odd world, it was an imperfect arrangement, to be sure; but at least with the making of furniture, that which served well was the balm for its shortcomings. I girded myself by leaning on my male side like a brother, and held space as best I could for the female core.

With the gift of well-earned age, I'm learning, finally, to align myself with what reflects my inner landscape, rather than feeling compelled to construct—especially with my own hands—an outer landscape that's relatively suited to it. Three times I rallied my male side through marathon runs to complete homes which would be a fine nest for me to soften nicely into—only to live in them briefly while awaiting the next phase of life.

For the duration of those long, stressful periods of rebuilding, I was living in a way which was the exact opposite of what I was creating that place for, and it's taken until now to realize that intense will directed toward physical effort provides at best an agonizingly circuitous route there—that I can't experience how I want to Be in this world of form by focusing on Doing. Peering into the periscope of retrospect, I spot the obvious hiding in plain sight.

There is a call in the afterlight for compassion for who I was, and where I was on the arc of this evolution. We simply have more energy when we're younger, and are more inclined to seek out ways to apply it in the world. We're driven to make a mark—to accomplish, to make a difference somehow—and the grander and nobler the better.

In the midst of radical change, I chose to climb mountains of work—some more, some less creative—for the rootedness of a place that was home, and the opportunity to merge with spirit and create beauty in the studio within it.

I see now in the wash of space and contemplation, how the gist of my way in the world has shifted from unabashed enthusiasm to simple acceptance and passionate joy. And my priorities have evolved along with it: I'm much more open to the revelation of that which serves *my* higher good, and thereby *the* higher good; and to being a vehicle by which others tap more deeply into the creativity of their own Being.

Releasing instead of building; spaciousness instead of ambition; these ways seem a finer fit for me in middle age. And where better to come home, finally, to Self than here in Bali, where Spirit is palpable—where it's seduced to Earth by a constant stream of incense- and flower-laden offerings.

What Flies Must Land

From the high of the residency at the dunes, re-entry into what constituted normal life was jolting, to say the least. I'd made a major mistake when balancing my checkbook before I left home, so I returned to find that instead of having a small cushion of cash to come back to, I had less than none. Resolving the need to work creatively with Earth back there in the dunes certainly hadn't resolved the need to continue working with it in terms of livelihood.

During the past school year, I'd taken on a few small furniture and lighting commissions through a designer in Providence, Rhode Island, and that had been a big help financially. But suddenly, I was scrambling to raise some cash, and turned once again to those well-worn building skills. In a few short days, I went from the freedom of melding with the Elements while creating half-naked in the dunes, to building a very basic wooden deck. Still, it was a blessing to have those skills when I needed them.

Having left Madrid to pursue creative exploration and intellectual stimulation, after *DuneWorks*, I could have happily ended the process and considered it an exquisite success. Yet I still had a year in the program in which to explore and put together my thesis, and the creative journey had taken me right to edge of the physicality on which the program was based.

The passion for creating was still brimming, but my motivations and interests had leapt forward over the summer. I'd have some explaining to do to my graduate committee, which was charged with overseeing and guiding my work to its potential, and with which I'd already established a formal line of creative inquiry.

Lumenhorse

It wasn't as though I'd taken off on some random tangent: The line of inquiry I was pursuing had brought me directly to the *DuneWorks* breakthrough, and I simply had to be honest about where my heart, mind, and spirit were in the ongoing unfolding. That fall, I did a good deal of contemplation and writing to support the new work.

Although the early Lumenhorse work was done primarily in the second year, my thinking has changed such in the meantime that it seems eons ago. While there is considerable continuity in the underlying passions and concerns from the earlier to later phases leading to the present, my experience of them has evolved, changing my relationship with them dramatically...

For years I made objects that, although inanimate, would not "sit still." They gestured, rippled, and writhed out of their stillness, borrowing motion from the enticed viewer's perception. Looking over these pieces, I have found myself pondering their destination: To where and what do they gesture, and why? I have been asking this because the work will no longer be held to that phase of its journey. It's as if—having designed and re-designed a launching pad—I've finally found myself flung deep into space, beyond this limited relationship with object.

In leaving the studio practice in New Mexico, and heading off to see where creative spirit would take me, I had no idea it would lead me back to imagery. I had turned to my first full-fledged medium, photography, to record the work out at the dunes, but as I've noted, it was more than just recording. I saw it as a sort of co-medium in that the image of what was created was an art object—an arti*fact*—in itself. And since the original pieces were gone, it was *the* artifact from that point forward.

Along with the photography, I'd also used a video camera to record the pieces and some of the process. I was thoroughly intrigued with its ability to capture the essence of what photography had to offer, and to lend it fluidity of form—the element of Water—and with that, Time. With Time came Rhythm, which had been an important part of the work since the *Treebone Garden*, and now I realized the medium I was most passionate about was the rhythm of life—the pulse of Being in form amid the vast field of consciousness.

> *Having spent these years focusing on the release of matter into space, and more recently of matter into light, I find my attention evolving now toward the occurrence of light meeting matter. I am thinking not just of the phenomenon of light striking objects and both becoming apparent, but of light as a physical property of the sacred. I am asking: How does the sacred ripple into here? With this new work, my attention is on the occurrence of light meeting life.*

As the exploration into video unfolded, it also revealed some foreshadowing:

> *I am not so interested in the surface appearance of things, i.e. the visual image alone... Video, like poetry, uses imagery to engage the mind's eye, which is informed not just by the visual, but by all the senses—as well as our storehouses of memory, emotion, perception, and intuition. As with poetry, the mind's eye is not ruled by linear time, but rearranges sequences and emphasizes some to serve the deeper streams of thought and meaning. I am dissolving the surface phenomena—letting some of those other layers "percolate" into the visual and aural fields of perception.*

Lumenhorse

In the process of completing the program and thesis, it certainly didn't help that in the final year, the school made a major move to a new site. The disruption was challenging for everyone, but the most difficult aspect for me was that the Wood and Furniture department was put in the basement of the intensely renovated former department store, and had not a speck of natural light. From the sprawling, funky studio spaces we'd had, we were transplanted to what amounted to glorified cubicles. I'd make a lousy troll, and being cut off from Sky in my creative space was simply heartbreaking.

Under the circumstances, it occurred to me more than once that finishing the program in two years might have been the better choice. On the other hand, if I'd done that, I'd likely not have done the residency that led to the breakthrough with *Duneworks*. The choice had been made, though, and it was time to focus on the creative journey of the moment.

When those planes hit the Twin Towers on September 11th, I was headed to Boston to show my work to a gallery. The sky was strangely clear of air traffic, and people were rolling down their windows, telling others to turn on their radios. I didn't know what else to do, so I just kept going to the appointment.

When I arrived, it was a little surreal: The woman and I just looked at each other and shrugged. She said, *So, I guess we just do this...* and I said, *Yeah, but it certainly puts it in an odd light.* So we talked about art in the midst of the towers collapsing—though we didn't know it at the time—and as one might imagine, anything to do with art seemed pretty tenuous right then. But at that moment, and for a good while after, much of normal life seemed that way.

Back at school, one professor offered another view, though, when he said, *What we do is exactly the opposite of what those terrorists are all about...* We refocused on what we did: creating with nuance and grace, in the face of spectacular insensitivity.

To compensate for the lack of natural light at school, I set up a small studio in my sunny apartment, and did what I could there, including teaching myself the ins and outs of video editing. I blocked out the space at school with black plastic, and used it as a lab for experimenting with the subtleties of light—in the form of LEDs (Light Emitting Diodes)—and translucent paper. It was in this setting that I came up with my main thesis project: a video projection of imagery inspired by the seven chakras—bodily centers of energy—through a set of seven large, oval sheets of hand-made paper.

In sharing the *Duneworks* experience, I wrote: *The ongoing explorations with paper and light in the studio had suggested that materials that were translucent and/or fragmented could interact with light in a way that made it seem almost physical—they could be a meeting place between matter and light.* With *Seven Graces*, I now used this meeting place to hold evolving images of life melded with landscape, focusing for a couple of minutes on each chakra. Starting with the red base chakra and moving up through orange and yellow to the green heart, and through blue and indigo to the purple-white crown, it was light meeting life—held minimally in layers of fragmented form.

At the time, I thought of the world as my studio, and spent a fair amount of time going about gathering the imagery for *Seven Graces*. It was a wonderful reflection of two earlier times I cherished: wandering in nature as a child, and roaming the Bay Area as a budding photographer. Writing to a dear friend in New Mexico, I shared my elation:

> *After fifteen years of concentrating on form, I've come full circle back to image. And now it moves. I feel free to create with a grace that I've never had access to until now. I am six years old with my amazing kaleidoscope.*

Lumenhorse

Not surprisingly, it took quite some effort to bring the committee around to trusting that I'd come up with the quality of work in video—in the relatively short time available—that they'd come to expect with the furniture and more object-oriented sculpture. But since *Seven Graces* did indeed evolve directly out of the earlier work, and drew from the very elements that were central to it—intimacy, gesture, sequence, rhythm, layering, and light—in the end they came around to seeing it as part of the *Lumenhorse* work. Though I was based in the Wood and Furniture Design department, my thesis show had not a bit of either in it.

Endgame

In reading about the life and work of Robert Irwin, an artist working in Minimalism in the 1960s and '70s, I found his relationship to his studio process most poignant. He'd spent enormous amounts of time alone there, peeling back the fundamentals of painting in a classic Minimalist drive toward the essence of his medium. Years later, he described in his autobiography, *Seeing is Forgetting the Name of the Thing One Sees,* what happened:

> *...I had dismantled the whole thing: image, line, frame, focus, transcendability. I'd dismantled the art endeavor, but in the process, I'd dismantled myself... I arrived at this point with a real dilemma...all my questions now seemed external to my practice.*

The parallels with Irwin were almost eerie, though my situation was somewhat different. I'd taken the creative process past object making, and dismantled a major portion of the relationship I'd had with creating art in the studio. My practice had shifted, but I wasn't ready to take on the next medium. And I don't mean that it had become video—that was simply a vehicle to the next form of creative expression, which remained for the time being in the background.

When I graduated in 2002, it was not yet a year since the 9/11 catastrophe, and the economy was still weak. With good connections through designers and projects I'd done alongside the *Lumenhorse* work, it made sense to stay in the area and set up a studio to take on commissions, and to use as a base for remodeling work.

The intensive writing of the thesis had put the creative process under a harsh spotlight, and I was left feeling that what was for me a deeply spiritual relationship had been over-analyzed. I'd run myself right off a cliff into mid-air, so to speak, and needed time to absorb the trajectory. In the conditions of the moment, settling into making some money the best way I knew how was a relief.

In the meantime, though, I still owned the place in Madrid, and while I'd been blessed with having the same lovely couple renting it for the three years I'd been gone, they were leaving soon to buy a house elsewhere. It was inevitably time to go there, prepare it for sale, and dismantle the massive storage unit as well. There was one creative project to engage, however, before heading out.

Along with a group of four other sculptors, I'd been invited to create landscape sculpture at a retreat center in western Massachusetts. A three-day workshop had been set up, in which people would practice making with us for several days.

My piece incorporated perhaps 250-300 pieces of copper wire of various thicknesses—some quite thick—that needed to be hammered flat on one end. Each piece required perhaps twenty to thirty strokes, so there was clearly a lot of hammering to be done. Most of the people who signed up for the workshop were women, none of whom were used to manual labor. It was far more than I could do alone, so I found myself teaching them one by one how to hammer for long periods without hurting themselves.

Lumenhorse

I set up a fairly flat granite stone to use as an anvil, positioning it a little below elbow level. The hammer was a steel-working version—substantially heavier than a carpenter's. I showed them how they didn't need to put any effort into swinging it downward—the combination of its weight and gravity would provide plenty of impact. All they had to do was guide it to the wire. They also only needed to apply a very small amount of effort to raise the hammer, since, without any downward thrust, it bounced nicely off the wire if they just allowed it to happen.

Lastly, I told them to pay close attention to how much grip they were applying to the handle and to keep it as light as they could while maintaining control of the tool. They were stunned at how little effort was needed, and not a single one of had an aching arm the next day despite hammering for at least a couple of hours each.

I'd often thought of this approach to working with tools and materials as *moving like the samurai*, because it conjured a fine sense of presence in motion, with an expenditure of energy in direct relation to what was required to perform the action. A question I often asked myself in and out of the studio in those days was: *How much is enough?*... enough, without being too much. It brought to the work itself a sense of being performance art... In this case, labor as an art of presence in motion.

A sixty-something year old woman who'd recently survived an ordeal with cancer told me with tear-filled eyes that this practice was the first time in many years that she'd felt confidence in her body. She was my most dedicated assistant, turning out well more flat-ended wire than everyone else combined. It was, she said with a grin of a six-year old, *Easy as pie*.

When it was time to part, she said, *I'm going to go home and think about this*. The welling in her eyes suggested she'd been weighing for some time her release from a lifetime of pushing for things not so important after all; it seemed that in this experience, she'd felt the spaciousness in her bones.

A lovely hug later, I gathered my gear, hopped in the truck, and made my way down and across the rolling Appalachians, into the vast stretch of dry beyond to Santa Fe.

Having settled into my friend Brooke's house, I set out for Madrid to reacquaint myself with the land and house that had been companions for those seven years perched in the sky. As I pulled up into the driveway, there was a strong sense of meeting up with an old lover: We'd aged apart, but the memory of deep embrace still resonated.

As the couple and their baby were still there, I didn't get to just be alone with the place. But clearly, I'd moved on, and there was no hesitation in getting to the few things needed for readying it for sale. In the brief round of work on this place with which I'd been so seamlessly familiar, I felt the evolution of my way as a maker in the wash of the three explorative years away, and it seemed that a lifetime's creative work had been compressed into that narrow time.

By far, the biggest project at hand was the dismantling of the massive storage unit. It had come to a point at which, for most of what it contained, the value of its absence surpassed the value of its presence in my life. I invited friends who were building homes to come by and take away the collection of architectural details, the now very well-seasoned wood, landscaping tools, and so on.

Rather than selling the stuff, it seemed better energetically to simply give it away, and with the exception of some gorgeous artwear traded with one friend, most it rolled away in a big, dusty truck to be ensconced in a spectacular straw-bale home. The last of the earlier furniture I'd made went to the gallery in Malibu. What remained beyond that either returned with me to Massachusetts, or landed in the Purgatory of Stuff—the local transfer station. Freedom was indeed an act of letting go.

In the midst of the month's sorting and disgorging, I thought of perhaps settling back there and doing some teaching, but Brooke just shook her head and said it'd be a dead-end. I knew in my heart she was right, and soon thereafter, I was loading the last bits from storage into the truck.

Lumenhorse

Flowing the Coop

Upon returning to Massachusetts, I started looking for a studio space to rent and soon found an interesting prospect: a former chicken coop. Months later, I described the tentative arrangement in gritty detail:

I spend a portion of most days in a chicken coop. The chickens, straw, and attendant smells departed some years ago, and what remains is a ramshackle shell—a utilitarian hodgepodge resolutely devoid of grace. At some point between the birds' departure and my arrival, it had been resurrected as a ceramics studio, with a minimalist approach to workmanship akin to its original construction. The result was a seamlessly shoddy environment, and an oddly antithetical backdrop for the work of a perfectionist.

Longish and low-slung—the pitch of its ceiling a paltry eight feet from its crumbling floor—it has the redemptive virtue of southern exposure along its thirty-eight foot length. The four long windows are a blessing, indeed, especially in the low winter sun, and a major selling point in my taking over the disastrous space, considering that my prior studio—located in the basement of a massive arts building—had no natural light whatsoever.

The outside of the building is quintessential "shack": deeply-grayed, curling shingles, and matching wood trim replete with green fungus, protruding rusty nails, and flecks of an ancient, deeper green paint. This authentic humbleness, however, is not at all problematic: Firstly, because it's not my building, I'm not compelled to fix it; and secondly, it looks to the passerby highly unlikely to contain anything of value—like, say, a small fortune in power tools.

A reasonable person might well wonder why I'd choose to work in such a place. I'd respond that it's pretty cheap, in a pretty good location, and, after clearing out the debris and poorly made shelving units, patching the floors, stripping out the ancient florescent lighting, insulating the ceiling, and hanging my own lights, it's now a relatively not so bad place. And I don't intend to be there for more than a year.

Locally, most artisans rent workspace in old, multi-story mill buildings. I looked into that, and realized that there were too many really good reasons for staying away: fire hazard, pollution from other studios, noise, dealing with freight elevators, unpleasant landlords, and the urban environment. Worst of all, I felt depressed in those massive structures.

Given the alternatives, a funky ol' coop nestled into a grove of pines looked downright inviting... One might alight, peck around awhile, and take wing again on a fresh wind.

In a way, taking on that coop was a rather like my life in general at this time: It was a period of limbo and making-do, and its rough edges were there to keep me from getting too comfortable in maintaining that mode any longer than I felt compelled. I was a creative mercenary again, though I didn't mind. I'd taken creative exploration for an extraordinary ride and was a little burned-out, so it didn't feel like I was sacrificing by focusing on simply making beautiful things and spaces for hire for a while.

In fact, I didn't work in the coop for quite a year, after all, and I didn't make anything there I'd consider to be art. It seems I just needed some time to absorb what I'd gleaned from the previous three years, and ease into what would come next. After a severe winter through which I remodeled, built furniture, and shoveled snow to get in and out the coop, I'd had enough—well more than enough.

The house in Madrid had sold quite quickly, producing some cash and lending some flexibility. From a financial investment point-of-view, it was a toss-up as to whether I lost or gained in the process of rebuilding it. As a soul investment, though, it paid dividends beyond any sort of linear or rational measure: It was the finest sort of companion, and the warmest kind of relationship, in that we held each other, and grew truer together, in the grace of mutual becoming.

Looking to another sort of creative life in which I wasn't leaning on my building skills to make a living, I wanted to focus on writing, and leave the dusty, paint-splattered clothes behind.

Lumenhorse

Sometimes I've left a place to be gone from there, and precisely where I landed mattered less. Other times, I've been drawn to a pointed elsewhere on the map that I think, or know, or at least hope, will suit me better. This time, the initial impetus was the leaving.

Moving the tools and materials through the difficult winter suggested that there had to be a better way, and in a warmer place. Unsure where such a place would be, I asked my dear friend Brooke in Santa Fe if she had any thoughts on the matter, as she has an uncanny sense of my way in this world. She didn't hesitate, and just said in her wonderful, knowing way: *Portland, Oregon!*

The Masterwork

This physical world seems a roughhewn realm. One may experience profound openings toward wholeness with seemingly major ramifications for one's expression of essence, yet find that years have passed before it's evidenced on the ground—if indeed one sees it at all. But perhaps that's one of the allures of coming to this earthly plane: that what we'd known of our higher Selves is strained through the varying densities of landscapes and objects, karma and circumstance, perceptions and beliefs—and what passes through of this grace, and becomes entwined with our days, is the more potent for the distillation of that rub. And it seems this grace is only evident in its resplendent fullness when one has left the gravitational pull of physical form, and one parses this evolutionary passage from a lighter beyond.

Meanwhile, how we balance the spaciousness of the inner landscape with the circumstance of our lives describes our artistry in the medium of living, and what that entails in practice is an inherently subjective thing. To connect with a deep sense of Being that we know is our own truth, and then to file the worldly engagement of it away for later, is rather like feeling a deep attraction to a practice in painting, but not following through with getting the paints and brushes; or acquiring them, but not setting aside time for their use.

This raw world requires that we engage the *stuff* of it—in whatever form—to get the real benefit of our callings, or risk exiling them to the realm of longing for the remainder of our stay. Longing can be a sublimely powerful motivator, but the essence of creativity, and one of the finest exercises of Being, is the introduction of longing to Doing. Perhaps one finds those dusty paints and brushes in the back of the closet one-day, and realizes it's time, at last, to paint.

A lifetime unfurls one moment at a time, yet only in the broad sweep of retrospect do we see if we've been drowning in days and months and years of circumstance of our own making which has dampened our unfolding—that we've perhaps entangled ourselves in modes of survival, and forestalled the onset of thrival. If only we'd really get what we "learn" as we go along life's path, our lives, and this world, would be very different, indeed.

But it would be a disservice, too, to bemoan our limitations in absorbing and applying what we're here to learn. What's important is that we show up for *this* moment, and *this* one, in the ongoing Now, with one eye on What Is, and the other on what calls us to the core of our Being.

I've shared how this equatorial life can seem like the after-life in its barely discernable seasons. It feels like that, too, in looking back over the myriad ways in which I've averted the potential benefits to my outer life of the breakthroughs in the inner landscape; I count among my teachers the stress and hardship that spilled from that reticence. Yet I know most profoundly, the joy and sense of homecoming gleaned from my eventual surrender to the inevitable unfurling of another, and yet another, aspect of who I am in the world.

That much younger me who gazed around, senses wide open, taking everything in unfiltered at the 4th of July parade, reaches right across the years in which I couldn't bear to see my own truth so clearly, and embraces my walking now in presence. The desire I had as a young artist for a rich life palette from which to draw, has been wrought over the years at times in less creative labors, dark nights of the soul, as well as moments of artistic discovery and sublime fulfillment, and it arcs onward into the realm of potential. Like the longing for touch dissolving in the embrace of a lover, the physical trauma of becoming, and the stress of those self-indentured years, recede in the calm of these lighter, more spacious ways.

From here, too, I see that there is plentiful rub with this plane left in my aging form, and that by the blessing of awareness, there is in every moment opportunity for allowing the grace to which I open within to have expression in the world.

In the reflection of so much making, it's become clear that, regardless of what one may create in the realm of form, one's true masterwork is the revelation of one's higher Self. In contemplating the unfurling masterwork in this arc of lifetime, I'm reminded of those words I wrote of the studio process nearly ten years ago:

I try to stay out of the way of the flow of potential.

7

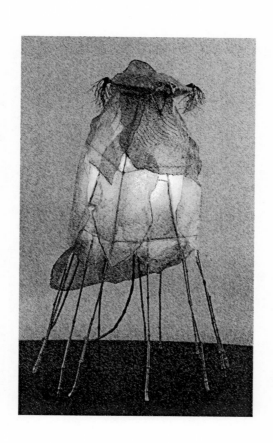

Rose City

Back West

Having moved a full woodworking studio and household from California to New Mexico eleven years before, I was all too familiar with the cost (in every sense) of traveling so heavily. I wanted flexibility this time, which meant making some hard choices about sentimentalized things with which I'd resettled numerous times. It was a pleasure, though, to sell off the bigger power tools and whittle the rest down to a portable kit.

Weighed against freedom of movement, the essentials became all the more clear: clothes, sculptures, hand tools, and small number of favorite books. I'd amassed once again a too-large collection, and donating most of the architectural design books to the local library nearly made the wide-eyed librarian cry. I was determined to fit everything I owned in a rental trailer and the back of the pickup.

Heading out in a chilly mid-April, I had mountains and a wide country to cross in the early spring with a four-cylinder engine and a dense load. The northern Appalachians weren't high, but proffered long uphill climbs that seemed for a long while to be without end. They broke, finally, and the freeway spilled out onto the plains to Chicago. The rain was nonstop most of the way across Nebraska, and every time a trailer truck passed, it kicked up such mist I couldn't see the road for long spans as it pulled into the gray ahead. I just gripped the wheel and muttered, *Go with the force, Luke.*

Approaching the Rockies, I saw rows of snow-capped peaks like shark's teeth, and couldn't help but think of Lewis and Clark going over them on horseback in winter with little food and wearing moccasins. My biggest concern was keeping the truck and wagon on the icy road and maintaining enough speed that I didn't get rear-ended by trailer trucks driven by seemingly craven men with a death wish and the means, at last, to bring it on.

On the far end of the range, near La Grande, Oregon, the road suddenly pitched upward and turned completely white, as if it lead right up into some heavenly realm. I had enough room to pull over and lock the wheel hubs into four-wheel-drive mode, and it was a good thing I did, as a winter squall had just left the road covered with several inches of icy hail, which amounted to driving on ball bearings.

I've done a good deal of difficult driving, but this was perhaps the most terrified I've ever been behind the wheel. Climbing up the through the twists and turns with a slew of other vehicles, I was most concerned about the other side: going steeply downhill with an awkward, heavy load and little chance of stopping or even slowing on the sheer mountain curves.

Blessedly, the squall had hit only that side of the mountain, and as I approached the summit, the hail faded quickly. Just over the top, the view opened out onto an emerald green valley far below, ringed by a crown of shimmering silver-white-tipped peaks. The sudden release of terror overlapping this stunningly beautiful counterpoint shimmering below brought me to tears, and made quite a welcome to my new home state. It was a breathtaking glimpse of what the early settlers must have felt after slogging their way through those layers of jagged mountains.

The next morning's drive was an inspiringly beautiful run along the winding Columbia River Gorge that led right into Portland. I'd moved there sight unseen, and the first time I laid eyes on the city, I knew Brooke had been right about it being a good fit: Green hills formed a lush backdrop for a compact downtown of old and new buildings glistening as the sun burned through. I was smitten at first sight.

Rose City

After a few days of looking around the city, I got an apartment near Laurelhurst Park in large part because of its proximity. I wrote at the time:

> There's a park a few blocks from the apartment that's become a second home. Soon after arriving in Portland, I bought a handsome red city bike, and nearly every day carry it down the flight of stairs, hop on, and ride the short distance to this Eden: thirty-five acres of towering trees, rolling lawns, ducks in a pond, and winding paths. Partly for exercise, but mostly for the shear joy of it, I pedal around those paths for a while, then stop to sit in the grass and read and write.
>
> Rarely are the same people there; the city seems to provide an inexhaustible supply of picnickers, Frisbee throwers, dog walkers, duck feeders, and sunbathers, as well as a regular stream of folks practicing music, martial arts, yoga, dance, and tightrope walking—sometimes even sword-fighting. There was an Irish wedding a few days ago, complete with bagpipes.
>
> I'm still amazed to be living in a city that's so easy to enjoy. Downtown is twelve minutes away, yet the area I live in seems like a big town. And with the park so near, I don't feel cut off from nature. The apartment—with its paper-thin walls, noisy neighbors, and unfortunate brown carpet—is less than ideal, but for now it's fine enough.
>
> For many years I've known that at some right time I'd comb back through the journey of this lifetime. The time would have to be right, and the place, too, as I'd need to be settled enough—in the world, and in myself—to take on the work. I've heard it said that writing one's story changes the outcome, so I've waited for a clearing—a time and place with room to unfurl.
>
> Already, I'm finding that the recounting, itself, is an odyssey. To write honestly of the past is to relive it, and while the mind is stirred by memory, so is the emotional body. This evening, as I contemplated salad dressings at the natural food store, a flood of grief washed through me. It seemed that the writing of the day had caused a storm

at sea, and the waves had taken a while to roll ashore. I've had plenty of practice with gathering my emotions before they cascade through my body in public from those earlier times racked out on massive amounts of hormones, but it came on so quickly, my eyes began to water before I could focus and let it go.

Pedaling slowly through the park on the way home, surrounded by green and growth, the cool air swept around me—a gentle, welcome salve.

☐ ☐ ☐

Back to the Wall

Failing to take into account the highest unemployment rate in the country, I'd arrived in Portland with an uncomplicated plan: a simple life of writing, and working at some basic job to pay the bills. But basic jobs were hard to come by, having been filled already by the over-qualified willing to settle for less until something better came along, or the economy decided to get up off the couch and go back to work.

A quick survey of the employment landscape suggested a more serious approach, so I pulled together a pretty resume that might persuade someone looking for a high-end furniture salesperson that I'd be just the person for whom they were looking. With many years of furniture making and an MFA degree behind me, I knew furniture—I *really* knew furniture. But it's darned near impossible to get interviews for jobs that aren't available. And when they were perhaps hiring, there was the unrelenting fact of my androgyny, which hadn't been a hindrance as an independent operator, but was apparently an issue in terms of me representing them.

So I took a hint, and did what I've done for most of my life: I hired myself (*...why yes, I'd be more than happy to vouch for the quality of my work, and the upstanding nature of my character!*). I'd seen some gorgeous natural wall finishing materials at a green building show a couple of months after arriving, and thinking it would be good to know about, had taken some information.

Rose City

The first few months in town had been a lovely time of settling in, resting from the onslaught of the work of pulling up stakes in Massachusetts, and exploring, but with the job prospects looking dismal at best, I went to the green building supply store that carried the materials. Janet, the woman in charge of the natural finishing supplies, was called from the back: Out stepped a woman with shimmering energy and an easy smile; we knew instantly we'd be friends. We talked as specifically as we could about the various mediums, and she sent me off with an armload of samples and literature.

I turned the apartment bedroom into a studio, and moved the bed into what most people would have used as a dining alcove. Over the next couple of months, I experimented and found my own approach and aesthetic with the materials.

Janet loved the sample boards, and asked if she could put some on their display stand. As they started getting more attention from customers, one thing led to another, and soon I was making a wall-mounted display unit to hold rows of my sample boards at the store—and, happily, my business cards as well.

Out of one finishing project came a commission for a nine-foot wide set of five large, hand-made paper leaves backlit by a serpentine strip of neon-like LED lighting. Working on it whetted my appetite for the medium again, and soon I was creating complex copper-wire armatures and overlaying small leaf-shaped pieces of paper. The wall finishing was for livelihood, but the sculptures—while still potentially remunerative—were created much more out of a sense of aesthetic passion.

While things were shaping up in the realm of livelihood and hands-on creativity, that *simple life of writing, and working at some basic job to pay the bills* had been neatly sidelined. One might reasonably ask why I didn't pursue the writing more intently alongside the finishing, but the reality was that the subtly of the writing process was overwhelmed by the challenge of working in several new mediums at once, and the physical intensity of moving equipment and applying the materials.

There was a resonant sense of the potential of language waiting just below the surface, but it's clear now that I lacked sufficient spaciousness—inside and out—for the daunting task of a major expedition to the Land of Retrospect.

Cusp of Unfolding

I've heard that a writer needs to get herself out of the way by writing her own story—whether it's to be seen by the world or not—and back in Portland, I felt the truth of this in my bones. I intended to comb through all the challenges, changes and Doing along the road of Becoming, to integrate it all and release what would follow. But then and there, I wasn't fully tempered for this work, or its outcome. The turmoil of facing old ways—and the suffering they spawned—flooded through the telling and left this teller far afield. It was clear I wasn't light enough yet that it would unfurl as the journey of true healing I knew it could be .

I was doing some writing, at least, which kept me tethered—tenuously—to the space I'd hoped would open up for far more, but the confluence of temperament, psycho-emotional space, and lifestyle wasn't there to usher the process into, and through, this sort of recapitulation.

Now, here in Bali, I feel in the background the dawning to come, as if it's waiting for me to apply the final punctuation. And the effort I brought to the studio all those years finds expression each day in the Writing Womb—though I wouldn't say that *effort* is the operative term, any more than an expectant mother sees the growth in her womb as a result of her exertion.

Slowly, I've come around to accepting that the arc of this life reveals its own way and time, and that desire and will are often not, by themselves, enough to fund the resolution of my intentions. It seems that divine grace has the ultimate say: I might find success in having set up the conditions, but the inner harvest of those efforts comes along on its own course of fruition—and at a deeper rhythm that takes the timing of my aspirations as advisory, at best.

I've mentioned the insight that suggests *the writing itself changes the outcome of the story.* As an artist, I know the truth of this, as I've seen with every creative endeavor that the making changes what was initially being made, and what is made next—and this, in turn, what comes after.

One of the blessings of the practice of art is that the conscious experience of a single act of creating can comprise a tremendous arc of learning and growing at the level of essence. Left to the circumstances of life, the value of that experience might take years or decades to unfurl—and even then, might not be appreciated while on this earthly plane.

Yet, endeavors in the creative practice of life often do unfold over years. I write now to wipe away the gathered dust, to reveal and contemplate what has been—the better to glean from its reflection a clearer sense of the value thus far in this unfolding. I think of the creative arc of the Lumenhorse work, in which I needed to work yet more deeply with density—with Earth—before I could release it in the dunes; I needed more discovery in the realm of density to reveal the more rarefied.

Seven years later, Agua Wingen perches in my inner landscape—at the threshold of old ways and those to come—and ripples through my days.

Reunions

When I was transitioning twenty years ago in San Francisco, it felt natural to share what was happening. It's said that there's no fanatic like a recent convert, and I was indeed a convert-in-process, and a recent one at that. But I don't know that *fanaticism* is quite the term I'd use for my motivations in speaking to groups, but surely something akin to it is necessary to share one's inner process with a roomful of strangers. The dictionary suggests that *excessive enthusiasm* marks one as a fanatic, and I seems it's the *excessive* part with which I'm uncomfortable. I was enthusiastic to be sure, and inclined to express what enthused me—traits which in part mark me as an artist, and who I am more broadly, to this moment.

After four years of gender limbo at school in the East, I wanted a sense of community which unabashedly included gender variance, and living in a progressive environment again, it felt not just safe, but welcoming, to get involved in educating the public about trans issues.

In being an activist this time, it was more about returning to openness and engaging community—both the trans and queer communities, and the wider community on our behalf. I'd been blessed with an easy time in being myself over the years, and applying the self-acceptance that made this possible to making more room for others was one way of expressing gratitude for the grace of this ease.

There was a group at Basic Rights Oregon putting together trans educational programs and presenting them, and for a while I was involved with that outreach. Since it's been demonstrated over the years that people are much more supportive of gay and trans rights when they actually know gay and trans people, the educational effort was focused on sharing information which was very much underscored by our presence.

In this work, there was of necessity a great deal of focus on the outer aspects of gender-shifting—on the ramifications of one's changing, or changed, body and expression in the workplace; in housing; and medical care. I had done a great of inner work in the realm of gender, and this was a balancing way to be of some service.

I'd like to think I brought some value with my presence, while I know for certain the camaraderie was a blessing for me. Eventually, the mounting studio workload and a sense that I'd shared what I could for the time being came to the fore, and I bowed out.

Rose City

For a large, annual ceramics show at the Convention Center in late April, the store and I collaborated on a set of six large panels to act as a backdrop for three display areas. The store built them, and I did the finishes: natural Venetian Plaster, European Beeswax Glazing, and pigmented Cellulose Plaster. It was a wonderful opportunity to jump-start the process of getting the word out, and I spent every hour the show was open talking to people and sparking interest. I remember looking around in a quieter moment at the throngs of visitors in the vast space, and thinking, *Well, this is certainly the antithesis of solitude!*

On Saturday night, I was exhausted after presenting the work repeatedly under artificial lights all day. The show closed at 9:00, and as I reached down into the hutch to get my things, I heard an oddly familiar voice right behind me saying, *Shannon Belthor, is that you?* I turned around to see my old friend Nancy, whom I'd known back in Madrid, but lost touch with for ten years when she moved away. I'd been in Portland for one year to the day, and suddenly I had an old friend in town.

We met at a cafe a couple of days later, and though we had some catching up to do, it was as if the conversation were a seamless continuation from all those years before. She said she'd bought some land in eastern Washington and spent what time she could out there working on a cob house and reveling in nature—which brought me right back to the folks building straw bale homes and earthships out on the desert land around Madrid.

A year or so later, I helped her erect a large greenhouse over the foundation of the cob house to extend the working season up there in the mountains where, unlike in Portland, they get a real, snow-saturated winter. She later installed a wood-burning stove in the greenhouse, which gave it enormous seasonal flexibility.

One of the finest Thanksgivings I've ever had was held in there in the midst of an ice storm. Some friends joined us, and we feasted on a duck they'd raised and slaughtered themselves, gorgeous vegetables from their organic garden, and wine. Best of all, we shared this with the sheerest of walls letting light in all around, while snowy rain fell and the stove radiated splendid warmth. Sky was there in abundance, and we feasted on its presence along with the lovely food.

Early one morning in the dull gray of dawn, I was aware in the earliest stages of waking, of *Being* consciousness reentering the body and circumstance I usually call *me* and *mine*—as if, after a night of freedom from density, I was returning for duty out of a confluence of assignation and choice.

I was floating down a list of qualities—age, sex, marital status, number of children, functionality of body, location, and so on—and it seemed that of all possible lives, *this* life was the one precisely fitted for this chapter of evolution toward mergence with higher Self. But it felt like it could have been any number of other existences under different conditions, and that this one was being given/chosen from outside of time.

I lay there in this well-formed Now, feeling the spaciousness from which I had entered, knowing that I am not this body, not this mind, not these feelings or emotions—that these are the means of Being and evolving here, in this indefinitely short stay.

Within six months of moving to Portland, the course of my life had reactivated the accustomed lifestyle of living with a studio—the arrangement seemingly arising out a field of inevitability. But I did love having the sense of potential around me in the form of materials and projects in progress, and it lent a quiet, familiar kind of companionship.

Getting the tools, materials, and ladders in and out of the second floor apartment for the site work was awkward, though—especially in the chilly mid-fall through spring rainy and icy season—and I clearly needed more and better space in which to create. Once again, it made economic sense to find a place to live and work, and I wanted to buy a property to build up some equity. A friend generously said she'd lend me some money to put down on a place, so I started a search for something that felt right.

Among the traits reverberating through my life was this combination of a tendency to lean on my studio and building skills for livelihood, in tandem with a desire for owning a place where I could live with my work, and it was readily activated here in Portland. Like so many others who work with their hands, I could support myself with my output, but in terms of "getting ahead," the best chance I saw for this was in buying a property, and hoping that rising real estate values and the worth of my sweat equity would provide for the funding of some better options later.

The alternative I was most interested in creating was an extended period—in a fitting place—in which to stop, dissolve the physically ambitious modes I'd embraced to support myself, and re-approach Creative Spirit in ways which were in alignment with my unfolding—in whatever form that might be.

□ □ □

Hitting the Walls

In the process of finishing a couple of rooms for a family in the Southwest section of the city, I realized how much I liked its small town feel and proximity to Downtown and the Eastside. The couple and I hit it off immediately, and it turned out that they were selling the nearby house in which they'd been living. I knew as soon as I saw it that it was for me: a 1926 bungalow on a double lot with a large, single-room addition that would make a wonderful studio.

A friend had said long before that when it comes to taking on fixer-uppers, you have to let enough time pass between them that you forget how much work is involved. It had been four years since the onslaught of labor in Madrid—suggesting that in taking this on, I was either short on memory, long on ambition, or some combination thereof.

In the midst of buying the house, I was talking with a designer who was working with a lovely couple building a state-of-the-art solar green home out at Cannon Beach, about ninety miles west of Portland. It was a gorgeous location up on the cliffs, with views out over Haystack Rock and the coastal mountains descending into the sea. It would be a huge project, entailing a fresco-like beeswax glaze finish on the gypsum plaster walls, as well as a natural oil finish on the wood floors.

The clients loved the palette and custom finishes I had developed, so about a month after I moved into my new home, I set out for Cannon Beach on a trip reminiscent of those forays back to the Bay Area in the first few years in New Mexico. Here, I was a lot closer to home, of course, but since it was barely set up to live in, it only marginally qualified as that. Over the very chilly winter, I camped in the house at Cannon Beach while doing the work, and stayed overnight perhaps three times at the basic encampment I called home.

As I often have with my work, I lived and breathed the project to its completion. And I do mean *breathed* literally: Normally, one would leave after a day of work and go home, but here I went to the loft and shared the air off-hours with the rest of the place. It simply wouldn't have been feasible if not for the natural materials I was using, and even then, I'd time the floor finishing for just before I headed out to Portland for an overnight visit and to stock up on groceries.

The glazing process was particularly intense, in part because it required that the walls be dampened—allowing the pigment to bleed into the surface watercolor-like. But they were also extraordinarily absorbent: Behind the gypsum plaster surface was a rougher plaster base coat, and behind this were the concrete and woodchip blocks at the core of the green construction. Since all of this was highly absorbent, keeping the walls sufficiently wet was a massive challenge. I'd soak a section repeatedly with a tank sprayer, and fly into action with the glazing.

Using a large brush on an extendable poll—often on a twelve-foot ladder—I was using my whole body in what felt like an aesthetic contact sport. About a month into the project, I came to the undeniable recognition that I wasn't in my twenties or thirties anymore, and that the sidelined pull to a lighter way of life was more than a desire—it was indeed becoming a physical necessity.

It certainly didn't help that, although it was being tweaked, the solar heating system hadn't yet been fine-tuned enough to really warm the house. The temperature was a quite steady 62-64 degrees, and with the added factors of a very wet climate, the humidity released from the wall work, and my being quite lean, the chill took its toll.

The previous winter, I'd gotten some painful swelling in my hands, which I suspected was set off by the damp chill in Portland, and at Cannon Beach, it was considerably worse. I never realized how much emotional energy I had in my hands until the swelling came on. So much of my relationship with the world had been expressed through their engagement with making, and to have them become so painfully swelled was saddening to the core.

We humans often require suffering to get our attention, and if the overall strain on my body from the intense work wasn't enough, this pain surely brought the point home.

The architect and I had a lovely rapport. This eco-home he had designed was temporarily an artist's studio, and he reveled in the bottles of dry pigments, cans of natural oils, and brushes of various sizes and shapes. I'd worked with many architects who were pretty uptight about color being introduced to "their" buildings, so this was a particularly pleasurable turn for me.

After a wonderful visit near the end of the project, he left the house and headed out to the driveway. A few moments later, the door opened, and he walked back in with a big smile. He looked up at me perched high up on a ladder and said, *I just got, this is performance art!* We had a good laugh, then he turned and walked back out the door. A fine thing, indeed, to be clearly seen.

When I returned to Portland in late winter, I had spent two and a half months living at the coast—far more time than in my own house. For the next six months I split my time between projects—for the house at the coast, and new ones—and working on my own place. In buying the property, I'd wanted the roots of a more settled life in rhythm with growing things, which I hadn't had for the five years since leaving Madrid.

But I knew it wasn't for the long-term—that I'd be there perhaps three years, or maybe as long as five. It was an investment, and a pit stop on the road to the hopefully much lighter next phase, which I'd begun thinking of as a more consciously artful way of life—one in which the spirited creative focus I'd put into the studio work was applied more directly to my way of Being in all aspects of my life.

Sometimes, surrendering to change means letting go of things we no longer want, and at others, it means letting go of something we love. I loved living in Portland, and had wonderful friends there—and still do. It's a beautiful, unabashedly progressive city abounding in parks and tress, and as far as I'm concerned, the perfect size: large enough to have plentiful things going on and resources for creating, yet not so large that it feels oppressive.

But the chilly rains that span half the year and swelled my hands forced me along my way sooner than I'd anticipated. Too, I *had* to finish with the intensively hands-on livelihood, and I sensed the next phase would require a less urban setting in which to unfold.

Rose City

For All Intents and Spaciousness

Things have so often turned out to be different from what I've intended, which isn't to suggest that I'm a victim—of circumstance, or a universe with a twisted sense of humor or fair play. It seems to be a given in the world of form that intention often translates poorly into effect—rather like computer translations between languages lacking the suppleness to account for idioms and cultural nuance, turning simple phrases into odd mal-approximations.

On the upside, it makes for adventure along the way in that, by declaring what we want, we set a benchmark from which to acknowledge the participation of the unknown in our lives—at least in regard to those intentions. On the downside, we may not want such adventure in a process that we'd simply like to see come to fruition.

Indeed, if there's an opt-out mode for the interjection of the unknown into even the simplest—let alone high-minded—intentions, it remains well hidden from me. It may well be that the reason many people don't invite more adventure into their lives is that they feel—consciously or not—as though they're already up to the neck in a sea of risky unknown.

It seems that this condition is not something that starts upon our arrival on this space-traveling orb. It begins, perhaps, in our contemplating residing again in human form: I imagine that from a state of formlessness, it seems exquisitely alluring to exercise one's light with physical form and senses. But we get here and quickly become sidetracked by the density of it all, forgetting how extraordinary it is to experience—to *Be*—manifest existence amid the background of Silence, Stillness, and Space. There is, after all, laundry to be done, random thoughts to be incessantly had, that spreading rash to be concerned about, bills to be paid, kids to be fed, and on and on...

A quick scan back across my own odd arc evinces no shortage of intentions lost in translation: I heard the call of the feminine for so many years, and in responding to it at last, I certainly intended to land closer to the center of that camp—but the hormones and my essential nature revealed a tool-wielding, soft-butch dyke in lieu of that sleeker fem. And though I had no conscious intentions as to a time frame for the surgical side of my gender becoming, had they existed, they'd certainly have been far shorter than the outcome that was akin to that vaporous mirage down the desert highway that always stays just ahead.

I think, too, of the years of studio production—driven, and limited, in creative scope, by the necessities of livelihood—and how I intended to make room in time and space to work my tools toward creating far more from the visions my soul would express; now that the room is here—beyond even the structure of the grad school exploration—I no longer see myself primarily as an object maker, and find that language has taken its place at the head of the media table. Naturally, this too may well shift along the way—perhaps to a wafting balance of writing and making similar to the time in the dunes of Cape Cod.

Along this circuitous way, I've come to see a willingness to set out toward some destination knowing the road there may lead somewhere else as the price of admission to a joyous, adventurous life. Intention is, after all, of the mind, and Being is so much more.

Slow Burn

In the fall, I turned more seriously to focusing on the house, with a goal of having it ready to be put on the market in August. There was a great deal of physically intense, and sometimes dangerous, work to be done, so with apologies to the feminine, I leaned into it from the male side as I'd done in Oakland and Madrid.

Again, I felt a little like a serial abuser who keeps promising that this time it'd be different—with this fresh version pleading that there would be open-ended freedom this time on the other side of the mountain of labor. I had a vision for the house and yard that would yield extraordinary space in my life relative to what I'd known, but in the meantime, I'd have to invest more than everything I had.

Rose City

With the calling to that lighter life on the aspirational front—and more pragmatically, concerns about the timing of finishing the house—fueling my motivation, I worked 10-14 hours a day, seven days a week for most of the next year. With little money to invest relative to the scope of the project, I did everything I could myself, but hired help with some of the basic prep and painting, and specialties like plumbing and tiling. I started early and worked late to have time to be in the flow without having the distraction of overseeing others' progress.

Even as I worked those exhausting days, the writing was coming forward in the form of poetry. I turned to the threshold—the meeting place of inner and outer landscapes—for refuge. With so much emphasis on the outer, turning inward and feeling the balance in that meeting was an exquisite counterpoint—a salve for the soul in those exhausting months.

I turned, as well, to the gardens surrounding the house for refuge. As I turned the compost pile that Christmas Eve, a wave of connection with raw earth swept through me, and I felt the stirrings of words joining in:

Ode to The Heap

Though I am the least serious
imperialist I know,
I govern the vast colonies
of glistening red worms
and unseen, yet nonetheless
darling microbes
in this restless, feasting pile.
As would any self-respecting monarch,
I demand huge sums of taxes
for the privilege of living
in my garden kingdom,
and I exact them
in hefty forkfuls of mulch.

On this newly winter day,
I am the peasant queen
outfitted in yard finery:
mossy scarfed neck under wearied coat,
muck-proof shoes over fat cotton socks.

My leathered hands pull the
weathered handle from the heap,
comb aside the drier,
still-leafy surface.
With rusty fingers
I pierce its tender flank,
lift, and turn once more
another serving.

Clouds of warm exhale join
shy plumes steaming from the gashes,
befogging this fibrous potpourri
of spring and summer's tender greens
turned crumbly umber browns
and charcoal golds
baking slowly beneath.
Worms writhe at the sting of chill,
as slender tines slide again,
heft whole worlds of humus
into the wheelbarrow,
waiting openmouthed
to serve its humble purpose.

I push the pregnant mound
around the yard,
sidle up to hibernating gardens,
leave on each
a fresh, duffy skin of Kali,
goddess of destruction and rebirth.

Despite My Efforts

August passed, though, without the house being done, despite my Herculean efforts. It went on the market with some details left to complete late in September, just as the real estate market began to show signs of weakening. It's easy to look back with the aid of hindsight and see where I could have made better choices, but I know I did the best I could in the midst of exhaustion, and with the inner tools I had at the time.

Twice I thought it was sold, only to have the prospective buyers back out within two days of closing. It took eleven months to sell the house, and in that time, between the overhead and the amount I had to reduce the price, I ended up with less than a quarter of the equity for which I'd hoped and planned. I'd likely have made as much if I'd just sold the place having done nothing at all.

I'd been disappointed years before when, after all that effort, the house in New Mexico hadn't sold before I left for grad school, and kept me from resolving the energy I'd put into it—but it hadn't prevented me from going on to the next phase. In Portland, however, those months of waiting were a slow burn as I watched the equity stream away by the day. To have a sense of resolution finally fixed on a date, only to have it ripped away at the last minute—twice—was simply wrenching. The circumstance was difficult enough in itself, but it also fed into a backlog of life-long inner work waiting to be resolved—and which was awaiting the very space that was just out of reach.

The last eight of those eleven months were an extended dark night of the soul, and I turned to the only thing that brought a sense of peace, hope, and understanding: I wrote, not so much out of a desire to express, but as a lifeline to my essence. Those months laid me bare and tempered my Being. I focused every fiber of my awareness on staying present and true to the vision of freedom in this seemingly interminable, purgatorial condition.

I was thinking of that vision of freedom—how finishing and releasing the house was like creating wings on which to soar to, and in, that new life—when I wrote *Icarus Moans*. Delving into the nuance of the inner landscape, and finding there some measure of resolution in the form of surrender to What Is, brought consolation and a sense of creative connection with the vision amid the winter darkness.

Icarus Moans

I'd planned to fly,
done all I could to
leave the ground behind:
gathered feathers
dropped by careless birds,
and lashed them overlapped
side by side in long, neat rows
on wispy canes of bamboo
with leather straps attached,
precisely fitted for my torso.
I'd scouted the countryside,
and found one shimmering June day
the grassy, sloping hill from which
to launch into outspread sky.

A date had been set, or rather,
I'd aimed for the middle of the month
proposed by the Muse,
but August came and went
while I sired those fine wings
each day from early to late.
It seemed for a time,
the tiers of bindings might be endless,
that those sails were cursed
with being always almost done;
and then their blue and green iridescence
was flashing in the cool October light.
I stood exhausted on that yellowing hill,
anxious for the tug of straps
against my chest.

Every desire, every gesture
of those labored months pressed in,
left me drawn like a bow;
I wanted only to be alone with Sky.
Perhaps in a parallel world
a lofty wind leapt me into flight
just then,
but in this one,
the air was calm.
The lift for which I'd hoped
was somewhere else:
chasing leaves,
billowing sheets,
gathering curses from the hatless.
Better wind tomorrow, I thought;
then tomorrow
and tomorrow,
until one day I woke
and knew the season for soaring
had departed without me.

Like a wheel seduced
by a curving wave of momentum,
I held vigil for the telltale flutter of trees,
yet they remained as placid as the wings
leaning ready in the corner.
The willful drive
that ushered that constant effort
still clutched my mind
and prodded these thread-worn hands
with fussiness over bindings
already well-done.

My desire, it was clear,
bore the clout of a drop in a torrent,
and the least where the calendar rules,
so I surrendered,
finally,
to the ranks of the waiting,
and started breathing
as if I had flown.

Though I haven't gone,
much less returned,
I am, it seems, a prodigal child:
welcomed,
despite my capricious intentions,
yet more fully within
earth's firm embrace.
I will glide some soon day;
until then,
I'll lay fallow with the gardens,
gather strength in the deep night,
and arise

when the zephyrs come passing.

□ □ □

Left to Me

When the first potential buyers backed out two days from closing, I suddenly regressed from the cusp of freedom to waiting once again for the place to sell amidst the draining away of equity. The studio had been transformed into a living and dining room, leaving no space in which to be productive—besides the bitterly cold garage—so I took on some site work to help offset the outflow of cash: wall finishing projects and the remodeling of a friend's kitchen. Regardless of the setback, I was starting to get a clearer sense of the next phase, and felt deliciously—though painfully—perched at the threshold.

Deliverance, and the Art of Reinvention

Just over that horizon's cusp,
crouched, waiting:
a new life...or at least a new
way of going about living.
I see it more often,
more clearly now
peeking up over the edge,
staring back, brilliant,
alluring as the last
fleck of sun setting.
A younger me would
shed it all now and run headlong
toward that liquid glow pouring,
always pouring down
that curving other side.
Older me knows
that such fickle pursuits
are inclined to leave one
entangled with windmills,
exhausted,
naked in the cold night.

Older me knows to take
the loose strings of these last days
in this most beloved home,
wrap them around
the bundle of remains,
and tie a neat knot.
To purge the pregnant rows of files,
sort the wanted and essential,
let go of the unwanted
and easily found.
And keep just enough flotsam
of those days past for ballast.

What has coursed through this mind,
these veins,
these hands across those years
for better or worse,
will be boxed and placed
in safekeeping,
or left as molted husk
to crumble with the grasses,
when I slide away fresh-skinned
and shiny-hearted.

Where better than the threshold
to sublime the raw with that implicit,
to nourish and prune a planted life
into something more joyous,
exquisite...transcendent?
And none finer a medium I've found
for one's masterwork
than the way and form of oneself,
wrapped in fibrous days,
clothed in well-spun years.

I stare out over the chasm,
and through time's haze
that life beyond this platted
speck of world gazes back.
We eye each other
like potential lovers
across a crowded room weighing
the form,
the fit...
that flighted what if?

Left to me, it would be
one of those old dances
with couples circling around,
exchanging partners with grace,
in time to the greater whirling.

I release and spin away,
while the next ones join this place.

Holding

My friends had a good sense of what I'd invested in the place on every level; they shook their heads, and said they didn't know how I was *'staying so balanced'* in the process of seeing the payoff draining away. I knew how I maintained that tenuous balance: I kept my focus on the calling of a roomier new life, and turned to the evocation of words for mooring.

With the poetry, I was finding my balance energetically, and trying to get myself out of the way of the house transitioning to the next owners. In a sense, these were prayers. And having those friends that shook their heads and asked, kept me feeling less alone, and let me know I was loved in the midst of the slow-motion nightmare.

Earlier, I wrote of those difficult days of transitioning and working the studio in West Oakland: *"Perhaps most essential to my ability to hold it all together was that, since childhood, I've been aware of some of the deeper rhythms of who I am. One might call it a spiritual identity—a sense of who I am beyond personality and circumstance. Not that I was in touch with it all the time, but there were sublime moments of exquisite satisfaction, and when I despaired, there was a profound spaciousness that seemed to hold me."* In the midst of this new transition, my awareness of those deeper rhythms—all the more honed by the intervening years—was the means and source of the writing. And the spaciousness was far more palpable—waiting, it seemed, to enter my life more fully just beyond the awaited unbinding.

I was holding it together, but also skating right along the edge of despair. Fortunately, that late afternoon in Madrid when I slipped into Void had provided a benchmark experience of being utterly beyond hope. Having that marked indelibly in my Being lent perspective to the helplessness and frustration of being stuck and watching what I'd worked so hard for gradually slip away—despite having done everything I knew to move on.

Yet, what I was called to was not impossibly out of reach. It had thus far stayed in the distance like a mirage, but while the financing for it was in fact rapidly diminishing, it still remained in the realm of the possible.

Another critical factor in maintaining a reasonable balance was that in renovating the house, I'd drawn on the experience of many years and projects to create a space that was supportive of a sense of wellbeing. It was a celebration of light, warmth, and beauty, with curving walls and ceilings that evoked playfulness and delight. And not just for me: Everyone who visited was enchanted. Indeed, part of the frustration was that it was so appreciated, but remained unsold.

I wondered more than once if—despite my being done with the house—perhaps the house wasn't done with me. In the meantime, though, I got to revel in its charms, and this was at least some semblance of an antidote to the shadow of despair.

As a counterpoint to the grim circumstance, I focused my attention on the other side of the spectrum by making a list of what brings out my joy. In looking back, I find that I didn't put a single object on it. It was completely experiential, and every experience had to do with aspects of expansive connection beyond form: transcendence, beauty, love, freedom, friendship, writing, creativity, meditation, presence, nature, essence, dance...

I had directed everything I had—in will, energy, skills, time, experience, and money—with the best of intentions toward a reasonable outcome, and it simply hadn't manifested. While doing everything I could to maintain a sense of balance in the face of losing most or all of what I'd hoped would fund the freedom I dearly wanted, I often felt like I was being charred to the essence of who I am.

All that was superfluous burned away; in the midst of that extended small death, I was left naked with only the persistent calling to spaciousness.

After finishing the house, I'd taken a lovely day-trip out to the coast. In a colorful little kite store in Cannon Beach, I bought one in celebratory anticipation of freedom. But in the intervening months, I couldn't bring myself to set it to flight; it seemed too sweet, too much like what I wanted, but which was floating just out of reach.

A couple of months later, the house went under contract again. *These Last Days* was written while waiting for that closing. I had drawn a calendar and hung in the kitchen; each morning I colored in the day before, watching and feeling the closing—and the next phase of life—inching forward.

These Last Days

On the wall
of this creamy-yellow kitchen:
lines of a calendar drawn
on grainy paper advertise,
stark as naked bones,
the dwindling days remaining
for sleeping
waking
pacing
waiting
in this, my beloved home.

Because the Muse replied,
when I asked the price
of my freedom in the world;
because the Muse said,
if you forge this old worn house
into a nest you would truly love,
then leave it...
then you'll be free.

From the box of colored chalk
by the stove that's made me
a better cook,
I choose a hue
while the morning tea steeps
and mark yet another
yesterday's passing.

To discern with my own eyes
these days arcing;
to rub with these aging fingers
between lines inked
on white fiber floating,
a slow-motion tsunami of colors
spreading down and across,
engulfing in its wake
my old worn ways.

Amid this warmth and light
and green, fine-tuned
to grace my sense of being:
waves of lighter ways,
and faraway living flooding through
these last days here.

Because I accepted,
and whole-heartedly wielded
the mallet one year more.
Because I'm yielding
these lovely walls' embrace,
and releasing myself to the world.

Surrender

These buyers had shown up suddenly, willing to pay a decent price and wanting a quick closing, but backed out just as suddenly at the last moment, too. Not long after, as the real estate and financial markets took a decided turn for the worse, I called my realtor and told her I just needed to be done, and was ready to cut the price to the bone and move on. It was, quite simply, an act of exhausted surrender.

The property sold almost immediately to a lovely family who'd seen it during an Open House only because they happened by while going to see a neighbor's house that had been on the market some months earlier. They'd loved it—the woman actually cried because it felt so right—but they couldn't afford it at the time; suddenly they could, and we closed in two weeks.

I stayed a few weeks in the neighborhood with my friend Cyndy and her two beautiful greyhounds while sorting out the remnants of that life, and readying myself for the road. The last days—and especially hours—in the house had been hectic to say the least. There hadn't been time to quietly extract my energy from the place, so I went by some days later, parked the truck on an upper street that afforded a view over the property, and did then what I'd done in New Mexico: breathed in the stray remnants of my energy and made peace with the arc of my Being there.

Rose City

Freedom Psalm

Let freedom ring...
let it peel from clock towers
and steeples,
spill from flagpoles onto sidewalks,
drift down rivers and roads sojourning.
May gravity conspire with levity,
seducing bones young and old
along byways
onto highways,
out to ports and waiting seas.

Let liberty rise...
let it unfold in thunderous skies,
and dwell
like umbrellas over each of us
sodden and thirsting still.
May we, in our own ways,
be Mary Poppins:
each floating, arm outstretched,
sailing again in splendid form
to where our biding hearts would be.

Let freedom ride...
let it wield a steering wheel
and saddle,
pierce headwinds with its certitude,
slice air with its greyhound gait.
May its gusty stride sweep fettered lives
along jet streams and ocean swells,
like sacred breath toward home to reside
with delight
in lands more spacious still.

Hobbling Toward Redemption

Over the two years of working on, and trying to sell, the house, I told friends I wanted to go to a warm place with lush vegetation that would also be inexpensive to live, so I could stretch out and get my bearings on Being in the world in lighter ways. But things often do, indeed, turn out differently from what one might intend, and obviously, the traumatic, draining resolution lacked the grace with which I'd wanted to leave.

Now, with the place finally sold, I was yearning to go abroad, but I knew I wasn't ready energetically. I needed a place to recoup for a while, and Lorraine—whose home I'd colored thirteen years before—generously opened her house to me to stay for as long as I needed.

I headed for Santa Cruz, with a pit stop in Ashland, Oregon, to visit the friends from whom I'd bought the house, and help with some painting so they could move on from a disastrous fire which had taken a serious toll on their belongings. Ashland is a wonderful town, but in the October chill, I felt as if I were being pushed southward, and as soon as the painting was done, the truck and I rolled toward Santa Cruz.

A happy twist it was to be going as a guest this time, and when I arrived, it was hard to believe it had been seven years since I'd created the *Anomalons* lighting. It was an ideal place from which to launch my new life, surrounded by a spectrum of my work from over the years: coloring, furniture, and lighting. Lorraine gave me a large room away from the main part of the house with a lovely view out over the lowlands and bay, and I went about setting it up to support the nurturing of my equilibrium.

The nonstop stress of the prior two years had caught up with me, and I began to realize that the depth of its effect was greater than simple rest for a few weeks would heal. I'd moved beyond the ordeal, but not by any means unscathed: Despite the focus on staying consciously connected to my essence and deeper rhythms, I still walked away with what felt like a mild case of Post Traumatic Stress Disorder.

Since the latter part of the waiting with the house, I'd been waking up exhausted after sleeping ten hours a night and was still feeling stressed and deeply tired. In my mind, I knew the ordeal was over, but the low-grade, long-term trauma still reverberated in my body and psyche. In

Rose City

all, I stayed for two months at Lorraine's. Though far from healed, I could see it was likely going to take a good while to rebalance my system, so it made sense to just get on with getting out into the world.

Packing was a challenge, as I'd never traveled abroad, and wasn't sure where the road would take me, or for how long I'd be gone. When I had headed out for coloring projects, my approach was *if in doubt, take it,* but I had a truck in which to put the bulk and weight. This time, I'd be carrying it all, so my mantra became: *if in doubt, leave it.* Rarely is there such opportunity to weigh precisely the balance between possessions and freedom, as when heading out into the unknown with a backpack.

The medium that required heavy tools and bulky materials had transmuted into one lighter than air, and the studio had been transformed into a laptop computer opened wherever I landed. What mattered more than anything was that I was, finally, ready enough for flight at last.

There was a quote from John Wooden taped on Lorraine's kitchen cabinet that said: *Things turn out best for the people who make the best of the way things turn out.* And the way things turned out, I didn't have nearly the financial resources I'd hoped for making space in my life, but I had enough to fund a good span of freedom. How could one not be filled with profound gratitude for such bounty?

I left the truck under a cover in Lorraine's yard, and the things I'd brought, in the loft of her garage. She dropped me off at the airport, and as we finished hugging goodbye, she said in her sharp-humored way, *Well, after all this fuss, if you're back in less than a month, don't come knocking on my door!*

Don't worry, I laughed, *I have a feeling it'll be longer than that...* It was time to spread my wings and see where I'd alight.

Blessing of Refuge

From the sanctuary of these tropical gardens, the Writing Womb, and the stillness within, I scan the years and find amid the massive effort, streams of refuge that open into this here and now: nature in the wild, the gardens, and materials; the love affair with Creative Spirit; deep, abiding sense of Being; the splendor of loving touch; joy of friendship; the power of graceful language; clarity of solitude; the sublime silence, stillness, and space of meditation.

While refuge may be seen as shelter or protection, I'm inclined to focus on what that sheltered space provides: room beyond the density of form for one to open and expand—to *Be* from a finer balance of form and essence. Given the distracting entanglements of the outer world, I've come to see *refuge* as the room I make—in attention, presence, and physicality—for my higher nature to unfold. I see, too, that allowing this space by choice is not only a conscious act of self-love and compassion, it's the finest gift one can bring to the world: the brightening of the inner light of consciousness.

For many years, I entangled intense labor with the refuge of creative connection with All That Is. It was the expansiveness of that fulfillment—artistically, and in the form of my body—that made it so alluring. Yet there was, as well, a deep sense of retreat—of self-protection—in pulling away from the programming of the human world, and attending instead to the necessity of focused will and work. I've learned at last to ask of something I turn to for supposed refuge: If this were an invitation, would Joy, Peace, Love, and Fulfillment feel welcome and at home?

I certainly could have been more gentle—less inclined to take on staggering mountains of work when I most needed room to freely explore—but I know now with unflinching clarity the price paid for seeking solace in endless labor, however constructive and noble; and the heavy toll for choosing the wheel of suffering as a vehicle home. I know, too, like a prisoner just released into a new life under wide-open sky, the joyous unfurling of bountiful space.

8

Bali

Spirit in the Air

After a month in northern Thailand—most of which was spent up near the Burmese border in the mountain village of Pai—I came to Bali on a 30-day on-arrival visa. I'd been exchanging emails with Barbara, a friend of a friend from Portland, who'd written of the wonderful community in Ubud, and the colorful, exotic landscape and constant ceremony. I had no idea how long I'd stay, and was thinking of perhaps going back and visiting southern Thailand.

Looking back now at the journal I was keeping during those early days of travel, though, it's clear I wanted to strike a balance between stability and exposure. Still feeling worn-out and sleeping ten hours a night, I wasn't in tourist mode as much as expansion mode. I wanted to open up my world, but didn't have the energy or desire to keep flitting about.

It was clear almost from the start that I didn't need to keep moving around to feel wonderfully free; the freedom I cherished was at least as much about time as space. I soon found that having a sense of spaciousness in an intriguing landscape was a fine balance, and having time to absorb and contemplate the rub of it all lent so much more delicious depth.

I didn't expect to fall in love with Bali. Thailand had been fascinating and beautiful, but something was missing—rather like a date who's lovely enough, but with whom one simply lacks great chemistry. In Ubud, there was an immediate feeling of home: a thick, rich spirit of artful making, and a palpable sense of spirit in general in the air.

Energetically, I felt as though I'd slid into a warm bath. Bali seemed to hold a space for me in the realm of making, whether it be a calling to do so myself in some easygoing way, or an opportunity to just relax into it already happening all around. And while the Earth element was in lush flux, Spirit was constantly called forth and fed with offerings. Within days, I was walking around with my heartspace beaming and wondering if this was the place to which I'd been called to recover and unleash whatever would come next.

Before the end of those thirty days, I made arrangements for a longer visa and made a quick trip to Singapore to secure it. When I returned, it was time to start looking for a more settled place than the guesthouse where I'd been staying. And though it was a frightening prospect, I'd need a motorbike to get around.

I started asking everyone I met about a place to stay. When I told a woman with whom I'd had some lovely exchanges at a cafe what I was looking for, she smirked and said, *I think I might have something for you...* and proceeded to give me a name, a number, and some background.

It was in a Balinese family compound, and the mother had just recently died of cancer at the age of thirty-six. An American woman named Amanda had rented a building there for many years, and had a deep connection to this family. Since she lived primarily upstairs, and was gone most of the time, she wanted someone in the space below to help bring some extra income to the family. She was looking for someone with the right spirit as well—preferably a creative one, as the father was an artist—to be a good presence for them at this difficult time.

I met Amanda the next morning on Monkey Forest Road, and there was an immediate, warm connection. We walked down a long alley, and as soon we passed through the brick portal into the richly gardened yard, I knew I'd found my home—for a while at least.

Just before moving in, I rented a motorbike. I'd never been comfortable with the exposure of riding on what amounts to a motorized seat inches from rushing pavement, much less in a place where what passes for normal driving would get pretty much the entire population taken off the streets for serial Reckless Endangerment back in the States.

Bali

From the start, every trip on the bike was an exercise in mild terror at best. For many years I'd used extremely dangerous tools, and knew how to replace fear with focused attention, but my nerves hadn't recovered, and I didn't have the energetic wherewithal to access that once-deeply familiar zone.

Being the Medium

Those many months of hopeful waiting in Portland had provided—despite the anguish—plenty of room to contemplate the essence of what might be revealed in bringing the element of discovery to the forefront of my life, though the specifics remained steadfastly and alluringly obscured. The next steps in actually living this in the moment and day-to-day, however, required more inner work than I had energy for back in Portland, or when I first arrived in Bali.

With the periscope of hindsight, I could in the meantime at least make an honest appraisal from the vantage point of this new phase, and move on from there. I needn't look any further than the constant tiredness I was still feeling to see that I'd worked myself beyond exhaustion more than physically with the house renovation.

Beyond that, because I thought I had earned what I hoped would come in return, I'd transposed this potential into expectation. I then made decisions about the sale of the property out of fear of loss, which turned out not to serve me well. The fatigue from the work and repetitious waiting had left me vulnerable to old fears about lack of money, and to the increasingly rational fear of what I expected in return for my intense output slipping mostly or completely away. Most of it did slip away, and I paid a steep price—physically and psycho-emotionally—for the stressful situation I'd set up.

In this process of honest appraisal in Bali, I felt surprisingly calm and light, despite the grim remembrance. This was certainly not the first time I'd noticed that even when what the truth reveals isn't pretty, there is beauty in simply seeing the unpleasant truth clearly. And oftentimes, there is even an oddly sublime undercurrent of joy that spills from this acceptance. It seemed the light of clarity burned away the shadows that would otherwise have crept in—bringing with them retraction—and the joy amid the difficulty arose from the space retained.

Having observed so recently that things unfold on their own schedule—and that desire and intention may well bring about an outcome, but not necessarily what I had in mind—I gradually surrendered to the larger process of allowing things to unfurl of their own accord. If ever there were a time to let go of willfulness and ambition, and let the medium—the art—of life play out naturally, this was most certainly it.

Thus, I spent the first six months in Ubud enjoying a decidedly unstructured life: I'd get up when I felt moved to arise, do some yoga and meditation, have breakfast, then spend the rest of the day doing some combination of writing poetry, journaling, walking, reading, studying Indonesian, contemplating, napping, doing a bit of sculpture, and hanging out at cafes talking to people from all over the world. Those amorphous first months started to dissolve the long-ingrained stress, along with old ways of living, and I finally felt as though I were floating slowly back toward wholeness—and to a more expansive version than I'd ever known.

There was all the while in the background, like rumblings of distant thunder, a hazy sense of a new medium emerging beyond the poetry. I'd opened to new media so many times; for my own clarity I wanted to draw from this experience, so I started journaling about what this sort of engagement involves. Though I didn't intend it at the start, I soon had a short guide to taking on a new creative medium, written from the point of view of entering a relationship. I put it aside, thinking of it as a good exercise.

Bali

Foreign Fringe

Leaving the United States, I had no expectations of how I'd feel being out in the world on my own, especially given my penchant for solitude. What I've discovered is that it's utterly familiar terrain; I know this landscape well because I'd nearly always felt like I was alone in a foreign land—on the outskirts of humanity even in my own country. I don't know how much of this is inherent in my nature, and how much is due to my off-putting rearing, or those formative years of stuttering, but the ongoing, curiosity-tinged reception to the betweenness of my gender has certainly underscored this sensibility.

Being a tourist abroad is easy compared to being a foreigner amongst those assumed to be of one's own kind. Out in the world, it's at least clear what one's role is, and there are myriad industries set up to receive strangers. There's plenty of company in Being—and feeling—foreign at a crossroads like this, and that I'm a bit strange even amongst the strangers is but a matter of degree. Day-to-day, it feels like I'm living in a shared metaphor of my odd life on the fringe.

The grounding of interactions with Westerners—the rub of the familiar amongst the foreign—strikes a good balance for me. But it can be challenging, too, in that one often meets people who are just passing through, so the continuity of wonderful connections is often broken— or punctuated by considerable periods of absence.

Sometimes the absence is mine; the calling to create is for me like the whisper of a sweet lover: *Be with me now... Humanity will still be there when we finish our gorgeous embrace.*

Space of Poetry

I was immensely grateful for the lovely heartspace pervading my days, and the passion flowing through the writing. Poetry was the perfect medium for this phase: As in the dunes—when the writing was integral to the creative process—it was the touchstone of my unfolding.

Starting in Portland, it had reached back across the arc of years to childhood—to the devastating humiliation of stuttering that quietly bred a deep sense and appreciation of the rhythm and vibration of language, and a love of cadence and flow. I wrote much earlier: "I want to reach back to him, hold him, and whisper: *You may find this hard to believe, but what terrifies you now turns out to be a hidden treasure.*" Much later, the stuttering that had hemmed in my early life blossomed in blessed counterpoint into a love of sharing evocative language.

Poetry is the sculpture of language; as a sculptor of words, one stands at the threshold between one's inner and outer landscapes, and invites them to meld through breath and bits of meaning-laden sound. Of particular joy for me is that seeing sculpting in this broad way allows for a seamless interplay of practices in the merging of physical form and realms beyond. Again, I think back to the work in the dunes: the wafting back and forth between materials and words—each medium its own realm, yet reflective of the essence of the other.

The grace of poetry ushered in the element of Space in the highest, clearest way I'd ever experienced with a medium. This melding and holding of Earth, Fire, Water, and Air through language, rather than the density of physical form, was wonderfully similar to the later phase of the *Lumenhorse* work. There, I was exploring with meetings of fragmented, translucent materials and light in which the material dissolved into the light, and the light in turn seemed physically present. With poetry, I could evoke meetings of impressions from the realms of form and formlessness, revealing their entwinement.

Those aspects at the core of my sculpting practice were there—gesture, rhythm, light, intimacy, layering, and sequence—but with the added ability to speak directly of the rub of essence and world. The lightness of the medium was a homecoming, as well, in that whatever

Bali

the materials seducing my attention to the studio over the years, the underlying medium had always been the field consciousness: the ultimate in spaciousness.

Much as I created armatures in the *Lumenhorse* work, and used those as undulating structure to support and define the form of the overlaid paper or wire-cloth skin, the lean, skeletal form of poetry laid the foundation for the more fleshy exploration in prose. Without the poetic practice in focusing on the form-fleshed essence of the circumstance at hand, I'd likely not have had the grounding or wellspring of motivation to comb through the years—or if I had, it would surely have been a very different exercise, and outcome, indeed. It's been a blessing to have both to call upon: the lean, incisive essence of verse, and the sumptuous landscape of paragraph—whichever best serves the translation.

The dark night of the soul in Portland had presented an opportunity to make peace with grief and despair more deeply than ever before. As my energy began to rebalance after several months in Bali, the healing of—and *from*—this difficult time merged with other trying times and healings along the way, and spilled out in a piece exploring embracement of the whole of oneself—shadows, wounds, and all—and the lightness and freedom therein.

In the Forest

In the forest of earthly being
I wander on paths well-formed,
well-worn by lovers of light
sojourning,
caressing into wisdom
old scars re-borne,
gathering like Spanish moss
by virtue of presence
furrowed souvenirs
of gravity's lingering claim.
Among trees of towering grace,

plants of sustenance and giving,
creatures of knowing and belonging:
waters of mothers ever pouring,
murmuring with smoothened
stones of fathers,
halcyon
and holding.

And everywhere,
waves of supple progeny
unfurling among strewn remains
of the full-grown now fallen;
young and old alike,
left to the gristmill of seasons
to crumble back to soil,
dark,
ancient
and lush.

Under canopies densely arching,
I meet sometimes in deep shadows
my viscerous twin
clothed in swathes of sorrow,
rags of seam-splintering grief,
or shards of fear and doubt,
or in near-naked loneliness
abiding.

I do not stray
from the heartfelt path
into thickets of worldly life
coursing all around,
but greet her as one would
the closest of friends.

I embrace her
as the dearest of lovers,
and with soul blazing disrobe her,
welcome her once again
into these gossamer pleats,
tear-cleansed
and unburdened.

At the threshold
of wholeheartedness waiting:
flocks of meadows rimmed
in tangles of branches and vines,
generous in profusions
of grasses,
flowers
and flighted ones wild
in vast,
unfolded light and sky.

I touch the clouds with joyous kites.

Just after typing the last line into the rough draft, I walked out onto the veranda to finish the morning yoga. Stretching these well-worked hands up over my head, I looked beyond the cascading treetops and saw a huge red kite against a pristine blue sky. Kite season had just started with the coming of the winds, and this was first I'd seen. For months, there would be dozens in the air over Ubud on any given day, and every one of them felt delightfully like siblings. And with this constant stream of sky-touching, the Balinese and their easy delight found a yet more special place in my heart.

□ □ □

There seemed a lovely symmetry between the poetry from Bali and from the last couple of years in Portland: What began as a wafting between connection with Earth and a longing for Space—for a lighter sort of Beingness—spilled across a small death into the living of that lighter way.

I wanted to gather these pieces in the world of form, and let them be physical sculpture, too, in the form of a book. At a store just off the soccer field, I found some pineapple leaf paper for covers and bamboo paper for pages. In a grounding mergence of hands and materials, I made a set of hand-bound copies, and called them *Thresholds*.

It felt as if the gorgeous interplay of language and form that permeated those heavenly days at the shack in the dunes of the Cape had come spiraling around once more. This time, the flight and form melded, and in the union some circuitous karmic thread felt—if not wholly resolved—nicely along an inevitable creative arc.

⬜ ⬜ ⬜

Solitude

A friend who is focusing on the more spiritual aspects of her life remarked the other day—in a shorter than usual visit—that she's become increasingly aware of how much energy talking requires. She's finding that the more she opens to a deep quietude within, the more apparent the outflow of energy from interacting with others. She's always been quite a social person, but recently she's taken to excusing herself mid-conversation, going home, and having a much more self-nurturing and clarifying time there. Seems my friend has discovered the value and richness of solitude.

I nodded a big smile of recognition, as we'd had quite a few marathon talks in the few weeks since we'd met, and she'd been astonished when I told her I've spent a good deal of my adult life living and working in solitude. *Now that's hard to believe!* she'd said, laughing and shaking her head in disbelief.

We'd just met, so she didn't realize I'd made more room beyond my usual quietude in both time and energy because we clearly had a great connection. As we've found in numerous ways since, we're working on similar themes, but heading in opposite directions: She's finding a new sense of social balance that provides more room for aloneness, while I've been gradually opening to a more people-inclusive life.

I'd have preferred, though, that my solitude over the years, like my friend's, were more clearly chosen. She's being pulled toward quietude by her spirit and deeper rhythms, while my relationship with it has been much more complex, woven as it is into the fabric of my life since childhood. I've certainly been pushed and pulled from inside and out toward quietude, but it's also in my nature to find and know my bearings there regardless. These days, it's much more a matter of creative and self-loving choice, less a withdrawal for self-therapy.

We're enculturated to recognize and value the companionship of humans and pets, and when these aren't present, to fill the gap with feelings of loneliness. But aloneness and loneliness are very different things: To be alone is to be apart from humans; to be lonely is to be apart from the awareness or appreciation of other, more subtle realms of companionship.

I'm naturally contemplative and introspective, and this side of my nature relishes the uninterrupted rub of time against stillness, of knowing against silence—and this will always call me to aloneness. I'm pulled there now by spirit far more than pushed by worldly circumstance, and in that there is freedom—sweet, blessed room to simply Be.

There were things in my life that certainly projected me toward solitariness, yet as long as I spun around in old patterns of retraction, those aspects of my solitude amounted to self-exile. One of the joys of putting on some years is that, with the wash of time, I've dissolved in the light of awareness the ghosts that chased me into a smaller part of my inner mansion, and I'm exploring, finally, the greater extent of my estate.

In this place of deep, gentle spirit, I've lovingly unraveled myself from the entanglements of that self-exile. Loosened from the hurt, its facets polished, I find glimmering past the remaining threads the jewel within that is pure Being. The choice of solitude is a gift to myself, to be sure; but much more, it shines far beyond my inner world.

⁂

As my friend is discovering, with aloneness and quietude we have the opportunity to focus on the deeper and higher rhythms of our Selves: on the quieter stirrings and voices within, on our relationship with the grace of nature, and on just Being—on presence. We have the space then to let awareness blossom, to invite in more of what we would grow toward; and to let go, if we choose, of what makes us smaller.

By the grace of openness in solitude, we're able to interact with greater clarity and compassion because we know ourselves—our edges, and our blessed stillness—better. In choosing aloneness and quietude as part of a practice in creative Being, we grant ourselves the companionship of our deeper and higher realms. We allow our presence to come forth into the community of humanity, not out of neediness, nor in avoidance of loneliness, but bearing spaciousness and graciousness—gifts of the spirited heart.

⁂

Poetics of Space

The ramifications of the right question at the right time can be quite extraordinary. Soon after the *Thresholds* volumes were completed, a fellow expat who's involved in hosting many sorts of yoga and movement-oriented workshops asked if I'd be interested in presenting ones more oriented toward the arts. As teaching had been in the periphery for quite some time, I naturally said, *Yes, I'd love to!*

Bali

I knew instantly that I wanted to present workshops from the perspective of living with a greater sense of creativity. They'd focus more broadly on Being in touch—in the studio and out—with the creative rhythm of All That Is, rather than on the specifics of a particular medium. Participants would leave with much more than a creative high: they'd have a deeper sense in daily life of the arc of their lives as art. I envisioned the workshops, too, as openings to developing an ongoing practice of refuge in which they could cultivate spaciousness—perhaps in the form of a relationship with an artistic medium, or a deepening of one already established.

Over the course of the afternoon, a workshop outline poured out as if it had been waiting for release. I started fleshing out notes for its presentation, and realized several weeks later that there was still much more to share. At which point I also realized I'd inadvertently started a book, and decided to put the workshop idea on hold to allow the flow of words to continue unabated. The inevitability of this writing came especially to light when I realized the guide to taking on a new creative medium, which I'd written earlier and put away, was also an integral part of the book.

Much as one would naturally explore the qualities of a medium as part of the creative process, I began to focus more broadly on the qualities of Being—in and beyond this form-infused world. This wasn't a great leap, as I'd always sensed—as many artists do—that whatever the materials and processes calling one to the studio, beyond the form, the creative medium is, ultimately, consciousness.

Now, taking the practice beyond the studio meant looking more deeply at the materials of the medium of life, and being more aware than ever of their subtleties. I made a list of some of those "materials," knowing that, while they are not separate at all in the Oneness, there is value in this dense world in the unique view each offers, like various windows onto an infinitely broad landscape:

What Is / All That Is / Oneness / Divinity / God
Silence / Stillness / Space
Formlessness
Consciousness
Being
Spirit
Self
Essence
Knowing
Awareness
Life Force
The Unknown
Discovery / Revelation
Realm of Potential
Love / Heartspace
Threshold
Art
Presence
Landscape
Relationship
Ego
Mind
Personality
Patterns / Programs
Knowledge
Perceptions / Beliefs
Memory
Feelings / Emotions
Senses
Viscera / Intuition
Body
Form
Cosmos
What Is / All That Is / Oneness / Divinity / God

Bali

As I peeled back the layers of the creative practice of Being, and contemplated the interactions of these elements, the wealth of my own experience surfaced more clearly. In writing about the role of *discovery*, the image of driving the pickup truck in the desert—and hearing the author talk about writing from what you *don't* know about what you know—unexpectedly veered right out onto the landscape of my life.

I suddenly saw that, while I sensed more broadly much of the value in what I'd learned, it remained partially submerged in disjointed memory, and many of those memories had been absorbed during psycho-emotional turmoil and trauma. Only a careful, heartful parsing and gleaning would suffice in bringing more fully to awareness what had been obscured along the way, and there was clearly much to be discovered.

In looking back across the arc of it all at this point, it was clearly all too easy to downplay or disregard whole swathes of experience because of its psycho-emotional baggage, and to get to the heart of what I had to learn and share, I'd have to move past this dismission and reclaim those gems left behind.

With roughly a third of the book on artful living written, my own story began to pour out. I felt to the core of my Being the value in interrupting the initial writing, and shifting my attention to the unfolding story as a means of unearthing the deeper rhythms of what I'd gleaned in and out of the studio over the years. So *Shape-shifter* didn't spill out of the years-long intention to write it after all, but out of service to another calling.

Those first months here in Bali were a time of worldly expansion—a socially oriented, open-ended appointment with the unknown. But as the focus shifted to the unknown in parsing the arc of this life, and the daily gesture of its translation to page, I found myself gravitating to the womb of solitude once more.

Such is the path into discovery, that a simple question might reveal an opportunity to step forward and share publicly the value of what one has gleaned, and opening to that might in turn reveal another extended time of solitude. Yet, I've found that any creative practice—and the medium of life in particular—requires room outside of mundanity and society: One must make the room within one's life to open up to the Space beyond the banal.

I've seen over many years of practice that the arc of exploration with a body of work might unfold more quietly over months or years, then suddenly leap to a new level—and I could feel it happening here. Again, the work in the dunes is a fine example, in that the breakthrough took far longer than the two weeks I was there: It evolved naturally out the *Lumenhorse* work at school, that out of the *Treebone Garden* in the mountains of New Mexico, and that out of the play with color and architectural details in the Oakland studio.

One never knows what might activate a sudden shift, or in what form new spirit will arrive, much less its timing. Although grace of opening may be earnestly invited, I've experienced it again and again showing up on a schedule of its own.

□ □ □

Angel with Trigger

A single question had launched the initial writing on artful living, and the underlying trigger for *Shape-shifter* showed up at the same cafe. I looked up as a beautiful British woman with shimmering energy smiled at me and said, *I like your style!*

She sat down on the pillows next to me, and we talked for about six weeks. It turned out that Abi had experienced a pretty wild past, and had landed in southern Thailand to detox from that life. She had learned to read Tarot cards there and discovered she was quite good at it due to a talent for psychic insight. This ability eventually transcended the Tarot reading, and blossomed into what she called Soul Retrieval. While one might just brush this off as so much New Age hooey, there was something about her that suggested to me she was in touch with some powerful healing abilities.

We spent a good deal of time together, sharing our stories and insights, and it was a few weeks before I said I'd like to have a retrieval session with her. I'm reluctant to open up my energetic field to anyone

Bali

claiming to do energy healing unless I know their work through people I trust *and* I feel intuitively in alignment with them. Abi was still getting a handle on her ability—so every session was a learning experience for her, too—but it felt undoubtedly right to trust her and her work. We decided to do the session the next day on the balcony over the veranda—right above the spot where the Writing Womb would later be created.

She described her practice as healing with angels: They did the work of bringing the fragmented pieces of a soul back together, while she was simply a conduit—a facilitator in the process. She said that when we experience trauma, aspects of the psyche leave our core for self-protection, but don't necessarily return when the traumatic conditions subside. Immediately recalling that moment in childhood when my mother was using the leather strap on me, and I hurled my essence across the universe to get it safely away from her, I knew exactly what Abi meant.

The fragmentation of soul isn't something one normally does consciously, though, and as I looked back across my life, I saw multitudes of traumas which had scattered bits of me, and left me feeling less than whole. Among the more obvious ones were the many years of humiliating stuttering and psycho-emotional abuse in childhood; the prolonged schism between my male embodiment and the nature of my essence; the stressful marathon runs of building; and the repeated physical traumas of electrolysis and surgeries. From this viewpoint, I had to wonder how I'd maintained my core at all, while it also confirmed the power of persistence in homecoming to Self, whatever the state of one's inner resources.

I could also see much more clearly what made the experience with the house in Portland especially difficult: It was one more trauma on top of so many earlier unhealed ones. Those traumas had arrived from myriad sources: abuse from others' suffering, from limiting beliefs picked up from family and culture, from the rub of my sensitive nature with this difficult world—while others stemmed from the physical changes born of necessity in responding to the deeper callings of my gender-variant nature. Many of the traumas marked the turmoil of massive life-change: They were, in a sense, birth traumas as I entered a new phase of life.

In my soul retrieval session with Abi, I could see and feel in the inner landscape the fragments coming home—some in larger pieces, scores of other smaller ones tinkling in like bits of glass—to the brilliant sphere of Being: the unchanging core that transcends lifetimes. I had focused my attention inside and out for so long, laying the groundwork for broader integration—for wholeness—without which this work would not have been so transformative. She facilitated an opening that was primed with my readiness, and I flowed into a richer, fuller knowing of Self, which was revealed all the more in the following days, weeks, and months.

Even just outwardly, the shift was remarkable: That night, I slept eight hours and woke up refreshed—and have done so virtually every night since. The next day I found the fear of riding the motorbike was simply gone, and the haunting, long-term stress had dissolved, too. I'd been looking pretty haggard in the past year, and within days started looking much healthier. My body had been trying to recover from something it couldn't heal—as the dis-ease wasn't physical; now it was free to flourish. And along with it, my psyche was no longer limping along, compensating for those estranged parts.

We did a follow-up session some days later to deal with any missing fragments or lingering traumas. With the traumas gone and those stray parts back home, energy was no longer draining away from my Being in a constantly reparative mode, and I didn't need to focus to feel a sense of inner balance.

Closer to the surface—in the world of form—the story of my unfolding appeared to proceed directly out of the writing about creative process. Yet, energetically, this healing with Abi provided the opening to a more seamless integration of my inner landscape, and in that spaciousness, the journey of this life revealed itself. Rather than me bringing my story out into the world, it unfolded naturally of its own accord, and called me out into the mix of humanity with it.

Bali

When I took the first hormone pill twenty years earlier, it seemed as though a dam had burst; relieved of the weight of those traumas, I again felt washed into a new realm by a flood of held-back readiness.

I had sensed for some time that, while I was contentedly—and often creatively—engaged with each day in Bali, I was actually waiting for something. Over the years, I had tried again and again by the earnestness of shear effort to set up the conditions for the lighter way of Being I'd envisioned, and finally, in the midst of simply waiting, my invitation was accepted.

I knew I'd come around full-circle when I recalled those Zen books I was reading in my twenties, suggesting that surrender is far more effective than struggle. Certainly, I understood the concept at the time, but some things can only be truly known from living them. One's karmic wheel, it seems, just has to roll over some difficult ground on one's way to liberation.

Being the Soul

Several months after arriving in Bali, I was getting a few things at the health food store across from the Kantor Pos when one of the guys who worked there came out and waved for me to come over. I wasn't expecting anything, but he smiled and handed over an envelope as I thanked him for letting me know. At a glance, I recognized Lorraine's neat handwriting, and lit right up at the prospect of whatever she might have sent. It turned out to be a beautiful card featuring a Rumi quote:

Wherever you stand, be the soul of that place.

Inside, she'd written: *This seems like a thought worth presenting to someone who has taken a step to a different land.* Worthy indeed, as the words had woven themselves right into the fiber of my Being on the first reading. I loved the expansiveness of them—the sense of identity beyond the body, melded with landscape.

This card floated down to the white-tiled floor from its perch on the wall recently, as if to say hello and reengage an ongoing conversation. As I picked it up, I was taken right back to the lovely aspirational quality it had when I first read it, and I nearly cried with joyous gratitude for the openings that had occurred in the meantime. On its arrival, I was very much in a different land from the one I'd left; I was in the same place now, but I was vastly different in it.

I had started seeing beyond individual things—observing, instead, the flow of everything at once. With the realization that the center of the eye is used to focus on detail, and is much more mind-oriented, I brought my attention to the periphery, and became far more aware of the relatedness of things, and thereby their essence. With a little practice, I soon found I was literally focusing on spaciousness as a normal way of seeing. And then *hearing* joined in, with listening becoming less a reaction to distinct sounds, and more an experience of a full symphony of What Is.

Then this spaciousness blossomed into the realm of meditation, as I realized this expansive, peripheral seeing worked even with the eyes closed—opening the field of consciousness out beyond the inherent limitations of mind. As without, so within: As the experience of the outer landscape shifted away from the content of separate things, toward the context of interrelatedness, consciousness opened right out into it. This had been there all the time, of course, as if waiting for me to surrender to the simplicity of What Is. *Inner* and *outer* had blurred into a continuum, like those spaces in the *Lumenhorse* work that were neither and both interior and exterior.

An exquisite, pervasive, transcendent sense of unconditional belonging in the universe at large would surge through my whole Being, and as it opened, so did my heart. Suddenly, I realized with joyous laughter the undercurrent of why I often use the term *heartspace*: Heartfulness and spaciousness are the same thing.

From the view of consciousness, I'd become acutely aware of the mind's compulsion to attach meaning to every thing and circumstance: to analyze, judge, rate, and establish the value—and therefore the meaning—of literally everything.

Lying back for hours at a time, watching the palms sway in the wind as clouds sailed the sky, I'd observe thoughts arising from the field of consciousness, and began to more clearly recognize the extraordinary wealth of choice in every moment. I would let go of thinking altogether, and find that without it, the world burst into new levels of beauty and aliveness, and seemed to be arising freshly, ecstatically, from silence, stillness, and space.

In the unfolding Now of daily life, I'd waft in and out of states of joy and bliss. Old patterns of fear or negative emotionality would appear at times, but they no longer had any power; I'd found simple acceptance and the awareness of stillness to be most pleasant alternatives to suffering.

Joy spilled right into bliss as I focused outwardly, leaving behind identity with the body, mind, and personality—recognizing myself more fully as Self. Just *Being* had become so wondrous that absolutely nothing needed to happen for there to be a sublime sense of peace and fulfillment.

This arc of awakening lent the spaciousness that at last made this life-combing recapitulation possible; and like halves of a slow-spinning wheel, the writing and it rolled through that landscape together. For the grace of this journey, I am no longer a separate thing *in* a landscape...

Wherever I am,
I am the Stillness of this place.

Coffee and Salt

This morning I cried in my coffee,
not because it's an evil brown liquid
I should not be drinking,
nor because some old stray fragment
of hurt surfaced and grabbed hold.
No, these were tears of exquisite joy
for the blessing of sweet space inside and out.

A blur of pleas for freedom from back then
and then and then funneled through,
rinsing the moment in splendorous gratitude,
salting the warm cup in my lap with redemption
to a chorus of cicadas, roosters,
and palm-fronded silence.

9

Reentry

Pregnant Words

On an early motorbike excursion in Bali, I had found a large bamboo basket in the shape of a pregnant belly. When the making of the *Thresholds* poetry books was finished, I'd used the basket as a form, and over it collaged fragments of the leftover bamboo pages onto layers of the colored pineapple leaf paper used for the covers. The work took the words past their first step into the world of dimensional form—as book—and released them into pure sculpture.

In this new form, bits of word and page seemed to float in from ethereal Space at the outer edges, gathering density as they passed through the colors of the chakras, finally reaching the full density of book, in the form of a thick book cover mounted like a doorway in the center. During the months of the initial writing of *Shape-shifter*, it was a constant source of affirming inspiration—a visual expression of the writing process, which I titled *Calling to Page*.

In the six months following the first draft, I turned again to the grounding meditation of sculpting. I wanted to absorb, in contemplation-soaked motion, the freshly appreciated wealth of the creative journey; and most especially, the unfurling of awareness nurtured by the writing of the past months, which had transformed my way of Being in the world. As the practice unfolded through form again, the Writing Womb became a tiny studio, and in its exquisite light I made a family of similar, basket-formed sculptures incorporating fragments of the *Shape-shifter* text printed on the rough bamboo paper.

I'd often thought of art as a meeting of the deeply personal and the universal, and in this sculpting, I could take bits of the arc of this lifetime and meld them with sacred color, imagery, and form. I was literally creating out of the material of my life—working the bits into a series of rich, layered universes.

It was a joy to simply Be making: a lovely counterpoint to the writing, which had evoked imagery with words: Here, flocks of words seemed evoked *by* imagery, sending them arcing across the bellied forms. The work was a blessed manifestation of the seamless wafting of word and world I'd long seen waiting on the horizon. I called this series *Shamanic Seeds*.

With no preconception as to how many there would be, I kept working with them until they announced their own resolution. In the end, there were seven. As the last one, *Cadence of Blessed Surrender*, was taking final form, I suddenly knew I was about to return to the point of this tropical journey's departure.

□ □ □

Port of Entry

Six months after the initial writing, a series of long flights takes me across the sixteen-hour time gap from Bali to the United States. The Immigration Officer in Seattle inspects my intensely stamped passport and says, *Well, looks like you've been away awhile... Nice to have you back!* I've been gone for over a year-and-a-half, and it *is* good to be back.

There's an undercurrent of purpose in returning: Though I don't know if, when, or in what form, *Shape-shifter* will appear in the world, it's clearly time to retrieve some images to illustrate the creative work from over the years, and they're shelved in the storage unit in Portland, Oregon.

After a short flight to San Jose, I flop down into the seat of Lorraine's Prius, and head with her to Santa Cruz for a few-day visit. On the way we catch up on the many changes in our lives over much-missed Mexican-American burritos, and I find myself marveling at the blessing of friends with whom one can experience huge gaps of absence, yet pick right up on the ongoing conversation when reconnecting down the road.

Reentry

The next morning, I start going through the things left in her garage loft before I departed the States, and discover to my delight that, since I'd stayed with her for a couple of months before heading out, much of what I find is the kit of clothing and accessories I'll need to live in Portland for the summer.

Days later, having re-oriented myself to Pacific Standard Time, as well as driving on the right-hand side of the road, I repack the contents of this personal time capsule into a rented car and embark on the fourteen-hour drive to Portland.

Dialing In

Heading up through northern California, I'm surfing the radio to get a sense of what's being broadcast rural America these days. Amazed to hear the word "trangendered" coming from the car speakers, I leave the signal right there and sit back, certain this will be interesting in one way or another.

It turns out to be a Christian radio station, and the pastor is talking about how Christians need to become more aware of "transgendered," and how "transgendered" is going on below their radar. It seems from his repeated, oddly inflected use of the term—rather than something like "transgender people" or "transgender issues,"—that he's likely to be operating from a deep, theological abhorrence to opening up to real understanding and compassion.

Not surprisingly, he describes such people in "this hurtful lifestyle" as "wounded, damaged, and confused," and says it's a response to sexual abuse or poor gender role models. "Coming to Christ," he goes on to say, could only happen by "honoring the gender given by God." It doesn't seem to occur to him that the work of a soul on this plane might be to learn and grow from the process of aligning one's physical form with a deeply felt "given" gender, and that experiencing gender as a spectrum rather than a duality might be a path to greater awareness of the Divine.

He assumes that transbeingness is inherently outside the grace of God, and any suggestion of such personal transformation as a Divine calling is not only missing, but implicitly dismissed. He talks of necessary penance from the point of view that "choosing" such a "lifestyle" is an insult to, and a turning away from, God.

The pastor offers a hypothetical situation in which a member of the church confides that she was once a man. What should the head of the congregation do? Why, he should council "Joan" to return to being "John" by getting off the hormones and slowly transitioning back. The men in the congregation should open up to "him" and welcome "him" into their fold, even if others do not, as this would be "Christ-like."

The message here is that Christ's acceptance is most conditional: you come on *these* terms—even if they are antithetical to your deepest sense of Being and wellbeing—or you can just burn in Hell. Simply being accepting and welcoming of transpeople—as they are—is apparently out of the question. Though I don't consider myself to be a Christian, I feel in my heart the unconditionally loving message of Jesus, and the deep sense of separation in this pastor's words feel like one more example of how it's been perverted, and depleted of its true spirit, among Fundamentalists.

His God is one of judgment and punishment; by not turning to "Him" to "fix" the gender dysphoria in the first place, and choosing instead to engage in such "self-destructive behavior," trans people should have to pay a price. He speaks as if God is a separate existence out there, always at the ready to reward or punish behavior based on one's choices, and damned you are if you make the wrong ones. It seems that for this pastor, God is a kind of Cosmic Parent with a set of rules that must not be broken; His highly conditional love is a reward for strict obedience, and suffering is punishment for not going along with the Program.

I can't help but notice how the long stretch of hot, flat, arid land I'm passing through looks so much like this pastor sounds: Water—the element of the heart—is in short supply, and the lushness of joy has either dried up or scrambled off for more nurturing environs.

Reentry

What is missing in his words is any semblance of appreciation for the inherent presence of the Divine within each of us, for the unfathomably vast love that is there without condition, or for the grace of trusting one's heartful unfurling in this adventure called life. Missing, too, is any apparent awareness that a profound homecoming to one's Self opens out onto joy, peace and love, and is thus a doorway to Divine spaciousness and the freedom and light therein.

But then, freedom is most certainly not what this man has in mind, and it seems quite likely he'd consider my assertion—that being what and whom one truly is constitutes an honoring of the Divine in the highest regard—to be some form of blasphemy. For him, obedience to a rigid set of rules absolutely trumps authenticity of Being as a guidepost in opening to grace.

Instead, the pastor suggests intensive prayer, but doesn't, of course, bring up the possibility of its affirming one's calling to the gender path of unfoldment. Rather, he pitches prayer as a way to explore one's wrongdoing, and how one could find out just what sort of penance— acceptance of punishment—would be required to get back into alignment with an apparently displeased Almighty. I do not find validity in the concept of sin, but if I did, I'd nominate the steering of someone away from a profound inner calling to Self, and toward suffering, for such a list.

It is glaringly clear in the light of awareness that the ultimate power in the universe—call it what you will: God, Divinity, Oneness—is well beyond dualities of good and bad, of male and female... of all kinds of separation whatsoever. It simply *Is*. It simply loves; it *is* love. Yet some thought-bound humans project their limitations onto Divinity, then behave—and demand that others behave—out of those shortcomings as if they were divinely sanctioned.

If some insist on overlaying the blazing love and light of All That Is with a dense, theological construct and living within its confines, that's their choice and their business. They may claim to be simply acting out of their beliefs—as though that were some sort of divine license for the peddling of suffering—but when they insist that others live in that same prison, and prey upon the vulnerable seeking their own spiritual bearings, that is in effect spiritual abuse—regardless of higher intentions.

It seems that at the core of so much strife and suffering in the world is the tradition-bound supplanting of simple loving-kindness—within and without—with belief systems masquerading as the thoughts of God.

For me, one of great blessings of this earthly stay has been a natural attraction to focusing inwardly for guidance. At numerous turning points, I've said in my own sort of prayer, *Show me what I am, and I will live it beautifully—whatever it is.* At these times, I'm asking for the natural unfolding of my Being on this plane to be revealed.

I surrender within to What Is, prepared to show up and live it in the world of form. This invitation is more than just intentional: it is extended through the work of letting go of limiting beliefs, choices, relationships, identities, patterns... whatever no longer serves in this arc of unfolding. How could joy, peace, and freedom not show up, too, and spill right out of this ongoing meeting with one's higher Being?

As the landscape begins to rise south of Mt. Shasta, it slowly cools and takes on more green; sparse, scrubby vegetation gives way to the emerald tones of conifers. Leaving the pastor's grim message behind, I realize the calling to share my story has been unexpectedly spotlighted and honed. Flowing through my Being is a wealth of compassion for those operating from the limitations that confine the wonder of All That Is into rigid, ideological thinking—and even more compassion for those steered toward further suffering by such misguided, righteous piety.

Reentry

I had been unsure as to whether or not I would actually publish *Shape-shifter*. The value for me in its writing has already well-exceeded the ability of language to express, and the impetus in returning to the States was to simply follow the calling to have the images ready for whatever direction it would take. Yet the timing, and unlikelihood, of hearing the pastor's dark, unholy message seem to underscore the moment, and I sense a clear invitation to counterbalance it: to share my journey of transformation toward wholeness.

I see more clearly and deeply now that moving past one's limitations is a form of service inside and out: In our growing spaciousness, we can't help but make more room for others. And in counterpointing the darkness of rampant ignorance, we're called to the outer work of more fully embracing the inner Light.

Until now, I've been wary of really putting myself out in the world, concerned it would be a distraction from my inner process—that my unfurling risked being sidetracked by the whirl of worldliness. I knew I hadn't quite yet ripened into whatever way of Being would naturally take me beyond the harbor of solitude. Even now, the blessed quietude of the studio and the natural world remains alluring as ever, but a sense of higher purpose beckons me to create a balance of that and a more public life. It's become utterly clear that awakening is not enough: it's how I *live it* that matters.

In responding to the calling to be out in the public realm much more than has been comfortable, acceptance infers the surrender of ways that no longer serve my Being. It portends—by the grace of attention, awareness, and spiritual will—the letting go of old, habitual patterns of self-perception that have placed me outside the broader human conversation. And it welcomes the ongoing nurturing of new ways that balance inner stillness and outer engagement in this moment and this one and this...

After the long, hot drive through the lowlands, the mountain curves and cool heading into the Siskiyou Pass are sweet relief. I'd been feeling fried by the intense brightness of the outer landscape, and note with pleasure the signs counting down the miles to Ashland, Oregon. It's mid-June—nearly the Summer Solstice—and soon I'm stretching out into the roomy evening in lovely Lithia Park in the center of town.

There was a dearth of parks and trails in Bali, and the long-missed joy of strolling along paths entwined with nature envelops me like the presence of an old friend; it brings out the best in me, and I see in the eyes and smiles of passerby that I'm not alone in its sweet spell.

Later, I get some dinner, and watch a movie in a theater for the first time in nearly two years. Not looking for the razzle-dazzle of special effects, I pick the gentlest one on the marquee, which it turns out to be about a woman raising a family in a poverty-stricken village in Sweden in the early 1900s: A camera comes to her by way of a lottery prize, and her tentative embracing of it ends up enriching and warming her very limited, often brutal, life in extraordinary ways.

Déjà View

In the early morning, I find an open cafe, order a latte and muffin for the road, and step back into what feels like a cockpit with my stuff packed all around. Five hours later, I'm in my friend Nancy's apartment, and we're having a fabulous time—catching up and enjoying the long-delayed presence.

Nancy is having a party the following night to celebrate both the Summer Solstice and having made the final payment on her land in eastern Washington. Setting up for it the next day flows right into a grand time reconnecting with friends, toasting Nancy's many-years-long accomplishment with wine she'd made with elderberries from her land.

Later in the evening, I read a few poems and some pieces from this writing. Thus far, I've scarcely shared the writing at all, and the warm, rapt attention and glowing eyes affirm the value in delivering my words in my own cadence and voice.

I spend a few days motoring around Portland, getting things done while I still have the rented car. Among the priorities are fitting the stuff from Santa Cruz that's not needed for the summer into the already densely-packed storage unit, and getting from there the boxes of film and prints that record thirty years of creative work.

I've come so far on this mission, and I'm feeling nicely energized about getting on with retrieving the images to accompany these words. The artist in me wants to share through the eyes pictures, as well as words, from the spectrum of transformation.

My friend Barbara—whose emailed depictions had enticed me to Bali—has kindly offered the upstairs of the beautiful house she's renting near Mount Tabor—as in Mount Tabor Park, replete with extinct volcano, trees, trails, and vast expanses of grass only blocks away. It really is fine to be back in the States, and Portland in particular, with the haven of nature so readily at one's fingertips.

Oh, maybe thirty or so, I say to her when she asks how many images I need to get digitally scanned. She thinks it might be worthwhile to try out her scanner, which turns out to be a fine one. Starting out with better-organizing the negatives and prints from growing up, I look over the 3-ring binders packed with light impressions: as an explorative medium in itself; of furniture-making, interiors, sculpture, lighting, and self-portraits.

Flipping through the pages, I realize they're already in book form, as if suggesting their later purpose. It gradually occurs to me, too, that I've been called to undertake a far more extensive project than I'd thought; it certainly isn't the first time I've been seduced into a seemingly small effort which expanded exponentially once started. But then, these times seem to be fine opportunities to let those enthusiasm afterburners kick on.

I've returned from halfway around the world to unveil this dust-laden cache of images, and it dawns on me in a flickering of presence and memory, that I'd known all along I'd write this, or I wouldn't have recorded all those images of process and place and production over the circuitous course of making. I suddenly recall the countless times I'd said to myself over thirty years: *Might as well get a picture of this... might be good to have it some day.*

Surrounded by binders and stacks of prints, negatives, and slides, the wash of so much creative work pours through me as if this span of lifetime had collapsed into a single gesture. I glimpse my dismissal of mediums and modes which had felt less directly expressive of my essence—the earlier furniture, interior, and remodeling work—and now I see and appreciate in the sweep of it all that it was the work my soul needed to do in those phases of the arc, not simply as an artist, but as a Being on a passage of learning and growing.

I see, too, that my higher Self had always been setting up the groundwork for this blossoming, and that this rediscovery and re-union marks the resolution of those psycho-emotionally challenging years. In my version of an artful life, these recordings of light reflected from the content of those many moments across nearly fifty years are some of the raw material for the new medium that ushers me into the world.

Reentry

Yet it's clear in the light of this moment that this arc of living has always been my form of art. My body—my whole Being—vibrates with this truth, and I feel the frequency of the calling to this new way of opening amplified and fine-tuned.

Having recorded only in digital mode for the past five years, there's a familiarity-tinged awkwardness in working with the delicate, light-sensitized plastic again. Yet as I touch it, I recognize one potent aspect in the shifting of the recording of light from being object-oriented to being information-based: These strips hold material impressions of the very light reflected from the work, and are therefore the closest thing I have to most of it. I feel no compulsion to grasp onto the actual artifacts of all that Doing, but it's a fine reunion in sharing light with them again.

These were companions called through well-labored intention into this earthly plane from what I'd long envisioned as The Pool of Potential—the Unmanifest: Silence, Stillness, Space. The grace of creative spirit channeled through my essence, thereby inflecting What Might Be with these materials, forms, and colors from the spectrum of infinite possibility, and as I turn page after page, an intense feeling of kinship naturally ripples through.

Eyes of the Beheld

I had never realized how often I'd taken a moment to place my own physicality with the work when I was recording. I rarely had interest in self-portraiture for its own sake, but there was something most inviting about accompanying the objects I'd made; it was more like a family portrait. There I am, entwined with my offspring, and they are *of* me—who I am, translated into yet more earthly density. I see this body changing amid the evolving furniture and living spaces, and I can't help but see the body as a furnishing of Self—of the soul.

Looking over the images of my transformation in the last twenty years, I notice that I often chose to hold the wooden mallet that for me has always symbolized physical effectiveness. I see that—even while I gravitated to a female basis—the mallet was in part an expression of the inner Father, making the space for the Mother and Child.

The core of my version of grace in this world was indeed found and practiced in the studio: in the experience of wielding that mallet with love and strength—with an essential melding in the moment of my intention, the mallet's exquisite arc, and the wooden forms shaped by its momentum.

In searching through the photos from babyhood to near-present, I realize that I'd never been able to see these images clearly before. The person in them had always seemed to be a sort of parallel rendering of me—out of step with my inner sensibility. I'd often cringed, held back from embracing them because they didn't seem to represent me.

Now, I see in every one of these recordings, eyes ablaze with this Beingness that never changes, as if I'm looking into a mirror while my physicality shape-shifts: evolving in staccato sequence from infancy to boyhood and young manhood, from intersex-ness to androgynous womanhood. I look into the spectrum of portraits as if for the first time, while boundless love and compassion courses through my whole Being.

The vast gift of it all shines with sublime brilliance, while tears of love flow for every permutation along the winding way. I want to hold every one of them, and I do: Time shatters, falls away; and I am there and there and there, in the heartspace of the eternal Now.

A sense of those countless moments of difficulty wafts through; I feel the deep presence of something holding me, and recognize in the reflection my own loving Self.

When I think of freedom, images of birds and sky flit through me, though I know it's not these things per se. I'm sensing, rather, the vast space they inhabit. I've found in my odd unfurling in this realm, that freedom is a way of Being: that true freedom—the only freedom available in every moment and place—is the spaciousness of Awareness. And the landscape of this expansiveness is the threshold of one's inner and outer life, where one exists in the moment, with one eye on the Stillness, and the other on the world of form.

Whatever the path to, and amid, this landscape, it seems the wellspring of Joy flows from simply knowing one is, in this moment, on it: however ranging the terrain or many the steps, moving in form in the light and space of one's higher Being... of Self.

Were I offered a crystal ball in which to glimpse where this earthly path goes from here, I'd choose not to look at all. I want the adventure of discovery and revelation along the way, and I know already how it ends: I leave this body amongst the density, and go on to the work of unfurling in yet finer and lighter realms.

In the Now encompassing this gathering of words and that blissful dissolution, I want only to know that in looking out across the arc of this living, I see and feel a fine blossoming, indeed.

I recall being the old man dying in the vision when I was five years old, and feel in the depths of Self the crystallization of what I've wanted ever since: to be in rhythm with the pulse of potential... feeling the gesture of life unfolding in form like a seedling toward light, divinely undefined.

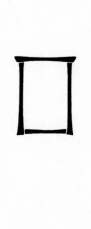

Reference

6
Lumenhorse 213

9
Reentry   323

Color images for each chapter are available at
shannonbelthor.com